T003B442

Praise for Peter Robison's

FLYING BLIND

A *New York Times* Business Bestseller

"The long train of events that led to the tragedies—and the subsequent reputational and financial trashing of one of America's biggest companies—is expertly dissected in *Flying Blind*. . . . A 'bottom-line mindset' prevailed. In rich detail, Mr. Robison chronicles the shortcomings of that approach at a firm where safety should be paramount." —*The Economist*

"[Robison] avoids simple explanations or scapegoats . . . resist[ing] the sort of pat causal explanations that many—including the government itself—have used to try to describe what happened." —*The New Republic*

"Vividly written and meticulously researched, *Flying Blind* is a story everyone—every consumer, every citizen, every worker in every industry—needs to read. Peter Robison brilliantly places Boeing's deadly downfall within the larger tragedy of an American business culture that gradually has smashed every altar but the one where the bottom line is worshipped." —Diana B. Henriques, author of *A First-Class Catastrophe*

"*Flying Blind* is superb reporting in service of a riveting story. Robison has crafted this tour de force masterfully, showing how modern capitalism's abandonment of quality in favor of quick bucks literally knocked airplanes out of the sky. As you turn each page in growing disbelief and anger, I guarantee it will keep you reading late into the night." —Kurt Eichenwald, author of *Conspiracy of Fools*

FLYING BLIND

THE 737 MAX TRAGEDY AND THE FALL OF BOEING

PETER ROBISON

ANCHOR BOOKS

A Division of Penguin Random House LLC
New York

FIRST ANCHOR BOOKS EDITION 2022

Copyright © 2021 by Peter Robison

All rights reserved. Published in the United States by Anchor Books,
a division of Penguin Random House LLC, New York, and distributed
in Canada by Penguin Random House Canada Limited, Toronto.
Originally published in hardcover in the United States by Doubleday,
a division of Penguin Random House LLC, New York, in 2021.

The Library of Congress has cataloged the Doubleday edition as follows:
Name: Robison, Peter, author.
Title: Flying blind : the 737 MAX tragedy and the fall of Boeing / Peter Robison.
Description: First edition. | New York : Doubleday, 2021. |
Includes bibliographical references and index.
Identifiers: LCCN 2021006584 (print) | LCCN 2021006585 (ebook)
Subjects: LCSH: Boeing Company—Management. | Boeing 737
(Jet transport)—Accidents. | Aircraft industry—United States—Management. |
Aircraft industry—United States—Employees. | Corporate culture.
Classification: LCC HD9711.U63 B6363 2021 (print) |
LCC HD9711.U63 (ebook) | DDC 338.7/6291300973—dc23
LC record available at https://lccn.loc.gov/2021006584
LC ebook record available at https://lccn.loc.gov/2021006585

Anchor Books Trade Paperback ISBN: 978-0-593-08251-5
eBook ISBN: 978-0-385-54650-8

Author photograph © Mike Nakamura Photography
Book design by Michael Collica

anchorbooks.com

Printed in the United States of America
2nd Printing

CONTENTS

FLYING
BLIND

INTRODUCTION

The scene before dawn at Soekarno-Hatta International Airport in Jakarta on October 29, 2018, was like that at any other big airport in the age of routinized international travel. In the concourses, bleary-eyed families and solo travelers clumped outside gates or gulped a hurried breakfast from Dunkin' Donuts or Burger King, the latter of which, in this majority Muslim country, offered a Halal-certified rice and crispy chicken combo (the King Deal). Others window-shopped for Kiehl's face cream or electronic gadgets. As the sun rose it was finally light enough to see the tropical gardens of narra trees, palms, and orchids outside—one of the few clues the traveler wasn't in Kansas City or Stuttgart.

Not many gave a thought to the machines parked beside the jetways, many of them Boeing 737s, the stub-nosed workhorses of airline fleets since the 1970s. Commercial aircraft are considered the world's premier expression of manufacturing excellence, designed by tens of thousands of people around the world who put their hands on them—at first figuratively, on the computer screens of engineers, and then literally when machinists climb underneath them to hand-crank stubborn fasteners to the desired torque. Before the planes leave Boeing's factory near Seattle, airlines send their own representatives to inspect every inch and reject the machines if they find, say, a loose bin or a fray in the forty miles of wiring (or, as sometimes happens, a forgotten wrench or gum wrapper).

The people gathered around Gate B5 that morning for Lion Air Flight 610 were about to board the newest and most advanced of more than ten thousand 737s Boeing had manufactured. It was called the 737 MAX 8. A far cry from the original 737, which had two tiny cigar-shaped engines tucked under its wings, this one had two massive turbofans. Almost six feet in diameter, they were so big they had to be mounted in front of the wings instead of beneath them, and the average person could stand inside the cowlings. The engines generated twenty-eight thousand pounds of thrust—double that of the first 737 models—while drastically lowering fuel consumption. The new jetliner was economical enough that Lion Air could charge sixty dollars for the one-hour flight from Jakarta to Pangkal Pinang, a city of three hundred thousand on Indonesia's Bangka Island.

A Lion Air subsidiary, in fact, had been the first to fly the 737 MAX, which was particularly popular with Asian airlines springing up to transport the continent's millions of newly mobile middle-class travelers. One of them, Paul Ayorbaba, forty-three, sent his family a choppy WhatsApp video of his mundane walk through the jetway and out to the plane, painted a cheery orange and white. In the minutes before the doors closed, twenty-two-year-old Deryl Fida Febrianto, a newlywed of two weeks, texted a selfie to his bride as he departed for a job on a cruise ship. Wahyu Aldilla sat with his son, Xherdan Fahrezi, after visiting Jakarta for a soccer match. A grieving family—Michelle Vergina Bongkal, twenty-one, her father, Adonia, and brother Mathew, thirteen—was heading to Bangka Island for the funeral of Michelle's grandmother. Twenty employees of the country's finance ministry, returning from a weekend in Jakarta, had caught the early-morning flight to reach the office in time.

Taking the MAX through a preflight checklist, the pilot, Bhavye Suneja, typified a new generation of pilots across Asia. At thirty-one, he had already flown six thousand hours, almost all of them on previous versions of the 737. His copilot, who went by the single name Harvino, was a decade older and had about five thousand hours. Neither knew that a tiny sensor on the left side of the plane, just below Suneja's window, had a twenty-one-degree misalignment in its delicate innards—an oversight by mechanics who had inspected it. The device, known as an angle-of-attack sensor, was basically a weather vane. It measured the angle of the wing against the oncoming air—too high, and the plane might stall. In the triple-redundant engineering of a product now more than a century old, dating to a pair of bicycle makers who hitched a 12-horsepower engine and a chain sprocket to a spruce wood frame, it wasn't even considered a particularly relevant indicator on most airplanes. Other dials measured the all-important airspeed, altitude, and pitch.

It was 6:20 a.m. when Lion Air 610 departed the runway. The nose gear had barely left the ground when Suneja's control column began shaking, the cue for a potential stall. Two alerts signaling bad altitude and airspeed readings blinked on. Flight data recorders don't pick up the expressions on pilots' faces, or the stab in their spines, when they sense their docile machine might kill them. Harvino, the copilot, immediately asked the captain if he planned to turn around. Suneja suggested they get clearance to a holding point to buy some time. "Flight control problem," Harvino radioed. As Suneja steered toward the new heading, the nose mysteriously dipped. He squeezed a switch on the control column under his thumb to push it back up. The nose lifted, but then it dipped again. For eight minutes, the tug-of-war continued. The blue expanse of Jakarta Bay filled the windows.

Harvino flipped through Boeing's Quick Reference Handbook, searching through pages of emergency checklists for an answer. Air Speed Unreliable. Dual Bleed. Pack Trip Off. Wing-Body Overheat. Nothing seemed to explain the ghost fighting them for control of the plane. Twenty-one times Suneja pressed the switch to keep the nose pointing up. The plane was cleared for twenty-seven thousand feet but had reached less than six thousand, the fishing boats in the sea below like toys in a tub. The passengers felt every sickening undulation in their stomachs. Harvino finally got on the phone to ask a flight attendant to come into the cockpit. "Yes, sir," she answered, replacing the phone with a ca-chunk (audible on the cockpit voice recorder) and opening the door. The captain asked her to send in a Lion Air engineer who happened to be aboard to help them figure out the problem. The chimes of the intercom sounded as she called him forward.

Suneja, preparing to brief his colleague and probably wanting a look at the handbook himself, told his copilot to take over the controls. The nose dipped again. "Wah, it's very . . ." Harvino muttered. He flicked the thumb switch, but not as firmly as the captain had. After a few seconds the nose fell again, and again he hit the switch. The jet tilted toward the water. Harvino exclaimed that the plane was pointing down. Suneja, distracted, answered, "It's okay." Ten seconds later they were plummeting at ten thousand feet a minute. Harvino pulled desperately on the control column, alarms blaring ("Sink rate, sink rate!"). The water was now immense and terrifying as the glare of early-morning light streamed into the cockpit. The copilot began repeating "Allahu Akbar, Allahu Akbar"—the Muslim expression of faith meaning "God is greater"—and a harsh robotic voice intoned, "Terrain, terrain." Suneja was silent.

At 6:32 a.m., the ghost won. Horrified fishermen on a nearby boat watched as the jet, carrying 189 people, hit the sea at a nearly vertical angle at five hundred miles per hour. Television stations soon began broadcasting images of floating debris and interviewing the victims' stunned relatives. "I'm sure Dad could swim his way out," said Nanda Ayorbaba, the thirteen-year-old daughter of the man who only hours before had sent the choppy video.

The crash triggered the well-worn machinery of accident investigations, dominated for decades by Boeing and American regulators. The National Transportation Safety Board and the venerable plane maker both dispatched teams to Jakarta, and at the FAA office near Seattle, a modernist edifice surrounded by embankments on all sides to deter car bombers, staffers began dissecting what went wrong. They called in Boeing engineers, who explained about automated software known as the Maneuvering Characteristics Augmentation System, or MCAS ("em-kass," as it was pronounced). Only a few people at the FAA had even heard of it. "What's MCAS?" asked one agency official.

It was immediately clear that the software was far more powerful than Boeing had suggested in documents submitted to win the plane's approval. The engineers had drastically underestimated the software's ability to move the horizontal stabilizer, the small wing on the plane's tail. What's more, it had fired because of bad data from the single misaligned sensor—a flaw Boeing's vaunted processes were supposed to find and root out long before the plane was in flight with commercial passengers.

At this point, in November 2018, the story went in two directions. There was a public narrative, the one advanced by Boeing chief executive officer Dennis Muilenburg, his top engineers, and FAA officials to convince airline pilots and passengers—and maybe even themselves—that the plane was safe. The problem (as they all but said) was one badly run airline from Indonesia. They insisted that an updated checklist was all it would take for any competent pilot to manage the unlikely scenario that brought down the Lion Air plane.

And then there was the private narrative. Behind the scenes, some of the largest and most respected airlines in the world were screaming that Boeing had hidden the existence of potentially deadly software inside their planes. Pilots for American Airlines in Texas were so distrustful that they recorded a tense meeting with Boeing executives. Whistleblowers got the attention of federal investigators, who opened a criminal probe into the plane's design. A Boeing manager asked pilots to come up with a list of airlines who might still struggle with the new checklist. Technical experts at the FAA privately questioned the assurances that Boeing and their own bosses were providing to the public.

Finally, the stories collided. On March 10, 2019, less than five months after the Lion Air crash, another MAX 8, this one operated by Ethiopian Airlines, took off from Addis Ababa. The 157 people aboard represented thirty-five nationalities. Twenty-one passengers were United Nations staffers, many of them heading to an environmental conference. Seven worked for the Rome-based World

Food Program. Four were from Catholic Relief Services. There was a Nigerian-born author of satirical essays, a Georgetown University law student, brothers from California having an adventure together, and two interpreters for the African Union. Six minutes after takeoff, they were all dead. The software—despite the confident statements from Boeing and the FAA—had again taken control of a plane even as the pilots struggled in vain to follow the new checklist.

The deaths of 346 people on a brand-new aircraft within five months badly shook the widely shared assumption of safety in air travel. There was the chilling fact that software had overridden humans. Then, too, it became clear that the FAA had abdicated much of its oversight to Boeing itself. Most disturbing was what the crashes revealed about the rotted culture of an iconic American company, as the plane's grounding stretched to almost two years, cost more than $20 billion, and finally forced the departure of Muilenburg. Once ruled by engineers who thumbed their noses at Wall Street, Boeing had reinvented itself into one of the most shareholder-friendly creatures of the market. It celebrated managers for cost cutting, co-opted regulators with heaps of money, and pressured suppliers with Walmart-style tactics.

In shocking emails handed over to congressional investigators, a Boeing pilot boasted of using "Jedi mind tricks" to convince airlines and regulators there was no need for pilots who'd flown the previous version of the 737 (like Suneja and Harvino) to undergo expensive simulator training on the MAX. An employee despairing of foul-ups wrote, "This airplane is designed by clowns, who in turn are supervised by monkeys." Other evidence showed that Boeing pressured pilots to skimp on testing and ignored engineers' entreaties for sophisticated flight controls that might have prevented the tragedies. The company even turned down a request from Lion Air itself for additional training. ("Idiots," a Boeing pilot grumbled to a colleague.)

The malpractice at Boeing is all the more distressing because it's been one of the most respected brands in American business for so long. Boeing is one of those rare corporations whose very name conjures mythic associations: the pioneering early days of flight, moon landings, World War II bomber missions, the awesome routine of the modern air transport system. Until the pandemic, a 737 was landing or taking off somewhere around the world every 1.5 seconds. In addition to making commercial aircraft, Boeing supplies the Pentagon with such military hardware as the F/A-18 Super Hornet fighter, the Apache attack helicopter, and the KC-46 aerial refueling tanker. The president himself flies on a Boeing 747 and is frequently called upon to close international sales worth billions of dollars. Barack Obama, who stood beside Lion Air's CEO in Bali when it signed a $22 billion order for MAX planes, once said he deserved a gold watch from Boeing.

When I visited Boeing's headquarters in Seattle for the first time as a Bloomberg News reporter in 1998, I was excited to meet the engineers who'd created these essential machines and the business leaders lionized in bestsellers like *Built to Last* and *In Search of Excellence*. What I found was a place at war with itself. The acquisition of McDonnell Douglas a year earlier had brought hordes of cutthroat managers, trained in the win-at-all-costs ways of defense contracting, into Boeing's more professorial ranks in the misty Puget Sound. A federal mediator who refereed a strike by Boeing engineers two years later described the merger privately as "hunter killer assassins" meeting Boy Scouts. At the time, with world-beating companies like General Electric in ascendance and the federal budget in surplus, it was hard to credit the engineers' dark fears about the future of the company they also so clearly loved. No workplace is perfect.

It's become sadly apparent that at Boeing—as at so many other places—the assassins won. Some of the very people who ran McDonnell Douglas into the ground resurrected the same penny-pinching policies that sank their old company. Borrowing a page from another flawed idol, Jack Welch's General Electric, they executed what today might be called the standard corporate playbook: anti-union, regulation-light, outsourcing-heavy. But pro-handout, at least when it comes to tax breaks and lucrative government contracts.

The Boeing that Muilenburg joined as a college intern a generation ago was created by driven engineers who wanted, as he did then, to design the world's best airplanes. They called themselves "the Incredibles." He rose through the ranks of a company that, instead, rewarded financial wizardry and aped GE's tactics—right up to the point where both became cautionary tales. Rather than investing in new aircraft, Boeing's leaders poured more than $30 billion of cash into stock buybacks during the MAX's development, enriching shareholders and ultimately themselves. Muilenburg made more than $100 million as CEO, and he left with an additional $60 million golden parachute.

What happened at Boeing reflects the same forces that have roiled corporate America since the Reagan revolution ushered in an era of imperial leaders like Welch, obsessively focused on stock market investors. The same year that Boeing bought McDonnell Douglas, the Business Roundtable, a lobbyist for the largest U.S. corporations, did away with any pretense that employees, customers, or communities also had important voices. The group declared that the first duty of any company was to shareholders; everything else would follow, as if by some natural law. In 1997, this new statement of purpose was uncontroversial enough that few newspapers even carried a story about it. It was the fulfillment of a long shift away from the communitarian ideals that had dominated American politics, economy, and culture from the New Deal of the 1930s to the Great Society of the 1960s. That consensus was just starting to fray when Milton Friedman, the Reaganites' favorite economist, argued what was then still the contrarian viewpoint in the *New York Times Magazine* in 1970: "The social responsibility of business is to increase its profits."

Fifty years later, communities are fragile, workers insecure, and families stressed. It isn't hard to see the connection to a half century's embrace of narrow corporate self-interest over collective responsibility. The federal government's mismanagement of the COVID-19 crisis was only the most visible sign of decay in American institutions—the effects are felt in virtually every aspect of life, from soaring health-care costs to skyrocketing inequality to wildfire smoke blanketing American cities for weeks on end because of escalating carbon emissions. All stem at least in part from the failed belief that corporations will police themselves and shower us in riches if they're just left alone to do so (and are lightly taxed all the while).

In just one example, the Agriculture Department in 2019 quietly cut the number of inspectors in pork plants by more than half. Finding defects—feces, sex organs, toenails, bladders—was mostly left to the companies themselves, much in the way that the FAA relied on Boeing's own employees to ensure aircraft safety. "If this continues across the nation, when you open your package of meat, what you're going to get for a pathogen is going to be a mystery," a longtime inspector said in December 2019. That same month, a pathogen of a different sort started sickening people at a market in Wuhan. Many other countries managed the crisis effectively, rapidly deploying widespread testing and contact tracing. The United States stumbled, with the Centers for Disease Control and Prevention botching a simple test that could have slowed the outbreak in its crucial early months. Just as the FAA had been eclipsed by regulators from other national and international bodies, the CDC was shown to be no longer the world's gold standard in public health. It's impossible to divorce these regulatory failings from the financial imperatives underlying them.

Under Dave Calhoun, the General Electric veteran who replaced Muilenburg as CEO in 2020, Boeing has said all the right things about returning to its engineering roots. The company's statement to shareholders that year mentioned the word *safety* 159 times. In this business, though, change comes slowly, and so do consequences. The deadly erosion of Boeing's safety culture began decades ago, and it was abetted by the creation of a conflict-ridden system that allowed the company to essentially certify its own products for safety. None other than Ted Cruz, the Republican senator from Texas who idolized Reagan as a boy, called the FAA a "captured agency."

A bipartisan aviation reform bill passed late in 2020 rolled back some of the tasks delegated to Boeing and provided for civil penalties for corporate managers who interfere with the FAA, among other measures meant to rebalance the power relationship. But some of those who are most knowledgeable about aircraft, including the very whistleblowers who tried to stop Boeing from pursuing a shoddy design, say that what's still missing is an insistence on bringing the 737's more than fifty-year-old airframe up to modern standards. In the absence of improvements, more people will find themselves waking up to the question Javier de Luis asked himself in March 2019, after learning that his sister, UN translator Graziella de Luis y Ponce, died in the crash in Ethiopia: "How unlucky do you have to be to die in an airplane accident?"

De Luis is an aeronautical engineer and the former chief scientist of a drone company in Cambridge, Massachusetts, that was eventually sold to Boeing itself. He's taught courses in aerospace systems design at the Massachusetts Institute of Technology. As he discovered when he dug into the data on the MAX, the answer to that question was: a lot less unlucky than he'd imagined. And a better one was: Why weren't government overseers doing more to slow the rush to put an obviously flawed plane back in the sky? The 737 remains the only large commercial aircraft without an electronic checklist to assist its pilots, who depend on heavy binders laden with step-by-step instructions to guide them in the event of an emergency. At the same time, Boeing has fitfully squeezed in software to guide some aspects of the plane, using two redundant computers with processing power that approximates a 1990s Nintendo gaming console. (Even the space shuttle, originally developed in the 1970s, had five separate computers.) That leaves passengers on the 737, in comparison to planes like the Airbus A320 or Boeing's own 787, more vulnerable to decisions made in the heat of the moment by confused pilots.

Accidents, thankfully, are still extremely rare; in 2018, there was a fatal crash once in every three million flights. But there were forty-one total accidents that year (including nonfatal ones), and eighteen of those involved the 737, more than the number for any other airplane, according to Boeing's own statistical summary. The Airbus A320 and its variants had four—even though the number of planes in service was similar for each model. That year, multiple Boeing

737s veered off runways. Others landed short of runways, or their tails struck the ground—all possible signs of pilots losing control of the airplane. In one of them, "during climb, control of the airplane was lost and it impacted the sea," as the Boeing summary of the Lion Air crash drily put it. Before its grounding, the MAX, in its limited service, had a fatal accident rate of one in every two hundred thousand flights—a frequency not seen since the early days of the jet age. By the count of a former Boeing executive who scoured incident reports for a congressional committee, one in twenty-five MAX planes experienced some sort of safety issue in the months after they were delivered. Despite that record, Boeing and U.S. aviation officials said the MAX was perfectly safe and let 157 people in Ethiopia file innocently into its cabin on a clear March day, just another routine flight.

How did a company that prided itself on its engineering prowess, that had perfectionism in its DNA, go so wildly off course? What were the forces, and who were the actors, that contributed to the fall of a seemingly insurmountable titan? Over a century in business, Boeing had become the biggest American exporter, with annual revenues surpassing $100 billion and a manufacturing line capable of shifting the country's balance of trade with a single sale. Boeing employed more than a hundred thousand people, and hundreds of thousands more at suppliers around the world owed their livelihoods to a company that literally connects the world. Its influence reached high in government, with Boeing veterans rising to powerful posts in the FAA, the Justice Department, the Defense Department, and multiple branches of the military. To the extent that ordinary people thought about Boeing, it was often with the same reverence accorded to elevators or light switches: the planes always seemed to work.

Given that defiance is at its core—the improbable belief that these machines weighing hundreds of tons should gracefully cross our skies without incident—it's little wonder that Boeing was born of grand ambitions. They first appeared in the mind's eye of a self-confident young timber baron who one Fourth of July took a fateful flight over the still-virgin forests of a raw new American city.

1

The Incredibles

Boeing occupies what feels like a city of its own to the south of Seattle. The company's footprint stretches more than a mile along East Marginal Way, the comically understated name for a street where so much of consequence has taken place for a century. Today there's a county airport known as Boeing Field; a museum that displays the original humpbacked 747; an aviation-focused high school funded in part by Boeing (instead of the ubiquitous 12 signs signaling support of the NFL's Seattle Seahawks, students there hang a $\sqrt{144}$); and block-long buildings where engineers and mechanics test and develop aircraft like the MAX. One massive building, in fact, *was* camouflaged as a town during World War II, when Boeing churned out bombers crucial to the war effort. Fake suburban streets were built atop the roof to confuse potential aerial attackers, complete with wooden houses and trees made from wires and chicken feathers.

War was actually the reason the American company would go on to dominate the jet age that brought international travel to the masses in the decades that followed. Days after Germany's surrender in May 1945, a Boeing engineer named George Schairer sent a letter from a forest near the town of Braunschweig. Schairer had joined a team of civilian advisers working with U.S. Army intelligence there to examine the research files of the Reichsmarschall Hermann Göring Aeronautical Research Institute. What he saw stunned him. The Germans, he realized, understood far more than anyone else about the potential of mating jet engines to swept-back wings. Most planes at the time still used propellers and perpendicular wings, jutting out from the fuselage at ninety-degree angles. Wind tunnel data that Schairer examined in the files showed a massive increase in speed and performance when wings were made to point slightly back, particularly when the engines hung beneath the wings in pods rather than being nested inside them, as had been the custom. The arrangement compensated for drag by making the wing itself more flexible in meeting wind resistance. Schairer sent seven cramped pages of mathematical formulas and sketches to a colleague in Seattle.

The timing was good; Boeing was then in the midst of a competition with three other manufacturers to build a jet-powered bomber for the U.S. Army Air Forces. The others soon got access to the same German data, but they all opted for fixed-wing designs, and Boeing won the contract for the B-47, whose mission was the rapid delivery of nuclear bombs to targets in the Soviet Union.

At $3 million apiece, the B-47 was the most expensive plane Boeing had ever built when it entered production in 1951. More importantly, the contract would give Boeing a crucial head start in technology that could serve as the basis of long-distance travel for generations to come—if the company chose to take such a gamble.

Boeing's president, William Allen, didn't have the appearance of a bold man of action. Before taking the top job in 1945, he'd been the company's chief lawyer and a board member for fifteen years. He never traveled without Triscuits and two pairs of eyeglasses. The night he became president, he jotted a series of resolutions into his diary. Among the promises he made to himself, in addition to daily sit-up exercises: "Be considerate of my associates' views"; "Don't talk too much, let others talk"; "Make a sincere effort to understand labor's viewpoint"; and "Develop a postwar future for Boeing."

Douglas Aircraft, in Long Beach, California, was then the acknowledged king of the skies. Since before the war, the propeller-driven DC-3 had been the backbone of commercial airline fleets, carrying as many as thirty-two people in graceful silvery skins that reflected the age's Art Deco aesthetic. The conditions inside were less graceful—bumpy, noisy, and, during storms, wet (the windows leaked). A cross-country flight took fifteen hours with three refueling stops. Douglas sold more than six hundred of them—trouncing a competing Boeing model eight to one—and during the war the United States ordered ten thousand copies of a military version. The California company had more of the same on its drawing boards—propeller-driven planes that were a bit larger, a bit faster, and a bit longer range.

Boeing was merely one among many airplane manufacturers in a business where gold-rush opportunity mingled with high risks. The youthful companies were controlled by dominant, strong-willed founders like Donald Douglas in Los Angeles, Glenn Martin in Baltimore, and James McDonnell in St. Louis.

Bill Boeing had been one, too. A wealthy timber heir who also owned a shipyard, he and a friend, a naval officer named Conrad Westervelt, got their first taste of flight at a 1914 Fourth of July fair on Seattle's Lake Washington. They took turns climbing into the open cockpit of a barnstormer's rickety seaplane, donning goggles to cruise a thousand feet over the hourglass of land between the lake and Elliott Bay. Afterward, Boeing, who'd studied engineering at Yale University, told Westervelt, also an engineer: "There isn't much to that machine. I think we could build a better one."

Boeing took flying lessons at Martin's school and bought his own Martin seaplane for $10,000. Flying it over Seattle, he tossed out missile-shaped leaflets urging military preparedness as the Great War raged in Europe. With help from a pontoon builder at his shipyard and others they hired, Boeing and Westervelt assembled the B&W Model 1, a seaplane made of spruce and Irish linen. Boeing took it out himself on June 15, 1916, taxiing to the center of Seattle's Lake Union and gunning the 125-horsepower engine. The plane skipped and threw spray before lifting into straight flight for a quarter mile. The navy transferred Westervelt back to the East Coast later that summer, but Boeing incorporated his Pacific Aero Products Company and converted part of his shipyard on the Duwamish River south of the city into its base of operations. In a wooden hangar—the famous "Red Barn" preserved in the museum near Boeing Field—some one hundred designers and carpenters worked on drafting tables and sawhorses to make an improved version of the Model 1.

The navy placed an order, the start of a rewarding relationship with the government that led to bombers and, finally, airmail contracts that were the industry's bread and butter in those days before passenger travel was widely accepted. By 1928, almost one-third of U.S. airmail was carried by Boeing Air Transport, and the following year Boeing merged all of his interests—by then including the engine maker Pratt & Whitney and the airline United Air Lines—into a single entity called the United Aircraft and Transport Corporation.

The vertically integrated juggernaut was not to be. Airmail contracts became an early target of President Franklin Roosevelt's new Democratic administration in 1933, and congressional investigators probed allegations of collusion in awarding them. Boeing himself was grilled for six hours by Senator Hugo Black of Alabama, later one of the longest-serving Supreme Court justices. In that miserable Depression year, with unemployment at 25 percent, Black made Boeing read out the profits from every sale of shares he'd made and the executive salaries at each subsidiary. The senator asked about former army and navy officers who'd gone on to work at the company, even insinuating that Boeing's friend Westervelt was responsible for its first navy contracts. His investigators dug up a copy of a Pratt & Whitney newsletter boasting of an employee who'd be serving as both a U.S. Marine Corps officer and a sales representative during a tour in U.S.-occupied Nicaragua. ("We all hope he has a good trip and everyone here has put in an order for a bandit's scalp," the item concluded cheerily.) "I do not know anything about it," Boeing said.

The next year, Congress passed a law barring airplane manufacturers from owning airlines and required a rebid of all existing contracts. Bill Boeing, at fifty-three, took early retirement and, in disgust, sold all of his shares in the newly separated companies. He spent his later years raising Hereford and Angus cattle on a five-hundred-acre farm, sailing on his yacht, *Taconite,* and smartly investing his tidy fortune as a silent partner in housing subdivisions around Seattle. (As was common at the time, his developments in such north-end neighborhoods as Blue Ridge and Richmond Beach attached racially restrictive covenants to the property deeds that barred nonwhite people from living there unless they were domestic servants.)

Now Boeing was former chief counsel William Allen's company. The safe bet would have been to milk the military business. It had roared back to life during the war, when Boeing was making more than a dozen B-17 Flying Fortress bombers in a single day, and fears of a descending Iron Curtain promised continuing military expenditures.

A commercial aircraft presented vastly greater challenges, for reasons still true today. Most obviously, there's no government contract putting a floor under revenue for passenger planes, promising a certain return if milestones are met. For a commercial plane, the capital to turn a blueprint into reality—the massive sums for machinery, tools, engineers, mechanics, pilots, flight testing, marketing, administration, regulatory affairs, customer service—all comes up front. After years of expense, the manufacturer has a single product, with no guarantee of sales. A plane maker's customers—commercial airlines—are often reluctant to commit until they see the finished item, so projects must be launched with a handful of buyers attached, in the hope that more will join later. Diligent market research only goes so far. It takes intuition, judgment, and ultimately, an iron gut.

British plane maker De Havilland thought it had the right combination. The maker of a celebrated World War II propeller-driven bomber called the Mosquito, De Havilland was already building the world's first commercial jetliner when Boeing was considering its own entry. Allen and his deputies took a close look at the British plane, called the Comet, during the 1950 Farnborough Air Show, just outside London. They concluded it wasn't ambitious enough, carrying just thirty-six passengers. The design Boeing would be implementing called for one hundred seats, which would allow it to generate more revenue—though some at Boeing argued the public would never stomach so many fatalities at once in the event of an accident.

Boeing had an advantage that its British competitor from a fading empire didn't: the financial support of the new colossus of the free world. Beyond commercial flight, the Boeing entry could be used by the U.S. Air Force as a jet-powered tanker. So in April 1952, Boeing's board agreed to invest $15 million—an amount four times greater than its total profits over the previous seven years—in a dual-purpose prototype. The marketing department already had the Boeing 707 in mind as a name; it sounded lucky. For the time being the model was known by a comparatively unmemorable moniker, the 367-80, Dash 80 for short.

Ten days after the board's approval, a Comet operated by the British flag carrier BOAC completed its first revenue flight from London to Johannesburg, with stops in Rome, Beirut, Khartoum, Entebbe, and Livingstone, in just under twenty-four hours—almost 50 percent faster than the typical forty-hour journey. This exciting new way of travel got a powerful endorsement from Britain's Queen Mother and her glamorous daughter, Princess Margaret, who flew in a "Royal Comet" to Rhodesia the following year.

The dazzlement soon faded. One of the elegant-looking planes ran off a runway in Rome, and two others crashed soon after take-off, killing fifty-four people. De Havilland had to redesign the leading edges of its wings (which hadn't benefited from German expertise: the engines were still embedded in them). Then, in 1954, two Comets went down at sea within three months of each other, causing another fifty-six deaths. After pieces of the aircraft were recovered, investigators determined they had simply broken apart. The designers hadn't accounted for the way metal expands and contracts with extreme temperature changes. Over repeated flights the skin had weakened, especially around the Comet's square windows, and the result was an explosive decompression. De Havilland made improvements, but commercial prospects for the Comet were finished. Jet travel was so compelling—effectively shrinking the world in half—and so much more comfortable than what came before it that people were willing to stomach some risk. But not if flying in jets looked like a death warrant. The stakes for Boeing had risen.

With years of B-47 flights behind them, its engineers had already chosen round windows and a thicker skin for its first jet-powered commercial aircraft. They welded pieces of titanium known as "tear stoppers" into the fuselage to prevent any tiny cracks from spreading.

The task of testing the new Dash 80 went to a onetime barnstormer from Kansas named Alvin "Tex" Johnston. He got his nickname in the 1940s when he showed up in cowboy boots for a job with Bell Aircraft in Niagara Falls, New York. It soon took him to the famous Muroc Army Air Base in California (now Edwards Air Force Base), where another pilot, Chuck Yeager, would fly the Bell X-1 past the sound barrier. In the fraternity of pilots, there is no shortage of ego. Tex wrote in his autobiography that he had a one-word answer when an attractive young female psychologist evaluating him for a job at Boeing asked what he liked better than anything in the world: "Copulation."

Johnston earned a place in company lore when, in 1955, at a time when skepticism of jets was still high, he executed a barrel roll of the Dash 80 over a crowd of three hundred thousand spectators—and a second one so that people who had missed the first one could see it. He hadn't told anyone of his plans before flying over the Gold Cup, a hydroplane race on Lake Washington that happened to coincide with a pair of industry conventions. Afterward, Allen asked what he thought he was doing. "Selling airplanes," Johnston replied. (As the pilot describes it in his autobiography, Allen gave him a mild dressing-down, then invited him for dinner with Eddie Rickenbacker, the World War I fighter ace who then ran Eastern Air Lines. Rickenbacker pulled Tex's Stetson over his ears and exclaimed, "You slow rollin' S.O.B.!")

Theatrics aside, what really sold the airplane was rigorous testing as well as design changes that Johnston pushed for later, at great expense to Boeing. Elaborate tests put the fuselage through thousands of depressurization cycles before it ever flew. The same year as the barrel roll, Boeing gave airline customers a film, *Operation Guillotine*, dramatically depicting the difference between its design and that of its ill-fated British competitor. The film showed giant steel blades penetrating the cabin of a pressurized test fuselage filled with seats, dummy passengers, and overhead bins. In the first test, of a fuselage similar to the infamous Comet's, the skin bursts and everything inside is blown out—even the floor. In the second, of the Boeing model equipped with tear stoppers, small puffs of air escape as the blade rips the skin, but nothing inside moves. A narrator explains that the occupants would be able to don oxygen masks while the captain safely lands the plane.

Pan American, Braniff, and even the U.K.'s BOAC, three of the foremost airlines of the age, ordered the 707, as Boeing now called its forthcoming Dash 80. But one evening in October 1959, Johnston was silently chewing his roast at home when his wife, DeLores, asked what was wrong. "Discussion time," he pronounced. Days earlier a 707 piloted by a Boeing instructor had plowed into a riverbank on a demonstration flight with a Braniff crew, killing four people. The crew had been practicing techniques to compensate for Dutch roll, an instability shared by all swept-wing jets that manifests as a kind of simultaneous bobbing and fishtailing. Survivors told Johnston it had been the instructor's mistake—he'd exceeded the maximum bank angle recommended in Boeing's manual. A copilot saw what was happening and strapped himself into a rear seat. But there had been earlier near-catastrophic incidents during training. Johnston believed the 707's design could still be improved.

He called for a meeting with the plane's lead engineers, among them Ed Wells (who also helped design the B-52 bomber). "It is obvious that training and establishing limits are not solving our problem," Johnston told them. He recommended a redesign of the tail and rudder. The tone in the room was unenthusiastic, even icy. What Johnston was proposing was no small fix; it would amount to a costly overhaul.

But Wells, as Johnston later described the scene, simply said, "We will fix it." In a Boeing-commissioned history, George Schairer, the engineer who had pored over Nazi jet research, said such a response was typical of Wells, for decades one of the company's most influential leaders. "When something goes wrong with an airplane, what should an engineer do? Send out public relations? The lawyers? Or the engineers?" Schairer said. "It's easy for the bean counters to call out the lawyers—and the lawyers will say, 'There was nothing wrong with our airplane—it was pilot error.' A manufacturer can go on for years this way. Wells wouldn't put up with that."

The test pilot went to London to brief BOAC, which had been spooked by news of the crash, and told airline officials the changes would eliminate the possibility of any more accidents of that type.

"Who pays?" the pilot was asked. Boeing, he answered.

Johnston, relieved to put the perilous issue behind him, summed up the decision in this way: "The one built-in marginal characteristic of the 707 would be corrected; the future of the airplane was assured."

The jet age had begun. In those days the leaders of airlines and the makers of aircraft saw themselves "as standing at the gates of El Dorado," as John Newhouse put it in his book *The Sporty Game,* a history of the jet age that became an industry bible for the way it glorified the men—they were all men—who took the bold gambles. Doing so was said to be "sporty," an insouciant thumbing of the nose at the deep risks of the trade. But if the costs were potentially ruinous, the rewards were great. Passenger travel was increasing 15 percent a year, much of it at the expense of trains and steamships. And in that era before deregulation took hold, airlines were either government owned or, essentially, regulated utilities; they could easily pass on the costs of equipment to passengers through higher ticket prices.

Ambitious young recruits began arriving in Seattle, transforming a rain-soaked hamlet into the epicenter of a glamorous new technology (much like the effect Amazon would have in more recent times). The Boeing workforce, which had been 50,000 in 1944, reached a staggering 142,400 at its peak in the 1960s, a decade whose *Jetsons*-flavored optimism was embodied in the Space Needle erected for the Seattle World's Fair. "We hire engineers and other people," went one saying around Boeing. It was an age when physical products, not software, defined economic success and national prestige. Boeing felt more like a scrappy startup than a hidebound bureaucracy. An early propulsion engineer, Granville Frazier, took the Dash 80's man-sized noise suppressor to a test hangar in the open trunk of his 1933 Plymouth coupe, a colleague standing on the rear bumper to balance it.

Boeing's designers worked at drafting tables clustered in groups of four, a swiveling telephone shared between them, in massive halls with bare concrete floors (until someone finally put down rugs). The manager sat at a low green desk. All reported to "functional fathers," experts of the various disciplines—such as structures, flight controls, and propulsion—who had wide authority over designs. They were encouraged to fight loudly for their views in the name of a better, safer airplane.

These headstrong men were epitomized by Joe Sutter, a legendary engineer who joined Boeing just after serving on a navy destroyer in World War II. The son of a Seattle meatpacker, he'd grown up watching Boeing test planes before pursuing an aeronautical engineering degree at the University of Washington. As aerodynamics chief of the 707—later a key contributor to the 737 and the chief designer of the 747—he went on expletive-laden rants that colleagues called "Sutter's runaways."

Another jet-age newcomer to Boeing was Peter Morton, a recent graduate of Rensselaer Polytechnic Institute in Troy, New York, who had read about Johnston's ostentatious barrel roll and followed Boeing's exploits in business magazines. Morton became an instructor in what Boeing called "the college of jet knowledge," with eleven courses on jet operations and maintenance. By 1963, the school had taught ten thousand students. Johnston required even Boeing's own test pilots to attend the courses (all except him), Morton recalls. At the time, Boeing put mechanics in the repair shops of its customer airlines, at airports around the world, to shadow them and ensure they maintained their new products correctly. Fast-paced as the industry was, "it was not the Wild West," said Morton (who, in 2020, was eighty-three and still sending memos, with increasing frustration, to Boeing's leaders after the MAX tragedies). He would go on to work as a salesman of the 737, a designer of flight controls on the 757, a manager of airline and executive training, and, finally, head of human resources for Boeing's commercial airplane business—making him what he calls Boeing's "Pug Henry," the Zelig-like character in a Herman Wouk novel who meets both Churchill and Hitler.

Back in California, Boeing's competition was kicking into gear, too. Douglas responded to the 707 with first its DC-8 and then its DC-9, which swiftly outpaced Boeing. The order came from Donald Douglas to "sell, sell, sell." His company gathered so many customers for the DC-8 that Boeing introduced the three-engine 727 to match it. By 1964, the DC-9, a twin-engine plane intended for short-range routes between midsized cities, had amassed two hundred orders.

Boeing had no competing aircraft. In the mind of its president, Allen, this was not necessarily a bad thing. The Douglas model was designed to take about eighty people around five hundred miles. The carriers who flew those routes were generally small and struggling—not exactly profitable customers. One internal study in 1965 estimated that Boeing could lose $150 million (equivalent to $1.25 billion in 2020) if its own competing entry into the market didn't sell. But some on Allen's board hated the idea of ceding *any* ground to Douglas. They argued it would be fine to build a loss leader—an entry-level model that small airlines could start with before moving up to bigger Boeing jets. It was the General Motors strategy: Sell young buyers a Chevrolet before they could afford a Cadillac. Reluctantly, Allen decided to design a new plane.

And so the 737 was born—quick and dirty. Most of Boeing's engineering resources were going into the massive 747, not to mention the hugely ambitious project for a supersonic transport. The company's first successful sales meeting, with Germany's Lufthansa in 1965, didn't have an auspicious start. Boeing had shipped to Cologne a hardwood box with massive hinges and a Yale lock, containing charts and diagrams about the plane's performance, for the airline's board to examine. It had neglected to include a key. The airline's chief executive had to pry the box open with a hammer and a screwdriver.

Two years behind the DC-9 in the race to put out a competing twin-engine plane, Boeing designed everything in the 737 for simplicity. The need to keep expenses down forced compromises, decisions that would one day hamstring Boeing's attempts to shoehorn in more sophisticated technology. But as airlines became increasingly cost-conscious, the lack of expensive frills was a big reason why the red-headed stepchild of Boeing's product line became its bestseller. "It's like a shitty pickup," said Gordon Bethune, a former Boeing executive who also ran Continental Airlines. "It's reliable and dependable and it may not be the most exotic thing but boy, it's what you want to be in if the weather gets rough."

For all their haste, managers stayed open to experimentation and change. Boeing pitted two engineering teams against each other to help hone the 737's design, and it was the "B" team led by the famously direct Joe Sutter that came up with the winning concept. The baseline proposal had engines mounted aft, just like the Douglas plane. Pondering a line drawing at his desk one day, Sutter pulled out a pair of scissors, sliced the engines off the back, and tucked them under the wings instead. It would allow him to squeeze in six extra seats, potentially a huge swing in revenue and profitability for a small airline.

The 737 was still more ungainly looking than anything Boeing had yet built in the jet age; Sutter's boss called it "the flying football." Compared to most commercial jets today, it had strangely square proportions, about as long as it was wide with a generously rounded fuselage—more like a squishable children's toy in an airport gift shop than the long, sleek machines that would succeed it.

Cockpits at the time were transitioning from three crew members to two, so Boeing devised simple controls that could easily be handled by one pilot if the other was incapacitated. Two handles on the floor were connected by pulleys to the landing gear. Either pilot could pull one and the gear would drop by gravity. In its mechanical simplicity, it was a feature not unlike cranking down the window in an old car. The manual trim wheel was another sturdy mechanical feature. Pilots had switches on their control column to keep the plane in what's known as trim, the condition in which air is flowing smoothly over the wing. But the manual wheel sat between the pilots as a backup and could be turned by hand to move the stabilizer. It mirrored the Cessna 172, the high-wing four-seater first flown in 1955 that was, and still is, a common trainer for young pilots.

Since the 737 was likely to be used by smaller airlines in more rudimentary airports, it was low to the ground, allowing baggage handlers to easily toss in bags without a conveyor belt. Passengers boarded on a short metal stairway that folded out from under the front door. To hold down costs, Boeing reused 60 percent of the parts from the 727. There were also fewer of them. The 727 had a complicated system of hydraulics and valve sequencing to open and close the landing gear doors. The 737 did away with those doors entirely. When it flew overhead, the retracted gears were plainly visible from the ground, a rarity for a big commercial jet.

As it had on the 707, when Boeing encountered issues, it corrected them. For instance, the thrust reverser's lack of stopping power bothered test pilot Brien Wygle during flight testing in 1967. (The reverser is what makes the "whooshing" noise heard during landing, as it sends engine exhaust in the opposite direction to slow the plane down.) Boeing had borrowed the reverser from the 727, and it wasn't particularly effective on the new jet; tucked under the wing, it actually lifted the tires and kept them from biting on landing. Wygle persuaded the program's manager to address the issue with a redesign costing $22 million (about $200 million today).

"I said, 'I know it's a big chunk to swallow, but the airplane's going to be around a while and I really think we ought to do it,'" Wygle recalled—to which his manager replied, "Well, if that's what you think, we'll do it."

With their matter-of-fact earnestness, it was a scene hard to imagine at a latter-day Boeing, for several reasons: the wide latitude afforded the pilot's authority; the lack of bureaucracy; and the willingness to break budgets.

Boeing debuted the 737 in January 1967, with stewardesses in miniskirts from no-frills PSA, Pacific Southwest Airlines, lined up along the wing. The San Diego–based carrier's business model helped inspire a Texas lawyer named Herb Kelleher to start Southwest Airlines at Love Field in Dallas that same year. Competing on short-hop flights within California and Texas, the airlines were beyond the reach of the all-powerful federal Civil Aeronautics Board that determined interstate fares and routes.

Months later, in California, Douglas landed in a cash crunch. It had intended to bury the upstart Boeing, drumming up a flurry of orders in response to its CEO's demand for ever more commitments from airlines. Instead Douglas choked on them. As the investment banking firm Lazard Frères explained in a report that year, Douglas suffered from "an overly sales-oriented operating management in the Aircraft Division which appears to be functioning with little coordination with corporate staff." With a backlog of orders, but without the funds to produce the necessary planes, Douglas was left with no choice but to sell to rival McDonnell Aircraft of St. Louis.

Spending freely was one mistake that James McDonnell, the imperious "Mr. Mac" who ruled the combined McDonnell Douglas Corporation, would not make. Then already sixty-eight, he kept a tight rein on expenses until his death at eighty-one in 1980. His company had an especially good relationship with the U.S. Air Force, making fighters from the F-4C Phantom to the F-15 Eagle. He preferred the more predictable returns of military programs, frequently scaling back investments in commercial jets. A self-proclaimed "practicing Scotsman," Mr. Mac once handed out egg timers to remind his executives to rein in their long-distance calls.

Undeterred, Boeing doubled down on the risk it had taken with the 707, betting even more money—ultimately the entire net worth of the company—on its massive 747. The gamble almost bankrupted Boeing before it was proven to be sound. The plane would become one of the most iconic in history. Three times bigger than anything in the sky, it required the coinage of a new term—"jumbo jet." It was the first commercial aircraft with twin aisles for seating, and even had a second deck in its distinctive hump. But what really drew early customers like Pan Am was the aircraft's range: at almost eight thousand miles, it brought transatlantic travel to the masses. Boeing president William Allen, still at the helm more than twenty years after his promotion, committed to the plane even as one of his directors, the DuPont chairman Crawford Greenewalt, tried to convince him to slow down. "You know, Bill, it took DuPont several years to decide whether to go into nylon," Greenewalt told him at a cocktail party just before the board met to approve the plane. When the director started probing the projected investment returns at the meeting, a senior manager replied that they'd run some studies but forgot the results. "My God, these guys don't even know what the return on investment will be in this thing," Greenewalt muttered.

Led by engineer Joe Sutter, the 747's designers pioneered fault-tree analysis—decision trees showing them how and when various systems might fail. The crushing pressure of meeting deadlines while building a plane with hundreds of thousands of parts brought the inevitable conflict with budget planners. Hal Haynes, the usually unflappable man who was then chief finance officer, said after a meeting one day in 1967, "Sutter, do you realize that your engineers are spending five million dollars a day?" Haynes left without waiting for an answer, but the engineer later recalled thinking, "We'd be doing a better job, and maybe saving Boeing some money in the long run, if we were spending six million dollars a day!"

Not long after, word came that he'd have to drop one thousand of his twenty-seven hundred engineers. In the meeting where he was supposed to lay out plans for doing so, Sutter carefully tallied up the work left to be done and asked for eight hundred *more* instead. Icy stares. "Hell, Sutter, you know you're not going to get any more engineers," declared Thornton Arnold Wilson, who was being groomed as Boeing president Allen's successor. Allen said he had a plane to catch, and the others followed him out without saying a word. The only person left was Sutter's manager, who had several choice words for his insubordination. Sutter figured he'd be replaced. But weeks went by, and word came back that Wilson had told people he was doing a good job.

They built and tested the first 747s in just sixteen months—right on through the moon landing. Boeing pilots and engineers at Paine Field in Everett, Washington, heard that the *Eagle* had landed on July 20, 1969, a Sunday, over the public address system as they prepared for an evening test flight. The team was in the air when the pilot came over the intercom to say that Armstrong was walking on the moon. In the same compressed time frame as the engineering work, thousands of machinists built a giant new Everett factory—the largest building by volume in the world—to assemble the plane. It's so big that clouds sometimes form in its upper rafters. The team called themselves "the Incredibles." The fact that the building remained in the misty Northwest was in part thanks to Sutter, who fought off a proposal to erect the plant in Walnut Creek, California, which might have added powerful political backers in a more populous state. "I told 'em point blank I thought it would be an unmitigated disaster," Sutter later wrote—coordination would suffer, costs would rise, logistical challenges would increase, and schedules wouldn't be met.

The profligate spending proved to be ill timed, coming just as government funding for the supersonic transport also ran out. Boeing's downturn was so deep that in 1969 it found itself two months from running short of cash. Wilson, by then having inherited the mantle of chief executive, laid off eighty-six thousand people and, at age forty-nine, suffered a heart attack. Fred Mitchell, a young Boeing worker then, remembers seeing desks stacked thirty feet high on the factory floor and swivel chairs piled unceremoniously in a corner. "Guys were walking through saying, 'Anybody want a house? Anybody want a car?' I know two or three guys, that's how they got their houses on Lake Washington, they just took over the payments," he said. In 1971, two real estate agents famously put up a highway billboard that read WILL THE LAST PERSON LEAVING SEATTLE—TURN OFF THE LIGHTS.

Early sales of the 737 weren't helping matters. The outlook was so bad, in fact, that Boeing offered to sell the entire production line to Mitsubishi; the Japanese company refused. "We were broke," a Boeing manager later summed it up. To eke out sales, engineers put a gravel-deflecting skid on the underbelly so that it could land on unpaved airstrips in places like western Alaska and Peru—not exactly the coveted markets Boeing might once have dreamed of for its new model. In 1972, just fourteen of the planes were sold. The next year, Boeing considered canceling the program altogether.

But the baby Boeing would have its day. While Boeing was preoccupied with other planes it considered more important, the 737 would lead one of the most remarkable product comebacks in aviation history.

2

Mea Culpa

The first crash of one of the new fully loaded wide-body planes was an international scandal, provoking newspaper coverage of shocking design lapses, televised congressional hearings, and even a full-length book exposé. Soon after the plane's takeoff from Paris Orly Airport in March 1974, an explosion blew out the cargo door, buckling the floor and severing hydraulic lines. All 346 people aboard died when the plane plunged into Ermenonville forest outside Paris, the worst airliner crash in history at the time. Debris was scattered for a half mile through wooded trails popular with Sunday hikers.

The plane was a DC-10, a slightly smaller wide-body McDonnell Douglas had developed to keep up with Boeing's 747. The engineers on the Douglas side in Southern California had struggled mightily for the needed investments, Mr. Mac holding the purse strings as tightly as ever. To save valuable interior cargo space, they broke with industry convention by designing a door that opened outward. At a stockholders' meeting a month after the crash, a McDonnell Douglas executive blamed an "illiterate" baggage handler at Turkish Airlines (who spoke three languages) for failing to latch the cargo door properly.

It emerged that Douglas engineers had known the design was vulnerable to a catastrophic failure, and indeed, two years earlier, a near disaster had ensued on a flight over Windsor, Ontario, which also lost a cargo door. The pilot had been able to land the plane in that case. Instead of fixing the issue immediately, McDonnell Douglas had convinced the FAA to let it add a support plate over time to the doors—a "gentlemen's agreement" revealed in the congressional hearings. Records at Douglas showed that the support plate had been added to the Turkish Airlines plane, when it had not. Three company inspectors had signed off on the nonexistent fix. "It was high summer," one inspector said, in trying to explain the discrepancy. "The Paris crash" became shorthand for scandal— "oh, the one where the door came off," as the journalist Moira Johnston put it in her 1976 book about the tragedy. "The press, too," she wrote, "had made the sprawling Long Beach plant that bustled with short-sleeved engineers seem a sinister fortress."

May 1979 brought another disaster. A DC-10 operated by American Airlines crashed in Chicago, killing 273, when the left engine and pylon simply fell off the wing on takeoff. A federal judge, acting in response to a consumer group's complaint that the FAA had taken "wholly inadequate" precautionary measures, ordered a grounding of the entire fleet—the first for a U.S. airliner since 1946. The FAA complied. (McDonnell Douglas, for its part, called the action "extreme and unwarranted.") The primary cause turned out to be an improper airline maintenance procedure. Still, the earlier crashes had damaged the plane's reputation, and sales lagged. McDonnell Douglas had to run ads with astronaut Pete Conrad to vouch for it: "The more you learn about our DC-10, the more you know how great it really is," one said. Deliveries fell to a fourth of their previous peak and production ended ten years later.

Under Wilson, Boeing kept up the pressure on its competitor by simultaneously adding two more planes to its line, spending $3 billion on the 757 and 767. Phil Condit, who would be a consequential figure in Boeing's later history, was chief engineer of the 757; the ubiquitous Peter Morton helped design the flight deck.

The plane was the first to use a kind of electronic checklist that sharply reduced pilots' workloads. It had computer displays known as EICAS, for "engine indicating and crew alerting system." Older planes—like the 737—showed the status of the plane's various mechanical systems with translucent buttons that had a comparatively primitive "yes/no" logic. When a button marked, say, LOW OIL PRESSURE, blinked on, it was the pilot's cue to turn to the handbook or a memorized procedure. The EICAS, by contrast, showed the fuel level, oil temperature, and other important indicators in real time. If a fault was detected, a message popped up giving pilots more detail about how to handle it. The system prioritized the alerts by color—red for emergencies, amber for cautions.

Over lunch at the Jolly Boy diner near Seattle, Morton and Condit mused about whether they could design the 757 so that its pilots could move up to flying the larger 767 without extensive additional training. If so, it would represent huge cost savings for airlines.

It became a question to explore, not a command. During the following months, Boeing's engineers worked out how to make the two cockpits appear exactly similar to pilots, despite myriad differences in their internal systems. (It's the reason the 757 has a broad snout: right up to the shoulders of the pilot, the smaller plane's cockpit is almost identical to that of its wide-bodied sibling, the 767.) At one point, the design team went so far as to bring in a psychologist to survey pilots about a slight difference between the control wheels of the two planes; the wheel on the 757 can turn about one-third farther in each direction.

"We were looking for somebody to say, 'Hey, this looks wrong,'" Morton said. "Nobody did."

Joe Sutter asked him to give a tour of the new plane at the 1982 Farnborough Air Show near London to the president of Airbus Industrie, then a loose collection of European aircraft makers that had only recently entered the commercial-jet market. The 757 was painted a sleek silver, with red, white, and blue stripes running down the fuselage and an American flag next to the italicized Boeing logo. Bernard Lathiere, the Airbus president, marveled at the computer displays in the cockpit and later sent Morton a poster of the competing A310, scrawling a note on it in French to "mon cher" Peter. The note said, "Votre EICAS est un beau jouet. Mais le financement de l'A310 est superbe!"—your EICAS is a nice plaything but the Airbus financing is superb. At unstoppable Boeing they had the luxury to laugh.

CEO Thornton Arnold Wilson went by "T.," and he could be as short as his name. "I know who the hell you are," he once snapped to a young executive meeting him for the first time. During a party to celebrate the renovation of the Red Barn, he said he'd prefer it had been dumped into the Duwamish River.

But if he was gruff and unsentimental, he also had high standards and the esprit de corps common to the postwar generation. Soon after joining Boeing from Iowa State University in 1943, he became one of the first officers in a union called the Seattle Professional Engineering Employees Association. The group, known as Speea, saw itself as more of a professional association than a traditional labor union; its first priority was eliminating a collusionary practice under which rival aerospace companies gave notice before hiring each other's employees. Long after he'd risen to become CEO, Wilson kept up a regular bridge game with his old Speea friends.

The Boeing chief was well paid, one of a dozen industrial executives in the country who earned more than $1 million in 1978. (Adjusted for inflation, his pay was equivalent to $5 million in 2019—less than a quarter of the *average* CEO compensation of $21.3 million that year.) But Wilson had little use for the trappings of corporate leadership, driving himself to work in a Chevrolet Camaro and living in the same house in a nondescript Seattle suburb that he and his wife had bought thirty years earlier. He kept bees and did crossword puzzles. Boeing had just a single small corporate jet and encouraged all but a handful of top executives to fly commercial to support its customers. A *New York Times* profile in September 1985 said Wilson was "putting Boeing in a class by itself."

Remarkably, the praise came only a month after the crash of a 747 in Japan that killed 520 people and became the deadliest single-aircraft accident ever, surpassing the grim record set by the DC-10 a decade earlier. A half hour into a short domestic flight, the plane's vertical fin had ruptured, and it plowed into a mountain ridge. Speculation began swirling that the skins of the giant planes were vulnerable to fatigue, the dreaded issue that had ruined the reputation of De Havilland's Comet thirty years earlier.

Wilson at the time was handing authority over the company to a genial lawyer from Boise, Idaho, Frank Shrontz, who became president in 1985 and succeeded him as CEO the following year. The Seattle plane maker surprised crash investigators when it issued a mea culpa just weeks after the crash. A statement said one of its repair teams had incorrectly installed a splice plate on the jet's rear bulkhead after a hard landing that damaged the tail section years earlier. Japanese officials, just settling in for a long examination and tough negotiations, were stunned at the company's transparency.

In a single stroke, Boeing had swiftly curtailed a drawn-out legal fight—and ended any doubts about the company's integrity.

That same year, another Iowa State aerospace engineering major got into a muscle car (a 1982 Monte Carlo, in his case) and drove cross-country to start work as a Boeing intern: Dennis Muilenburg. Raised on a farm outside Orange City in the Dutch-inflected northwest corner of the state, he had one goal, as he later told people: "To be the world's best airplane designer."

Boeing at the time had a towering reputation for customer service, a share of the jetliner market that surpassed 70 percent, and a stock that had been the Dow's best performing for a decade. "The Seattle Airplane Company was probably the most honest, reputable, best company you would ever work for," said Gordon Bethune, who was a customer training executive and division chief at Boeing from 1988 to 1994 before leaving for Continental. Soon after he joined the airline, it placed an order for a number of 767 jets at a price Boeing promised would be the lowest for any customer. The board was skeptical there would be any way of enforcing such a deal. Then one day, Continental got a $275,000 check from Boeing because, it said, Ethiopian Airlines had bought a 767 at a lower price.

Despite its hard-won reputation for prioritizing quality over cost, a more fiscally conservative approach began to shade Boeing's thinking. There also crept in an inevitable hubris, that of a company enjoying the fruits of what it had achieved.

Airbus, with huge subsidies from Germany and France, had been slowly making inroads into the commercial market then dominated by Boeing, McDonnell Douglas, and Lockheed. The European consortium approached the market with messianic intent. "We are fighting for our children," then Airbus chief Bernard Lathiere said in 1975. "If we don't have a place in high technology in Europe, we should be slaves to the Americans and our children will be slaves. We have to sell . . . we must fight and fight." Airbus clinched its first U.S. order in 1978, when Florida-based Eastern Airlines bought twenty-three twin-engine A300s. It was, as the *New York Times* declared, "the biggest foreign penetration ever made in the American market for airliners."

Eastern chief Frank Borman, the astronaut who'd commanded the Apollo 8 moon mission, told a reporter the value was equal to "less than four and a half days of imports of Japanese cars." (When a McDonnell Douglas executive called Borman to complain, the ex-astronaut asked him what kind of car he drove.)

Among those who didn't buy Borman's assurances was C. Fred Bergsten, then a U.S. Treasury assistant secretary. He convinced his boss, Treasury secretary Mike Blumenthal, to impose duties on the Airbus plane because of the financial help it had gotten from European governments: no-interest loans that didn't need to be repaid if the plane sold badly. Borman, he recalls, immediately "went to the White House and bled all over them"—telling Vice President Walter Mondale that his airline would have to cut jobs if it couldn't buy the planes. Foreign policy considerations also argued against a trade fight with European allies in the midst of the Cold War. Carter let Airbus in.

That same year, his administration pushed for passage of the Airline Deregulation Act, eliminating the government agency that had, since 1938, been responsible for setting minimum airfares. Prices at the time were soaring, and the Civil Aeronautics Board was painted as the culprit, a corrupt agency doing the airlines' bidding to keep fares inflated. The new legislation meant that the country's airlines would be run like the post office no more. Now they would be subject to the forces of the free market.

It took years for the effects shake out, with early experiments like Laker Airways fizzling, fabled names like Braniff and Pan Am disappearing, and the now-familiar Big Three—American, United, and Delta—finally consolidating their control. They did it with a strategy few anticipated at the time, funneling traffic from smaller cities into big hubs like Chicago and Atlanta, and from there directing fliers on to their final destinations. This would require many more small jets making frequent flights.

None of that was clear in the late 1970s, when Boeing went ahead with the larger 757s and 767s. The 737, again, was an afterthought, a model hotly desired by a single tiny airline in Texas, Herb Kelleher's Southwest. Boeing had produced two versions of the earliest 737s, the 737-100 and 737-200. For Southwest, it developed an updated model called the 737-300, featuring larger, more fuel-efficient engines. To fit them under the low-slung wing, Boeing moved the engines forward and rounded them off at the bottom. It gave them a unique flat-tire look. Internal forecasts at the time figured Boeing would sell three hundred of the new planes. Southwest kicked off the line with a modest order of ten.

United had been reducing its fleet of 737s, but as the hub-and-spoke strategy took hold, the airline unexpectedly bought back some of those it had sold and ordered large quantities of the new 128-seat 737-300. Other carriers followed. A valuable new market segment was forming, seemingly in spite of Boeing's decisions across the previous decade and a half.

It would be Airbus that rushed in with an altogether new product. The first of many times Boeing would underestimate its European competitor came in 1984, when Airbus began selling the 150-seat A320. Earlier Airbus models, like those sold to astronaut Frank

Borman's Eastern Airlines, had required generous discounts, or leases that made them practically free.

The A320, by contrast, was its first direct competitor to the 737. The plane had sophisticated technology known as fly-by-wire, borrowed from French Rafale fighter jets. Pilots controlled the aircraft with small joysticks at their side, connected to control surfaces through wires instead of the heavier network of cables and pulleys used by its competitors. This saved precious weight, as well as space in the cockpit—pilots in Airbus jets got a handy clipboard in front of them instead of the traditional yokes between the legs of Boeing fliers. (It was also a great place to eat their lunch.) The weight savings allowed the Airbus planes to be seven and a half inches wider than the 737, a difference that passengers would notice. Seats were up to an inch wider, and it was easier to squeeze past the flight attendants' cart in the aisle.

Most importantly, the flight control software included features meant to prevent pilots from climbing or diving too steeply, banking too hard, or otherwise stressing the aircraft. Though controversial with some pilots, who claimed the technology eroded their ability to "feel" what the plane was doing, automation led to a marked decline in accidents. By 2019, Airbus estimated the ten-year moving average of hull-loss accidents for so-called "fourth generation" fly-by-wire aircraft (also including later Boeing planes like the 777 and 787) was one for every twenty-five million flights. The rate for third-generation planes like the 737 was five times higher, about one in every five million.

Rudy Hillinga, a European salesman for Boeing at the time, sent telexes back to Seattle warning that Lufthansa, the airline that had partnered with Boeing on the 737's launch eighteen years earlier, was warming to the A320. At the time, most people at Boeing still considered the DC-9 and its successor at the merged McDonnell Douglas, the MD-80, the main rivals to the 737. They were slow to grasp the sweeping changes that deregulation had brought to the market. Airlines now needed smaller planes that could make frequent, short hops, and cheaply. "The 757 would sell beautifully if it had 150 seats," a Lufthansa executive said of the 220-seat plane while it was under development.

The legendary Joe Sutter, nearing retirement as Boeing's executive vice president of product development, viewed the latest plane from Europe as a quirky science experiment. "Sutter had a hate relationship with Airbus," one former Boeing executive said. "He just didn't think they could build a good airplane." Others at Boeing had no appetite for ripping up their product strategy to replace the baby of its lineup with yet another new plane. Phil Condit, who'd risen to sales and marketing roles, talked about leapfrogging the A320 with futuristic "prop-fan" planes (with engine blades whirling in the open like a submarine's rotors) that never came to fruition.

Sutter, by then the industry's éminence grise, visited the White House twice, in 1985 and in 1986. On the first occasion it was to accept the U.S. National Medal of Technology from President Ronald Reagan, who leaned in and spoke softly into the engineer's ear as he handed over the medal. (Asked later what was said, Sutter had to tell people Reagan had explained where to find the footmarks on the floor to pose for photographs.) The next year, he was named to the White House commission investigating the *Challenger* space shuttle disaster, alongside Neil Armstrong, Sally Ride, and other aerospace luminaries. NASA's organizational structure, Sutter discovered, was a mess, with competing fiefdoms, tangled reporting lines—and no top-level leader focused solely on safety. It would never happen at Boeing, Sutter declared.

Airbus, meanwhile, became the genuine threat to Boeing that some had feared. Lufthansa bought fifteen of the new A320s for $1 billion in 1985, and a year later Northwest Airlines placed a massive order for as many as one hundred, opening the door to sustained success for the European plane maker. Boeing eventually introduced larger 737s known as the 737-400 and 737-500, but it was too late to blunt the impact from Airbus. "In the aviation industry, you make these [new airplane] decisions every ten years, give or take a few," the analyst Wolfgang Demisch of First Boston said. "You then have to live with the consequences for the next fifty."

The revamped 737s still easily outpaced the Airbus plane at first. In spring 1988, Peter Morton, in oversized gold-rimmed aviators and a boxy suit, proudly called the 737 the "unsung prodigy of the Boeing family" during a gathering of test pilots and employees at the Museum of Flight in Seattle. The runt of Boeing's fleet had become the airline workhorse, with 137 operators around the world. By the end of 1991, the Classic models—the 737-300, 737-400, and 737-500—accounted for two-thirds of the almost three thousand 737s sold to that point. In spite of its rushed conception, the sturdy Chevy had proven to be the most indispensable product in the Boeing lineup.

But two crashes of the early 737s, a 737-200 in Colorado Springs in 1991 and a 737-300 near Pittsburgh in 1994, exposed the shortcomings of the more conservative strategy. After the longest investigation in the history of the National Transportation Safety Board, the authority finally assigned blame. The crashes had been the result of a faulty rudder design. One of Boeing's many compromises in its hasty design of the 737 had been the use of a single-paneled rudder. It lacked a device called a limiter, which made the plane more vulnerable to what's known as a hardover, an uncommanded deflection that appeared to happen only in extremely rare circumstances, such as when microscopic bits of grit got stuck in a valve.

The tragedies were the first evidence that the 737, coaxed into new iterations across the decades, was being stretched beyond its own limits. As Bernard Loeb, the NTSB's aviation safety director, put it when the agency released its report in 1999: "We believe the airplane is trying to tell us something."

3

"Jack Welch, Look Out"

If T. Wilson was the crusty Cold Warrior who defined Boeing's world-beating golden age, Phil Condit was the man from the Age of Aquarius who set the tone for its muddled era of risky acquisitions, New Age management-speak, and lavish bonuses that followed. He was an only child born on the cusp of the baby boom in Berkeley, California. His father was a research scientist at Chevron, his mother a photographer who traveled to exotic places taking photos that would one day decorate the walls of her son's homes and offices. Young Phil was a tinkerer. He took apart clocks, got absorbed in the latest mechanical inventions, and was regarded as technically brilliant by professors at Berkeley, Princeton, and the Tokyo University of Science, where he became the first westerner to earn a PhD in engineering. After joining Boeing in 1965, he would add a master's degree in management from the Sloan School at the Massachusetts Institute of Technology.

Condit stood out almost immediately. Working under mentors like Joe Sutter at age twenty-nine, he helped calculate the wake turbulence behind the 747, establishing rules on takeoff spacing still in use today. Rising to lead the 757 program, Condit impressed superiors with his ability to capably handle the complex trade-offs that might force designers to, say, lose three seats in order to make room for the overwing exit door. He tended to spot the elegant solutions that satisfied customers and regulators alike. As a manager, he inspired colleagues with a style that was less autocratic than that of the silent-generation types who preceded him. "No one of us is smarter than all of us," Condit would tell people. Burly and jug-eared, he often joked that the appendages made him a better listener. He wore chunky sweaters. One analyst described him as a cross between a teddy bear and a grizzly bear—"good on people skills, but furious in the marketplace."

Like his predecessors, Condit, who became president in 1992 and CEO in 1996, worked from a stolid building on East Marginal Way across from Boeing Field. The wood-paneled executive offices had the feel of a well-crafted yacht—or an episode of *Mad Men*. ("There are a lot of big swinging dicks around here," as one public relations official said to me in 1998.) Condit had just been divorced for a third time and would soon embark on his fourth marriage, to a former Boeing engineer. Another of Condit's spouses had been an executive secretary; among the possessions divided under the terms of their divorce were their 757-program commemorative glasses. A relationship with a customer relations manager in the early 1990s led to a settlement, kept quiet for years, after she was laid off. Condit's third wife was his first cousin, Jan. Marriages of such close kin were prohibited in Washington State, and they'd wed in northern California, where Condit sang, "Can I Have This Dance for the Rest of My Life?" Granville Frazier, the engineer who had once hauled a part in the trunk of his 1933 Plymouth (and who was then still married to Condit's *next* wife), was a groomsman.

None of these intra-office relationships slowed Condit's ascent. Boeing didn't have its first female director, the diplomat Rozanne Ridgway, until 1992, and women were a decided minority in the male-dominated ranks of engineers and machinists. In the 1970s, women made up less than 3 percent of the engineers, and that had increased to only 15 percent by April 2015. A lawsuit over unequal pay and hiring opportunities led to a settlement of a class-action discrimination lawsuit covering twenty-nine thousand female employees in 2004. But if there were whispers about Condit's personal life, many people at Boeing were too polite to linger on them. With his fleshy features and oversized wire-rimmed eyeglasses, it was easier to believe in a homely decency about him. On the Myers-Briggs psychology tests, Condit once said, he was an "INFP." In the lexicon of the commonly used personality assessments, this is an introverted and intuitive type whose shorthand is "the mediator"— not the commanding personality commonly associated with chief executives.

Early in his tenure he started rotating senior managers through a weeklong training course. The highlight was always Tuesday evening, when they would pile into buses and head to Condit's house outside Seattle, a Northwest-style lodge he and Jan had built on sixty wooded acres. A miniature train of Condit's own design chugged from room to room delivering drinks as the group listened to a British-born poet, David Whyte, tell stories about courage and integrity. Whyte had written a bestselling book called *The Heart Aroused: Poetry and the Preservation of the Soul in Corporate America,* and his remarks often highlighted the difference between "true power" and "fake power." Condit would close the evening by asking everyone to share their own stories about Boeing, both good and bad. Then he had them jot down the bad memories on slips of paper and throw them into the fireplace.

Condit had taken the helm at Boeing when its markets were in the midst of wrenching change, the end of the Cold War throwing defense budgets into turmoil while creating new sales opportunities in previously closed economies. Deregulation brought more travel but also cheaper fares, challenging aircraft manufacturers to become efficient volume producers. And it wasn't just in the United States; the European Union began liberalizing fares and routes in 1997, and even China allowed the establishment of multiple competing airlines.

Alongside the newly cutthroat airlines, it was getting harder for Boeing to escape the fact that Airbus was a real threat. A mid-1990s internal analysis came to the unthinkable conclusion that Airbus, a consortium of European manufacturers it had always derided as a glorified jobs program, actually had a cost advantage over Boeing. Its factories produced planes 12 percent to 15 percent cheaper than Boeing's, the study reported. Ironically, this was in part because of rigid labor laws in Europe, which made layoffs more expensive and, in places like Germany, forced the involvement of labor unions in management decisions. As a consequence, Airbus was quicker to adopt automated machinery, but also more likely to train and develop its workers rather than to fire them. Condit and his predecessor as CEO, Frank Shrontz, looked to Japan for answers, sending executives to study the lean manufacturing techniques of companies like Toyota and Hitachi. These managers came back to Boeing and implemented ideas they'd learned about there, involving workers in commonsense solutions like creating cutouts for tools at every workbench so it was easy to see if one was missing.

For employees like Stan Sorscher, who'd been a Boeing physicist since 1980, it was a moment to savor. Suddenly the command-and-control types of the postwar generation who had long ruled Boeing were out of favor. ("I *hate* this new culture," one dissenting manager told him. "I don't want to be anybody's facilitator, I want to come to work and kick some ass.") Sorscher worked on projects like X-ray machines to spot tiny cracks in components—things that had short-term costs but ended up saving money. Some managers resented him for ruining parts that seemed perfectly good; "you create scrap," they sneered. But more of them listened, asking him to explain his thinking and offer multiple alternatives. "It was a great problem-solving culture," he said. "You really have to know what you're talking about to lead that discussion."

The high point of the collective approach was the 777, still considered one of the most successful jetliners ever made. At the time Boeing proposed the plane in 1990, Airbus and McDonnell Douglas were both further along on similar-sized models, intended to eat into the 747's market for intercontinental flights. The A340 was to have four engines and the MD-11, an update of the DC-10, three. Boeing spotted an opportunity for a twin-engine plane using giant turbofans, then under development. It represented a dangerous leap because flying with just two engines over water was riskier: if both failed, there was no backup. "Engines turn or passengers swim," as the calculus went. It was also costly—Boeing would have to spend more than $5 billion to bring the plane into production, during a recession that had caused worldwide air travel to slump. But if the 777 succeeded, it would be so cheap to operate that airlines could open more frequent flights linking secondary markets, like Phoenix to London or Chicago to Frankfurt.

Condit, then the program manager, set the tone in an October 1990 deal with the plane's first customer, United. Teams of lawyers and salespeople negotiated at the airline's suburban Chicago headquarters for seventy hours. At 2:15 a.m., a United executive sat down and wrote an agreement on a yellow legal pad, in language that was anything but lawyerly. It said, "In order to launch on-time a truly great airplane, we have the responsibility to work together to design, produce, and introduce an airplane that exceeds the expectations of flight crews, cabin crews, and maintenance and support teams and ultimately our passengers and shippers. From day one: best dispatch reliability in history; greatest customer appeal in the industry; user-friendly and everything works." Condit and the United executive signed it, and the airline placed an $11 billion order for thirty-four 777s.

The phrase "Working Together" became the organizing principle of the project. "The culture of the 777 program was very, very intentional," said Morton, Boeing's Pug Henry, who was by then running the entire customer training operation where he'd started as an instructor. One saying went that every airplane development program has twenty thousand surprises; the point was to send a message that bad news was welcome. Trying to avoid confusion and costly changes, Boeing created a group of early customers it called the "Gang of Eight" and involved them in all design decisions.

Alan Mulally, a Boeing veteran later famous for turning around the Ford Motor Company, took over as the project leader for the 777 when Condit was promoted to company president. He welcomed and mastered complexity, right down to the fact that discarded salt packets from passengers' meal trays in the galley tended to corrode the aluminum in the belly underneath. Some people had the feeling that Condit kept his impressive colleague, only four years younger, at arm's length from his own superiors and board members to avoid being outshone. One former executive remembers Condit once telling Mulally there was no room on the corporate jet he'd be traveling on with then CEO Shrontz, when a seat was actually available. Mulally always projected enthusiasm; when Condit was promoted to president, he leapt across the table to grab Condit's hand and blurted, "Great choice!"

Mulally's perpetual half smile and straight, slicked-down hair (which stayed red, even well into his 50s) gave him the air of a character from the Sunday funnies. He grew up in Lawrence, Kansas, a churchgoing, small-town midwesterner, like so many men who rose to the top ranks at Boeing. One of Mulally's after-dinner speeches was about a near disaster he once had while piloting a small plane as a teenager; in his telling, the primary thought in his mind as he spiraled to the ground was fear of embarrassing his parents. His demeanor was intensely, almost manically positive, but there was an edge of menace behind it. He would frequently grab your arm or touch your knee when he wanted to make a point. Mulally often repeated maxims like "no secrets" and "the data will set you free." When his temper flared, he put it less delicately. "The only thing that will make me rip off your head and shit down your neck is withholding information," one engineer recalls him saying.

In a measure of his intensity, he frequently ended meetings by pulling out a marker to write down on one of the plastic transparency sheets under the overhead projector what each person had agreed to do and having them all sign it. "Accountability is huge with him," said a former lieutenant. "Burying things and letting them fester—Darth Vader comes out."

Communication among a team of ten thousand people is challenging; Boeing brought them together in person once a quarter. It helped that the 777 was the first plane Boeing designed using CATIA computer programs, allowing for three-dimensional images of parts. Akshay Sharma, who worked on the plane as a telecommunications consultant, was impressed that Boeing invested in sophisticated $100,000 IBM workstations for every engineer who tested software. "No expense was spared," he said. "There was this feeling of camaraderie."

The openness extended to the FAA. Airplane safety manager Paul Russell remembers a meeting in which Mulally hosted the agency's chief data officer in a hangar where one of the first aircraft was being assembled. Mulally introduced the FAA official to every person there—by name.

"My first project was the 777; that was fantastic," said Ken Schroer, who was lead program manager for the aircraft at the FAA's Seattle certification office and held that role for eight more Boeing models until he retired in 2013. As time passed, he had the feeling his Boeing counterparts were withholding information from him, keeping him at a distance, but not on the 777. "A lot of the Boeing management were engineering oriented," he says. "They weren't the money people, contract people."

When Boeing rolled out the first of the 777s in April 1994, an orchestral score by Dick Clark Productions swelled as the "Working Together" motto appeared on a 285-foot screen before thousands of employees gathered at the doors of the massive hangar in Everett. It was the first new Boeing model that didn't have the names of its test pilots, notoriously ego conscious, under the cockpit window. "Working Together" was scrawled there in cursive instead.

That spring, Morton, then in charge of the training business, finished construction of what he considered Boeing's crown jewel: a $70 million training center near Seattle for pilots, mechanics, and flight attendants who would use the 777 and other Boeing planes. He commissioned a local composer to write a piano and orchestra piece for the opening party. Several dozen airline representatives sat at banquet tables in the massive hall where full-flight simulators would soon be installed to hear the first movement, titled "Promise." (The piece was later expanded into a forty-five-minute piano concerto by its composer, Walt Wagner, who called it *The Miracle*—referring to his shock that an airplane company had commissioned a classical work.) The plane remains one of the safest ever to fly, going eighteen years before a single fatality was recorded.

"The 777 was Boeing's Camelot," Morton said. It was also expensive, ultimately costing as much as $12 billion, by some estimates. As with earlier programs, the sum was tough to swallow at first. But as orders rolled in—eventually more than two thousand—it proved to be the right choice. Time, inflation, and the lure of a well-designed product worked their magic, in the staggering arithmetic of an industry that completes tens of millions of flights each year. With list prices starting at $150 million, the value of the deliveries soared past $250 billion—more than enough to recoup the investment.

Just as spending on the new plane was ramping up, the 737 reached another major crossroads. In July 1992, a bedrock customer, United Air Lines, had stunned Boeing by defecting to the A320. United was one of the biggest carriers in the United States, and the lost order represented a massive setback for the runt of Boeing's fleet, by then a quarter century old.

Some at the company saw the loss as a cue to take the advanced electronic cockpit they were developing for the 777 and migrate it to the 737, creating a truly common fleet. In such an arrangement, pilots could switch from one plane to the other with little additional training, as they did with Airbus's growing product line.

The head of Boeing's commercial airplane business, Dean Thornton, convened a meeting of eight of his managers late that year to decide their course. He asked them to vote on whether to recommend an all-new aircraft—matching the A320—or to move forward with another derivative, a so-called Next Generation 737. Bethune, then in charge of training, recalls leaning toward a new airplane, but he knew that his friend Ron Woodard, who managed the 737 factory, much preferred the simpler update. "I was thinking we might have lost out to Airbus and we ought to get a jump on them," Bethune said. But under the table, he got a sharp kick from Woodard—"and I said, 'The next gen's the way to go, Dean.'"

The vote was five to three. Rather than a new plane, Boeing embarked on a third redesign of the 737.

Woodard, who'd started at Boeing in 1966, was among the more swaggering of its swaggering personalities. Meeting with engineers in the Speea union around the time the new planes were being built, he told them that Boeing's products had attained "theoretical perfection," a remark that led to a few smirks from the people who knew the imperfections all too well. Woodard's point was that the heady days of the jet age, when flying machines had shrunk the world with vast leaps in range and speed, were over. Airplanes were now a commodity, like most everything else. The physicist Stan Sorscher asked him about all the ideas they had to improve their products and processes: Wouldn't implementing those help?

Woodard, who stood six feet four, peered down at the diminutive engineer and said, "I have more leverage over outcomes with decisions that I make than all of you have with the decisions that you make." In other words, leave it to the corporate titans.

It was the first gusts of the headwinds soon to hit Boeing's product-focused, collegial culture. Still, by many accounts, this latest version of the 737 was the best yet. Bigger engines—now looking like soda cans clipped far forward of the wings—provided most of the fuel savings, though Boeing also added tiny "winglets," raked vertically from the wingtips, to squeeze out more aerodynamic efficiency.

Southwest, by now one of the biggest U.S. airlines, again dictated many of the specifications. The company had grown, but it didn't want to move up to the Cadillac, as Boeing market planners had once imagined. For its new airplane it wanted the same old Chevy, saving substantially on the ever-compounding costs of pilot training and spare parts. Bethune guaranteed that Southwest pilots wouldn't have to take more than eight hours of training courses to switch from the previous version, the Classic, to these new planes, the Next Generation models eventually numbering 737-600, -700, -800, and -900.

The team verified those conclusions with real-world tests, much as Condit and Morton had when they hired psychologists for the 757. Boeing agreed with the FAA that it would bring in thirty experienced line pilots for a check ride on the new models and measure how they performed. When Southwest proved resistant to giving up instruments resembling the old analog dials—the team called them "the steam gauges"—the Boeing engineers didn't simply concede. Other airlines *did* want a more modern display, with moving maps, and they figured Southwest would eventually change its mind. So Boeing designed both versions, writing software to allow flight displays to be easily switched. After the plane started flying, Southwest's representatives came to Boeing and asked how much it would cost for the new displays. Thanks to Boeing's prescience, all they had to do was push a button.

The troubles at McDonnell Douglas, meanwhile, were only deepening. After the death of founder James McDonnell in 1980, the St. Louis–based company was led first by his nephew, Sandy, and then by his son, John McDonnell. Neither showed a great aptitude for management, often reaching for off-the-shelf solutions. A quirky strain was said to have passed through the family starting with Mr. Mac, who had a lifelong fascination with the paranormal— his fighter jets had names like Voodoo and Phantom—and funded research on such personal passions as whether the human mind can bend an iron rod.

Sandy, long in waiting for the throne, developed multiple interests of his own: he was a sculptor, a born-again Christian, a bagpiper, and a social crusader. In an odd choice for a defense contractor, his central management message, which he called "The Five Keys to Self-Renewal," came from a book by the founder of Common Cause, a nonprofit that advocated for campaign finance reform and an end to the Vietnam War. The five keys were said to be strategic management, human resources management, participative management, ethical decision making, and quality/productivity. Executives displayed posters of the keys in their offices and held contests for the best examples of self-renewal.

In 1988, Sandy sent a survey to managers about a system of voluntary contributions he'd developed, in hopes of cutting the federal deficit. Participants would get "Modern American Patriot" certificates, lapel pins, and medallions stamped with President Ronald Reagan's signature for their participation.

"I sent mine back demanding a statue of Reagan that glowed in the dark," C. W. Bradshaw, a former McDonnell Douglas human resources manager, told the *Los Angeles Times*. "The St. Louis corporate mentality is amazing. They are suckers for anyone with a new fad that will put them at the forefront of corporate culture and make the business magazines."

Mr. Mac's progeny never had a great feel for the commercial market either. They opted for incremental advances like the MD-11, an update of the ill-fated DC-10. "Our investment is only a quarter of what it would be for an all-new airplane," John McDonnell boasted in 1987 when the project began. The 777 wiped out the market for their MD-11, outselling it eight to one. Then the end of the Cold War blew a hole in the company's supposed bulwark, the defense business. When air force procurement officials including Darleen Druyun (later to figure in a major scandal at Boeing) quietly expedited $349 million in payments for McDonnell Douglas C-17 cargo planes, critics said the company had been granted a secret government bailout.

John, James's son and Sandy's successor, tried to connect with employees, but he came off as patronizing. He recorded videotapes quarterly and sent them to the company's 113,000 employees, or "teammates," as Mr. Mac had always preferred to call them. The bearded, bespectacled Princeton graduate would offer advice about responding to change, quoting from books like Alvin Toffler's *Future Shock*. He cautioned his charges to avoid "petty competition, jealousy, and fear of losing turf." In one of the videotapes he told a story about a gardener he'd spotted on the grounds of the St. Louis campus using a rake that was missing most of its tines: "Obviously, this person was not being very productive," he sniffed.

And yet, as he cycled through various management approaches, he practically guaranteed turf battles. Even twenty years after the merger, the rift between the McDonnell and Douglas sides of the business remained pronounced. One day in February 1989, all fifty-two hundred supervisors from the Douglas side in California were ushered into a paint hangar and told they'd been stripped of their titles. They could reapply for their jobs—but one thousand fewer positions would be available. And before rejoining they'd have to take "Discovery" classes to learn about one more new corporate initiative: the Total Quality Management System, or TQMS. The bitter joke among employees was that it stood for "Time to Quit and Move to Seattle." Some did exactly that: Darce Lamb, a spare parts manager, called a friend at Boeing from the paint hangar that very day and was soon hired.

Rick Caldwell, then a young engineer, says he went six months without a first-level manager, as his superiors jockeyed for position. The classes put them through role-playing exercises to see if they fit the new culture, with judgment passed by a panel of under-graduates from Cal State Long Beach. James Douglas, a son of the founder, was among those deemed unfit and laid off. "We were fragged," he said.

When the dust settled, perhaps inevitably, a manager based out of St. Louis—the McDonnell end of the business—had taken charge of Douglas. Most of the nine highest-ranking vice presidents were also outsiders; the holdovers facetiously called them "the Divine Nine." Caldwell, who eventually rose to become the lead design engineer for the MD-11, met John McDonnell once, when the founder's son stopped by the nearly deserted offices in Long Beach one midafternoon shortly before Christmas. "Where is everybody?" McDonnell asked, with a mystified air. "And I just looked at him, like, what do you think?" Caldwell said. "He really didn't seem to get how hard everyone was working. I thought, 'Does this guy have no social graces?'"

The junior McDonnell was quietly planning his exit. In 1994, a year after Defense Secretary William Perry held what later became known as "the Last Supper" to urge the chiefs of America's compet-ing military contractors to consolidate, McDonnell and Boeing's then CEO Frank Shrontz began their first tentative conversations about a merger. The combination had a certain commercial logic: McDonnell's military programs like the F-15 fighter and Apache attack helicopter balanced out Boeing's jetliner franchise.

That same year, John McDonnell hired Harry Stonecipher, a driven protégé of Jack Welch, as the first outsider to run the family business. McDonnell cautioned him that a sale to Boeing was likely. Stonecipher, then fifty-eight, told an associate that if a merger came to pass, he would probably retire. As it happened, he wouldn't go nearly so quietly, ushering in a bottom-line mindset that would shake the proud Pacific Northwest engineering firm to its core. In fact, by the end of it, Boeing would be neither from the Pacific Northwest nor, to hear Stonecipher tell it, an engineering firm at all.

Stonecipher hailed from Scott County, Tennessee, where his grand-father had been a superintendent in the coal mines and his father a union electrician. The force of nature in the Stonecipher family was his grandmother, the aptly named Lillie Goad Stonecipher, a math teacher. She gave people the impression of having wanted more for her own son, and pushed her grandson Harry to excel. Harry's mother waited tables at a truck stop. He worked there, too, starting at age eleven, climbing on top of a milk crate to wash Coca-Cola bottles. After starting college at sixteen, he got married at eigh-teen and then worked for a few years as a technician in a lab in Indianapolis where the Allison Engine Company, then owned by General Motors, developed jet engines. Stonecipher finished up at Tennessee Tech and got a job at General Electric's aircraft-engine unit in Cincinnati, starting in 1960 as an evaluation engineer before rising through production and marketing roles to become the unit's president in 1984.

Stonecipher never lost the manner of the ass-kicking first-line supervisor he'd once been. He had a mien you'd call Trumpian if such a thing had existed then: a kind of deep-seated need for alpha displays, public humiliation, and conflict. "I'll tell you why you're all wrong," he once said to a junior Boeing sales executive, minutes after meeting him. "I know things you can't imagine, and I operate on a level you don't even know exists." In his "furrowed, weather-beaten face," the *Wall Street Journal* saw a cross between Karl Malden and Johnny Cash.

While at GE, Stonecipher was always the operator, never the visionary. That role was occupied by his British-born boss, Brian Rowe, the longtime head of the aircraft engines unit. Rowe pushed a skeptical Jack Welch to invest in a giant engine for the 777, called the GE90, and was ultimately fired in a standoff over job cuts. (When the engine later proved a success, Welch conceded Rowe's foresight.) By contrast, Stonecipher described his most formative experience with Welch as a meeting in the early 1980s, when he mentioned how proud he was that his team had won 65 percent of the orders in large engines. "Tell me what your profit margins would be if you had 45 percent," Welch said—implying that he was okay with losing some market share (and even leadership of an industry) if it could boost the all-important bottom line.

A month after taking the McDonnell Douglas job, despite the dire future prospects for the plane maker, Stonecipher authorized *increasing* shareholder dividends by 71 percent. He also used the company's shrinking war chest to buy back 15 percent of the company's stock. The message for investors was clear enough. "McDonnell Douglas Takes Actions to Enhance Shareholder Value," the press release said.

Buybacks of the sort Stonecipher had instigated were once considered market manipulation. They represent a technique in which a company uses its revenue to acquire its own shares on the open market, then cancels them. With fewer shares outstanding, the ones left are more valuable. Hold a single share in a company that issued one hundred shares and you own a 1 percent stake. If the company buys back half of the existing shares, you now own 2 percent, artificially increasing the value of your share and increasing your dividends, without any additional expenditure on your part.

For decades, the Securities and Exchange Commission limited how often companies could buy back shares, but a Reagan administration rule in 1982—a year after Welch became the chief executive at General Electric—did away with those restrictions. From the point of view of executives and board members at public companies, who are typically rewarded primarily in stock, it offered a virtuous circle: buybacks mean more money for their investors and more for themselves.

But the money isn't free. When companies buy back shares, they're forgoing other spending, like investments in their next line of products or pension contributions. McDonnell Douglas ramped up buybacks over the next two years; simultaneously, it cut its R&D spending 60 percent.

Far from seeing these maneuvers as the warning signs of a company approaching tailspin, Oppenheimer Capital in New York spotted opportunity, making McDonnell Douglas its largest investment in a $400 million fund. "Although production of aircraft was coming down, we thought they could reduce costs faster than revenue fell," Richard Glasebrook, the portfolio manager, explained in a *New York Times* market column in 1995. The stock had been the fund's best performer that year, gaining 50 percent.

The shares may have been soaring, but as an independent company, McDonnell Douglas was dying. Stonecipher in 1996 dispatched one of his top lieutenants, Michael Sears, to run the commercial aircraft business and take a hard look at its prospects. Its market share had declined to 7 percent, and Sears told Stonecipher it would take $15 billion over a decade just to pull even with Boeing and Airbus. That same year the Pentagon eliminated McDonnell Douglas from a $200 billion contest with Boeing and Lockheed Martin to build the Joint Strike Fighter, the only new U.S. fighter on the horizon for at least a generation. (One of those supervising Boeing's entry was a brash young manager named Dennis Muilenburg; he told a TV interviewer that he dreamed of shooting down the Lockheed entry.)

Given the perilous state of their business, Stonecipher and McDonnell decided it was time to get serious about selling to Boeing. They wrote down four items they considered nonnegotiable: the price, the number of board seats allotted to McDonnell Douglas directors, a leadership role for Stonecipher, and the combined company's name. It had to be the Boeing McDonnell Corporation.

That December, Stonecipher and Shrontz's successor Phil Condit met alone in Boeing's private suite at Seattle's Four Seasons hotel to hammer out an agreement. At first, Stonecipher recalled, they circled each other "like a couple of cats." The two had been friendly for decades, golfing in Sun Valley, Idaho, and other vacation spots at annual retreats called "love-ins" that GE and Boeing took turns hosting for each other. But where Condit was gentle and professorial, Stonecipher was abrasive and single-minded. Years before, the two had joined T. Wilson for dinner, Condit then a rising star at Boeing and Stonecipher, from GE, just another one of its suppliers. Stonecipher called Boeing arrogant, after a long discussion about wing design. "And rightly so!" Wilson shot back.

Condit and Stonecipher had one thing in common, though: they both admired and envied Welch, then the undisputed king of American industry. He had led what appeared to be an incredible renaissance at the old-line maker of lightbulbs, jet engines, and washing machines, the progeny of Thomas Edison. A vast financing arm, GE Capital, was bigger than most banks. Subprime mortgages would one day hobble the division, but in those years it powered earnings of which other industrial companies could only dream. GE met or beat Wall Street's expectations every quarter from 1995 to 2004. Welch was an innovator in the euphemistic art of "earnings management," relying especially on the opaque dealings of GE Capital. The unit might sell half a parking lot at the close of a quarter to juice earnings, then buy it back later. GE workers finishing a steam turbine generator once moved it across the street on flatbed trucks to meet an accounting rule that it be "removed from the property" before booking profits. (Much later, the Securities and Exchange Commission determined that Welch's successors had "bent the accounting rules beyond the breaking point" and levied a $50 million fine.)

Welch's raspy New England accent was a common presence on the business networks then proliferating—including the one his company owned, CNBC, where he could be seen dispensing catchy aphorisms. He believed in "rank and yank," firing the bottom 10 percent of managers every year regardless of the overall performance. Another motto was "fix it, sell it, or close it," reflecting the unsentimental speed he demanded of managers when it came to results. As GE's market capitalization soared, Welch's unflattering nickname—"Neutron Jack," for the one hundred thousand job cuts he implemented in the early 1980s—was all but forgotten.

In their meeting at the Four Seasons, as Condit and Stonecipher talked over the possibilities of the deal, they got past the awkwardness and within a few hours were acting like "giddy school kids," Stonecipher recalled. Condit wrapped things up by saying, "Gosh, I guess we should shake hands." At a meeting a week later, Boeing's board blessed the purchase, agreeing to pay $13.3 billion in stock.

The only one of those items Stonecipher and his boss John McDonnell didn't get: Boeing would remain Boeing, at least in name.

The merger brought gushing praise from Wall Street. The European Commission was so concerned the American monster would crush Airbus that it briefly considered blocking the deal. In the end it relented only after Boeing agreed to drop exclusive sales deals it had signed with three U.S. carriers.

"I love this deal," Lehman Brothers analyst Joseph Campbell said on CNN the day the acquisition was announced. "Jack Welch, look out."

Privately, longtime Boeing executives grumbled that they'd been played. When they took a closer look at the Douglas machinery in Long Beach that they had just acquired, they reported that it hadn't been updated since World War II. Boeing's factories had an extensive network of overhead cranes on rails; at Douglas, the workers were mounting engines on the planes with what looked like rented mobile cranes. Woodard told people their old rival "brought nothing to the table but a lot of headaches." He was especially upset that his exclusive sales deals—"the most beautiful thing we'd ever done"—were voided as part of the deal. "I took the position that we should just give them (i.e., Airbus) McDonnell Douglas, but nobody would go for that," Woodard said. (Indeed, the European company would have been Stonecipher's next call: "If the merger with Boeing hadn't happened, we'd be building Airbuses in Long Beach," he said years later.) Others took issue with the price Boeing had paid, saying it would have been smarter to wait for McDonnell Douglas to falter and buy its military assets at fire-sale prices.

Most galling to Boeing veterans was the influence amassed by what they saw as a failed rival: John McDonnell and Stonecipher became Boeing's two largest individual shareholders. They both joined the board, as did two other former McDonnell Douglas directors, giving them four of the twelve board seats—a powerful decision-making bloc. The others were Ken Duberstein, the former chief of staff to Ronald Reagan, and John Biggs, a St. Louis native who ran the investment firm TIAA-CREF. They brought government and financial connections, in contrast to the Boeing board, traditionally stocked with practical-minded leaders of Pacific Northwest firms like the timber company Weyerhaeuser.

Larry Clarkson, then a senior executive at Boeing, recalls running into T. Wilson after the merger in the parking lot of the headquarters building, where the retired CEO still kept an office. "McDonnell Douglas has bought Boeing with Boeing's money," T. said ruefully. The phrase was soon widely heard around Boeing, with few aware that one of the company's most legendary leaders had come up with it. T. told at least two of his former deputies that grooming Condit for the top job had been his biggest mistake.

Clarkson brought his concerns about Stonecipher's newfound influence to Condit himself. The Boeing chief was placating. Condit echoed Stonecipher's own prediction, the one he had made when John McDonnell had told him a merger with Boeing was on the horizon. Stonecipher would probably stick around no more than eighteen months and then retire, Condit assured him.

4

Hunter Killer Assassins

It wasn't in Harry Stonecipher's nature to fade away, not after forty years of hard scrabbling had finally brought him to the top of the industry. The executives who arrived with him, too, were skilled infighters, survivors of the very recent Cultural Revolution within their ranks.

When it came to the dark arts of corporate one-upmanship, many at Boeing were novices. Their products may have won in the marketplace, but the people who designed them were scientists and craftsmen, not sharp-elbowed operators. A wine club for employees drew such exacting hobbyists that it spawned more than a dozen commercial wineries, some regularly rated among Washington State's best. There was undoubtedly some fat to be trimmed; T. Wilson himself, asked once how many people worked at Boeing, had jabbed back: "About half." Hiking and camping around the Northwest's lakes and forests were surefire watercooler topics. "What you had at Boeing at the time of the merger was a very collegial, bloated, flaccid management structure," a thirty-year veteran later recalled in a University of Puget Sound oral history. "When the McDonnell Douglas guys came in, they just went through them like a knife through butter."

The deal closed in August 1997. In a parking lot near Boeing

Field the following year, two hundred engineers working on fighter jets gathered to hear from the Stonecipher protégé named to run the newly combined military aircraft business—Michael Sears, who'd determined the Douglas jetliner unit wasn't worth saving. A courtly Boeing VP named Frank Statkus introduced Sears as their "guest" and suggested they listen. "Frank, remember, you work for me," Sears pointedly replied. When the roar of a 747 overhead interrupted his remarks, he flashed contempt for "the Queen of the Skies," too. "Not one of ours," he said—in other words, not one this military team (or McDonnell Douglas) had built. Engineers at the edges of the crowd quietly registered their disapproval by walking back to their cubicles.

In the information systems department, Boeing executives found themselves told to adopt the "5-15 rule" imported from McDonnell Douglas: Memos should take no more than five minutes to read and fifteen minutes to write. One quirk Stonecipher maintained long after it was considered rude or insane was the all-caps email. "You know, when you do that, people think you're shouting," Morton gently told him at one point. "That's fine," Stonecipher replied.

He laminated a three-by-five notecard on which he'd written the list of things Condit had agreed to as part of the merger and told people he kept it in his top desk drawer. Stonecipher actually made more money than his supposed boss in the year the deal closed: $3.5 million in cash (including a $2.2 million payment to offset taxes on vested stock) and as much as $12.2 million in stock, compared with $1.3 million in cash and $204,000 in stock for Condit.

As board members and the largest individual shareholders, Stonecipher and McDonnell wielded outsized influence. "Michael Eisner, for all his excesses, could only dream of this level of power at Disney," said the analyst Richard Aboulafia of the Teal Group, a consulting firm focused on aviation, defense, and space. After a months-long series of meetings to plot how to rationalize their many duplicate facilities, labs, and administrative offices, the McDonnell Douglas team presented the lead manager on the Boeing side, C. Gerald King, with a plaque. It showed an *Economist* cover of two camels humping, the illustration for a story about the challenges of corporate mergers, with the added line, "Who's on Top?" Embarrassed, King put it in a closet.

One of Stonecipher's more idiosyncratic requests of Condit was that Boeing complete and enlarge an executive training center he'd been planning for McDonnell Douglas. It was modeled after GE's famed Crotonville center, where Welch held forth to his assembled executive team from a sunken auditorium called "the Pit." McDonnell Douglas had paid $8 million for a French country château in a wooded area on the Missouri River just outside St. Louis to house the new complex. (Boeing's own plans for training had been more low-key—a few conference rooms in the Longacres building that Morton had just opened south of Seattle.) Stonecipher hired away a former Crotonville deputy to run the combined training operation. It had 120 private residence rooms, a lecture hall (called "the Cockpit"), and classrooms where executives role-played negotiations and dissected business case studies during courses lasting as long as two weeks. Stonecipher gave the opening speech.

He frequently lectured people about how Boeing needed to be a "team," not a "family," the word people there had always used partly because it was true: sons had followed fathers, and grandfathers, to Boeing. Managers there always thought of it as a strength, said Fred Mitchell, the executive who'd survived the 747 bust when desks were stacked thirty feet high: "We fought like hell but when push came to shove we all came together." Stonecipher brought in a consultant who'd written a book about how Phil Jackson managed the divergent personalities on the Chicago Bulls to drive home the message. But the takeaway, for many, was that if you're Dennis Rodman—the team's disruptive, narcissistic power forward—it will be tolerated as long as you get results.

Stonecipher soon got ammunition to take even more control. Distracted by the merger, Boeing had let production problems fester in its aircraft factories over the previous year. Under Woodard, the former sales executive who ran the airplane division, Boeing had tried to bury Airbus with massive discounts, as the market roared back from the recession. He pushed through a doubling in production rates at the same time the factories introduced new computer systems to replace laborious processes relying on manual drawings.

It was the same mistake Douglas had made in the 1960s, the sales department charging ahead with no regard for the production team or its capacity. Factories seized up, contributing to $2.6 billion in additional costs and a $178 million loss in 1997—the company's first in fifty years. No one at Boeing could remember a bigger black eye, and for shareholders expecting a bonanza after the merger, the news came as a shock and a disappointment. Boeing faced a class-action lawsuit from investors, who claimed it had committed fraud by hiding the extent of the production setbacks to avoid reducing the value of its shares and increasing the price of the all-stock merger with McDonnell Douglas (the suit was ultimately settled for $92.5 million).

In Stonecipher's first appearance at Boeing's annual management retreat at a hotel in Palm Springs in January 1998, he asked the managers in charge of commercial aircraft production, among the two hundred attendees, to stand up. "They should apologize," he told the group, for falling behind in their commitments and therefore causing the entire company to miss its financial goals. The only threat to Boeing came from within—the failure to execute, he told them.

The contrast with GE's financial performance couldn't have been sharper. That same month Welch gathered his senior managers for a celebratory meeting in Boca Raton, Florida. GE's share price had risen 48 percent in 1997, its third straight year of increasing more than 40 percent, and Welch's company had set records for revenues, profit, and income per share. A bestselling book compiling the GE leader's wisdom, *Jack Welch and the GE Way*, put all of his statements in bold type, like the voice of Jesus in the New Testament. That day in Boca Raton, Jack said unto them: **"Price-share management has never been more important. Never. Productivity is critical to counteract this enormous price pressure. Assets are going to be worth less, rather than more. So the asset efficiency, inventory turns, receivable turns have got to improve."**

Continental Airlines chief Bethune came back to see his old Boeing colleagues that spring. He was now a big customer, and he had written a book about his turnaround of Continental, *From Worst to First*. Boeing hosted a party for him at the Museum of Flight in Seattle. Bethune shared a cocktail with Condit and Woodard under the airplanes of its illustrious past in a cavernous hall. Bethune knew Stonecipher from his days buying engines from GE, and in his view, the man had one mode: attack. "First he's going to kill this guy," Bethune said, pointing to Woodard. "And then he's going to come kill you," he added, to Condit. The CEO just laughed and shook his head.

Stonecipher and Woodard already disliked each other; one story went that Stonecipher never forgave the Boeing salesman for stealing a big Scandinavian Airlines System order out from under him while he was running McDonnell Douglas. After closing a desperately needed sale of MD-95s, Stonecipher had gone on vacation for a weekend, with orders not to be disturbed, according to a person told of what happened. Woodard swooped in with a lower offer for Boeing's competing model.

To be fair, Stonecipher's low opinion of Woodard was shared by plenty of others at Boeing. They said that by refusing to heed the warnings of his deputies, he'd bungled the production ramp-up, contributing to the company's nine-figure loss the preceding year.

That August, Boeing's stock was still plunging. Condit had to endure brutal conversations with Wall Street analysts in New York. Stonecipher was always deferential to Condit in public, and the two spoke often about what a great team they made—the visionary and the realist. Privately, though, Stonecipher relished the free rein that Condit's indecisiveness and aversion to conflict afforded him. Whenever Stonecipher said "it's time," he once boasted to an associate, Condit did what he wanted.

That's precisely what took place later that month. Proving Bethune's first prediction well founded, Stonecipher marched down the hall and told Condit: it was time to fire Woodard. "Phil was a mouse," said a Boeing executive who frequently interacted with both men. "I think Stonecipher scared the crap out of Phil because

Harry was really strong, really profane. He beat up Phil even though Phil was supposedly his boss."

Obediently, Condit called Woodard in on a Saturday, ostensibly to work on a presentation for a board meeting that Monday. After an it-hurts-me-to-do-this preamble, Condit told Woodard he was being replaced by Alan Mulally, the highly regarded leader of the 777 project; an announcement would go out after the meeting. Incredibly, no one so high-ranking had ever been fired so publicly at Boeing. That Monday, Woodard's top reports gathered in a conference room; they'd been told that some of them could expect to go, too. They waited hours with no word, then finally called headquarters, according to one person there. It turned out they'd been forgotten. With an "oh, yeah," a human resources manager was dispatched to fire two Woodard lieutenants, Dan Heidt and Harry Arnold.

That wasn't the extent of Stonecipher's culling. In the finance department, now more central to Boeing's operation than ever, he eased out the finance chief, Boyd Givan, then sixty-two. A Boeing lifer, Givan had never been a favorite of Wall Street stock analysts. He resisted sharing the information they wanted about expenses and investments. "Tell them not to worry," he was said to have responded to one such request. The board agreed to appoint Stonecipher acting chief financial officer. His first move was a familiar one: Boeing would spend as much as $4.5 billion to buy back 15 percent of its shares.

Amid all the turmoil, Welch couldn't resist sending a needling note to his old underling about his new role. "CFO??? Question: $2 + 2 = ?$" he wrote.

For all his hard-charging manner, Stonecipher recognized there were limits in his ability to get messages across to his staff. "Do you have any idea what it feels like to go in there and know everybody hates your guts?" he asked a confidant. To put a further jolt into Boeing, he recruited another outsider to take the chief finance job he'd temporarily assumed—a forty-four-year-old executive from

General Motors named Deborah Hopkins. She had also worked for Unisys and Ford, occupying unglamorous and not particularly high-ranking posts as an auditor. At Boeing, she was given wide latitude to press for a more shareholder-friendly company. Bethune at Continental grumbled about it at the time. "Have you ever seen a bean-counter build an airplane?" he asked.

At the Boeing management retreat in Palm Desert in January 1999, the group got what amounted to a scared-straight message. Condit started by telling them that the stock price was so depressed even mighty Boeing could face a takeover, perhaps in a leveraged buyout that would break the company into pieces. Then he handed the floor to Hopkins, the unusual change agent they'd recruited. Wielding a series of charts, she underscored the importance of financial benchmarks like return on net assets, or RONA, the metric Stonecipher had learned under Welch at General Electric.

That May, Hopkins invited Richard Glasebrook, the Oppenheimer fund manager who had done so well with his McDonnell Douglas shares, to speak to finance staff. Oppenheimer was now Boeing's biggest shareholder, with a more than 3 percent stake. Glasebrook had been tempted to sell before the merger—he was skeptical Boeing could compete with state-backed Airbus—but reluctantly remained an investor after a conversation with Stonecipher. ("I was comfortable with Harry," Glasebrook later explained. "He was essentially a financially oriented individual who wanted to achieve improvement in finances and returns and cash flow.")

So far it appeared the fund manager's first instinct had been right. Glasebrook told staffers at the meeting that Oppenheimer had made six times its money and a profit of more than a billion dollars on the stake in McDonnell Douglas. At Boeing, by contrast, "I have given at the trough," he said. "It has not gone unnoticed by my wife, who looks at my pay stubs, that my pay is down because our profit is down—a lot." He reminded them that Boeing, special as it was, had to measure itself against companies much further along in practicing "value-based management." The finance department transcribed the talk and forwarded it widely to Boeing employees, part of the heavy-handed messaging effort. Another thing they couldn't miss in the transcript: Glasebrook's comment that they had no more than eighteen months to fix Boeing's problems before someone else did. "You can imagine what [leveraged buyout] people are like or what Jack Welch is like," the fund manager said.

Hopkins distributed a "value scorecard" based on the RONA metric that showed which businesses were "value destroyers." The formula measures the ratio of income generated to the capital employed. The idea is to encourage efficient use of assets—what the boldfaced Welch was so insistent on improving in Boca Raton. In practice, the easiest way to make the number go up was by selling off plants. It was the Walmart model: Boeing would still get the parts it needed to build planes, but it would get them from smaller, more vulnerable suppliers, whose costs could be squeezed and union benefits renegotiated or eliminated.

Some longtime executives resisted, arguing that Boeing wouldn't get the same quality or level of commitment if it sold them. One senior manager who had to report quarterly on his asset utilization goals dragged the plant dump out as long as he could. Once, he found a plant making McDonnell Douglas DC-8 parts in Arkansas that had so little work it kept people busy painting rocks in the driveway. He suggested selling that one. Stonecipher, he recalls, was soon on the phone barking at him. "You dumb son of a bitch," he said, "don't you know who they know? They know Clinton! We're trying to sell military aircraft to the air force, and you're closing a plant in his home state. Close one of these other plants!"

In a place run for generations by phlegmatic men, Hopkins, a much younger woman, was an irresistible subject of feature articles in the *Wall Street Journal, Fortune,* and other publications. She delivered the same message in all of them—that Boeing had heeded Wall Street's message and was serious about meeting its demands for bottom-line performance.

Hopkins told staffers she and her husband had moved so many times that they kept boxes around unflattened for the next one. Now they were ready to get rid of them, anticipating a long stay at

Boeing. And perhaps those boxes were on her mind in one of those interviews when she reached for a metaphor to explain why the proud engineers at Boeing, always so focused on building planes that went higher, faster, and farther, needed to think more about profits. The important thing was not to get "overly focused on the box," Hopkins told Bloomberg (a line that, from the vantage point of two decades, has an ominous ring to it). "The box"—the plane itself—"is obviously important, but customers are assuming the box is of great quality."

It was heresy to engineers, to whom the box was everything. They were losing faith in the business plan, with Airbus coming on strong and customers complaining of declining quality. United called Boeing "dysfunctional" in one widely reported 1998 memo, writing, "We (United) do not trust you (Boeing)."

While reaching for financial glory, Boeing increasingly was ignoring the basics of customer support. A year earlier, Condit had approved turning Boeing's pilot training operations—the unit Morton was so proud of—into a separate, profit-seeking company. The unit was now known as Boeing FlightSafety, part of a joint venture with a company owned by Warren Buffett called FlightSafety International. At the time, Jack Welch was getting praise from Wall Street for turning GE into more than just a manufacturer; it was a "services" company that made money, for instance, on after-sales support of its engines for airlines in the field. In aviation, the centerpiece of Welch's strategy was the purchase of a British Airways engine repair shop in Wales that serviced engines made by GE as well as competitors like Rolls-Royce.

The Boeing strategy, again, was to be just like Jack. Condit at first tried to buy FlightSafety International outright. The company, based in Flushing, New York, trained pilots on more than a dozen different types of aircraft, from small business jets to military planes. The salaries of instructors at FlightSafety were lower than those at Boeing; the plan was to compete more aggressively for contracts to train flight crews, even if they weren't already Boeing customers. Some of the bigger airlines, like United and Northwest, also sold their training expertise to others. But Buffett's Berkshire

Hathaway outbid Boeing, paying $1.5 billion for the company in 1996. As a consolation prize, Boeing formed the joint venture, a Condit deputy telling stunned pilots at a meeting in March 1997 that they needed to reapply for their jobs with FlightSafety.

As its president, the new company recruited a Harvard MBA named Wake Smith, who would go on to become a partner in a private equity firm. Two years after the venture was formed, sales were growing 20 percent a year. But the effort distracted Boeing from supporting its existing customers. At first, engineers in the newly separate company couldn't even get into Boeing's computer network to access diagrams to answer customers' questions. Miscommunications led to complaints from carriers including Australia's Qantas, which told Boeing in July 1998 that the venture had been "completely unsatisfactory" in responding to a request for training material. Help arrived so late that Qantas had to delay putting an aircraft in service. It was the first time in memory that an issue seemingly so mundane—training—had forced a delayed debut for a Boeing customer.

Instead of reapplying for their jobs with FlightSafety, Boeing's instructor pilots found a labor attorney. They formed a union called the "Lazy B Pilots Association," a smirking nod to a nickname for the plane maker bestowed by fed-up employees long ago. The union negotiated for the training pilots to remain at Boeing and provide their services to the new venture.

It was the start of tangled reporting lines, conflicting priorities, and siloization of a segment of the Boeing workforce that knew perhaps better than any other how well—or how poorly—its far-flung customers actually flew the company's airplanes. In fact, it was precisely the kind of messy corporate structure that Joe Sutter had discovered at NASA a decade prior in the wake of the *Challenger* disaster—the sort that, he had declared with so much confidence, would never come to Boeing.

Resentments among the engineers, too, would soon boil over into open conflict. Many of them felt disrespected, especially after Boeing's offer of a new four-year contract to the engineers' union in 1999 failed to include a bonus. Members of its larger machinists' union had received bonuses. The company was also trying to save $25 million by standardizing benefits to match the less generous packages at McDonnell Douglas and other companies it had acquired.

It didn't help when Stonecipher blasted one of his shouting emails in August of that year: "FIRE SORSCHER," it said. Boeing had discovered that Stan Sorscher—the physicist and twenty-year veteran who, in his emphasis on perfection, had once been accused of creating scrap—had sent the Glasebrook speech, as well as a Condit employee newsletter, to reporters. Stonecipher saw it as a violation of company policy on disseminating proprietary information. Stonecipher had sent the email directly to Sorscher's supervisor, but Walt Gillette, the chief engineer, negotiated the firing down to a hand slap: a "corrective action memo" warning of further action if any more rules were broken. Sorscher filed a complaint with the National Labor Relations Board that argued the information wasn't proprietary and, as a union negotiator, it was within his rights to send it. (He eventually won the case and the memo was rescinded.) That October, Speea voted to join an affiliate of the AFL-CIO, a big step toward organizing for a group that had always been more of a loose professional association than a true union; even high-ranking executives like Condit and Mulally had once been members.

Sensing the tension rising between labor and management, Mulally recruited Peter Morton to become the commercial airplane group's head of human resources and asked him to see what he could do to mend fences: "Everybody knows you and everybody likes you," Mulally told him. Morton, a pilot himself, was lean and five foot six. He had a baritone voice, and hearing it frequently created the impression of listening to an audiobook, with his fully formed sentences—especially when he was explaining the finer points of flight controls. In his home office, Morton kept a list of "things to remember": Courage. Will. Perseverance. Skill. "And in flying, the superior pilot uses superior judgment to avoid situations that might require the use of superior skill!"

Soon after his appointment to the post, Morton had gone to see his new boss, Jim Dagnon, who'd been brought in from Burlington Northern to run Boeing's human resources team. Dagnon asked him to explain what Speea was. Morton told him it was really a "quasi-union," not the kind of labor union Dagnon knew from the railroad company. "They see themselves as the defenders of Boeing's virtue and values in a technical sense," Morton explained. "Hmm, sounds like a union to me," Dagnon had replied.

Now, with a strike appearing imminent late in 1999, Morton went to Dagnon again and told him it could be avoided. All the union wanted was "some respect," and a bonus like the other employees got, he told Dagnon. "No, Harry wants to break the union," the former railroad executive replied.

Speea was an open shop, meaning membership wasn't a condition of employment; only about half of the represented workers actually paid dues. On the morning of February 9, 2000, the day of a planned strike, Sorscher waited alone outside the 737 factory on the south end of Lake Washington, his only company three circling seagulls. Doubts began wheeling through his head, too: was it foolish to think highly paid professionals, many of them PhDs like him, would actually strike?

At the appointed hour of nine a.m., all was still quiet. Sorscher went over to a few guys sharing a cigarette in the parking lot and asked if they'd seen anybody around. Just us, they said. Ten long minutes after nine, hundreds of engineers streamed out. They were late because they'd marched around the factory, cheering and clapping, as machinists on the assembly line shouted encouragement. Thousands packed into a nearby football stadium, where the brainiacs finally looked like a real union, roaring chants like "No nerds, no birds!"

It was the largest white-collar strike in U.S. history, encompassing twenty-three thousand workers in six states. The difference in money that they were asking for was vanishingly small—one engineer estimated that Boeing's proposed cuts in medical benefits would cost him about $300 a year—but the engineers saw their strike as a referendum on management. "We're concerned about the viability of the company if we don't change the way they're running it," one twenty-year veteran said at the time. On a portable toilet near the picket lines outside Boeing's headquarters, a scrawled sign made the target of their anger clear: HARRY'S OFFICE, it read.

The dispute got so bitter that the engineers began writing to airlines to express doubts about the quality of Boeing planes. Others told university professors not to send their students to such a "terrible place to work," as one letter put it. Some promising young employees simply left. One such engineer, Maurice Prather, then twenty-eight, took a job at Microsoft Corporation that paid 10 percent more and offered stock options; he later started his own software company.

Three federal mediators were brought in to try to resolve the standoff. After one resolution attempt failed, one of the mediators shared his own doubts that the merged company could survive, said Cynthia Cole, a striking engineer who would later become Speea's president. The mediators were supposed to stay neutral but in a moment of frustration at the hotel where talks were taking place, he confided that he saw the partnership as doomed. The executives who'd come from McDonnell Douglas, he said, were "hunter killer assassins"—and those from Boeing, "Boy Scouts."

In late February, Mulally was due to host financial analysts from investment management companies—including its big shareholder, Oppenheimer—for an annual retreat at the Silverado golf and tennis resort in Napa, California. The strike was getting more bitter by the day, and Boeing stock had dropped 10 percent. Merrill Lynch analyst Byron Callan—hoping for a fuller airing of the employees' grievances, or at least some fireworks—suggested Speea come to the retreat, too.

The union rented its own suite at the resort as a kind of salon where the analysts could gather to hear its message. Sorscher came with the union's executive director, Charles Bofferding. In physical appearance, Bofferding resembled a character from a Gary Larson *Far Side* cartoon, six foot five, pear-shaped, and bespectacled. His first job at Boeing involved gathering live chickens to shoot through windshields for strength tests. He won two company awards for technical excellence. At one dinner, in a tuxedo with his wife, Diana, at his side, Stonecipher came up to them. "You're not half as bad as I thought you'd be," Stonecipher pronounced to Diana, who answered, "Is my husband bothering you? If he does it again, give me a call."

In their Napa suite, over a floral print couch, Bofferding and Sorscher tacked up photos showing throngs of picketers and put up computer printouts with Speea's key messages in oversized type: "People Matter" and "Airbus engineers are designing Product." A spreadsheet charted how far some of the most important measures of Boeing's success had drifted in just the five years since the last contract had been signed. Most strikingly, Boeing's 70 percent share of commercial airplane orders had dwindled to the mid-40s.

Mulally spotted them in the lobby the first morning, and he came over and shook their hands, smiling. The union leaders were cordial at first, but Bofferding couldn't resist a little gloating. He told Mulally the no-longer-docile engineers were standing strong. Then he raised a subject that most of us would need the Boeing acronym guide to decipher, but which immediately set off Mulally. "We're going after the P.C.," Bofferding said, meaning "the production certificate" allowing Boeing to deliver aircraft. It was an authority delegated from the FAA, and workers represented by Speea performed most of the required tests and inspections. If Boeing no longer had the necessary employees, it would lose a capability central to its financial position. Mulally spun as if to walk away, turned, then turned again, and sputtered, "You're doing what?" It was a shot at Boeing's basic competence. The conversation was over. (Ironically, it was an outcome the company wouldn't actually experience for another twenty years; at that point the FAA would be the one to pull Boeing's authority to deliver MAX aircraft, not Boeing engineers.)

Around nine p.m., after the analysts had spent a full day with Boeing's team for briefings, meals, and cocktails, they started showing up to hear Speea's pitch. Several of them hadn't wanted to meet with the union publicly, so Sorscher and Bofferding had scheduled them each for separate private chats.

Sorscher, the scientist, recalls telling Marie Douglas, an analyst from Lazard Asset Management, that the strike had been emotional. He said the feelings were far different from anything he'd ever experienced at Boeing, which now seemed ruled by anger, fear, and pride. "Really? That's my experience every day on Wall Street," replied Douglas, then twenty-eight. Blond, six foot three, and a countess from Sweden, Douglas would go on to marry George David, the CEO of United Technologies, another of the aerospace companies she covered. (Their divorce at the height of the Great Recession in 2009 became a tabloid sensation when, though the couple were childless, she asked for $53,000 in maintenance—per week. That included $4,500 a week for clothing, $1,570 a week for horse care, and $600 a week for flowers.)

The union team also talked to Heidi Wood, an analyst from Morgan Stanley, and Joe Campbell, from Lehman Brothers.

Then Richard Glasebrook, the shareholder from Oppenheimer, came in. Bofferding tried to explain why Boeing wasn't just another commodity business that needed to wring out costs. He talked about the complexity of aircraft, the heavy performance demands, and the skilled workforce required to produce them. He asked: "Which would you rather have—a high-performance work environment with high productivity, or lower unit costs?" He had meant that second option as the straw man, the obviously stupid choice. But the Oppenheimer analyst evidently took it as a real question. He folded his arms and looked up, thinking. Finally, he answered: "Lower unit costs." (Glasebrook doesn't recall this exchange but said, "If I had to answer that today, I might say I want a high-performance company with costs that are low versus the competition.")

As the conversation continued, the analyst got restless for specific numbers. The profits Glasebrook had made with Stonecipher were long past, and the Boeing shares in Oppenheimer's portfolio were a big reason its performance was now lagging Wall Street competitors'. "You're killing me," Sorscher remembers him saying at one point, and then asking, "What does it take to settle this strike?" Bofferding told him the difference between Boeing's offer and the union's demand in additional wages, benefits, and pension costs. It amounted to around $75 million. Oppenheimer's representative looked shocked. "That's in my roundoff error," he said, according to the two union leaders, then snapped his notebook shut, seemingly appeased. (Glasebrook said he doesn't remember this.) The meeting broke up soon after, and when he left, Sorscher had the impression the next person he wanted to see was Mulally.

Three days later, Speea got a call from the mediator: Boeing was ready to talk. The company soon acceded to their demands, and the strike was over.

The episode had cost Boeing $750 million—a figure Sorscher and Bofferding learned after convincing an ally on the board to submit a question about the strike's costs for discussion at the next meeting. Stonecipher had assured people it would cost Boeing nothing. When a finance manager revealed the number, it was on the corporate jet and Stonecipher erupted, telling him he was fired, according to someone who later relayed the conversation to Bofferding. The pilot came over the intercom and said he was preparing for landing and everyone needed to be seated; after the plane touched down, he said, "I think I saved that guy's job."

Morton retired a few months later, staying long enough to reach an even forty-two years of service. "I was coming home and my wife would say to me, 'You look green,'" he said. It bothered him to see professionals treated like "line-replaceable units" and the cavalier way Stonecipher and his lieutenants had welcomed the walkout. "They caused it and they didn't know how to fix it and all my buddies were at burn barrels in the winter."

Sorscher got one more surprise. When he sat down a few weeks later to go over the contract's hundreds of pages of fine print, he found lots of little benefit cuts—less coverage for periodontal examinations, chiropractors, things that people wouldn't notice right away. Boeing had promised no change in benefits in exchange for their return to work. Sorscher asked his Boeing counterpart about the cuts, and the response was "We had to take away something."

Within a year, Condit surprised the workforce with an even bigger takeaway: he was moving Boeing's headquarters to a city far removed from its workers and their communities, the better to make cold calculations about the future of the jet business.

Hopkins would need those boxes after all, but not to take part in the same move. She left in April 2000 for Lucent Technologies (fittingly, a spinoff of the old-line AT&T Corporation created in a fervent bout of value creation). She had made more than $6 million in stock and salary at Boeing in a year and a half. Hopkins lasted at Lucent until May 2001, an even shorter stint, leaving after accounting errors at one point led to a $700 million restatement of quarterly revenue. Lucent's stock cratered, and it was eventually sold.

Her replacement at Boeing only solidified Stonecipher's growing influence at the company, the merged plane maker he had once been expected to quietly retire from. He named his protégé from McDonnell Douglas, Michael Sears, the man who had been so quick to let the Boy Scouts know who was in charge.

5

"Everybody *Thinks They're Different*"

In public, Condit said the searing experience of the strike had been a valuable lesson. "All of us have a greater understanding of what is meant by the issue of 'respect,'" he said. "One day I hope we can all look back on this as a turning point." In private, he had a different view, telling one colleague that Speea now felt professionalized—no longer a loose formation of like-minded engineers, now just another business with a competing agenda.

He was drawn to the bold vision of capitalism presented by the corporate chieftains, academics, and consultants he increasingly sought out for advice. During a party at Bill Gates's house, as Sorscher heard it from one of the Wall Street analysts, Condit had met Clay Christensen, the six-foot-eight Harvard Business School professor who coauthored an influential paper called "Skate to Where the Money Will Be." Using the metaphor of hockey hall-of-famer Wayne Gretzky's uncanny ability to sense the puck on the ice, the paper argued that successful companies knew how to separate the commodity-like and the performance-driven parts of their business. The best of them, like IBM, could "flexibly couple and decouple [their] operations" in order to "thrive from one cycle to the next." Condit came away excited, telling the analyst, "We've got to do this."

Of course, after the bursting of the Internet bubble in the early 2000s, the September 11 terrorist attacks, and the 2008 financial crisis, even the wisest business leaders would have to acknowledge that they didn't know where the puck was going—and in fact, maybe it was going to be a basketball. Boeing's own history would seem to counsel humility, too, in the way that side bets and chance had ultimately sustained the company. The 737, for instance, had once been marked for cancellation—before it became Boeing's bestseller. The only constant was that investing in modern airplanes—"to let no new improvement in flying and flying equipment pass us by," the company motto enshrined by Bill Boeing—eventually paid off.

But Christensen's ideas suited both the moment and Condit's own need to tinker. It was the era of the imperial CEO, not only Welch but swashbuckling figures like Tyco International chief Dennis Kozlowski, "Deal-a-Day Dennis," who turned a tiny New England maker of security alarms into a conglomerate worth $120 billion. When Kozlowski spoke at Harvard Business School, he told people, he got a standing ovation. Even Washington bowed to the gods of capital. The Clinton administration downsized federal agencies and introduced market-based performance metrics as part of what it called "reinventing government." Before the 2000 election, Condit was holding forth from the podium at a conference, held in a downtown Seattle high-rise, when blaring sirens interrupted his remarks. Told it was Vice President Al Gore's motorcade passing by, he growled, "Tell him we're busy."

With the strike over and Boeing's assembly lines finally restored to health, Boeing's financial performance improved. When a *Fortune* magazine reporter visited Condit one day in mid-2000, his office was decorated with fifty-four white roses to celebrate the stock's recent closing price of fifty-four dollars, nearly double its low for the year. Condit began using the slogan "five in five" to motivate managers, telling them they could quintuple the stock over five years.

The main driver would be new sales markets, not investments in commercial airplanes. That business, with its maturing technology, would be flexibly "coupled and decoupled," as Stonecipher continued pressing for efficiencies. Condit paid $3.75 billion to buy the satellite arm of Hughes Electronics in January 2000, and he poured more resources into other new ventures he believed had higher potential. They included an air-traffic management unit—its vice president of engineering was a rising executive named Dennis Muilenburg—and, improbably, a project to beam digital movies to theaters via satellite.

The latter project, called Cinema Connexion by Boeing, signed AMC Entertainment as an early customer. AMC hoped to replace the film canisters and projection reels then still in use in its theaters with 50-gigabyte digital files transmitted via a secure network of satellites and ground stations. Stonecipher hosted a weird press conference at Boeing's headquarters in November 2000 featuring a video linkup with Ben Affleck, star of *Bounce,* the first Hollywood movie delivered via satellite to a theater through the new Boeing system. The movie was about an advertising executive (Affleck) who gives his airline ticket to a stranger—who is then killed when the flight crashes. Affleck, awash in guilt, manages the ad campaign to help the airline recover, while trying to summon the courage to confess his own role to the man's grieving wife (Gwyneth Paltrow). It was a mark of the plane maker's reputation at the time that news stories about the venture, and Boeing itself, breezed past the unlikely choice of subject matter. "It's more of a love story," a spokesperson said.

The movie venture was shuttered within three years, in part because of a limiting factor apparent from the start: theaters that survive on overpriced popcorn and soda can't afford technology originally developed for the Defense Department. Still, it satisfied Boeing's desire to project a glamorous image. During the press conference Affleck, probably at Boeing's request, put in an unrelated sales plug for the Boeing Business Jet; he claimed to be *thisclose* to buying the ultraluxury craft.

Condit and his wife, Geda (his fourth bride), traveled themselves in Boeing's new $50 million business jet. It had a master suite with a queen-sized bed; two bathrooms, each equipped with a shower and gold-tone fixtures; an office; a sofa-lined lounge area; and an array of leather armchairs facing a forty-two-inch flat-screen TV. Condit and Welch had come up with the idea of converting the ever-adaptable 737 into the world's largest and most luxurious business jet in 1996, after convincing themselves of a market need. They set up a partnership to build and market the planes. More than one hundred were sold, mainly to wealthy individuals such as Middle Eastern princes. Boeing and GE themselves took two of the first off the line.

Some Boeing executives privately criticized this ostentatiousness as not in keeping with the company's traditionally low-key image. When Condit arrived in his own Boeing Business Jet for an air show near London in July 2000, a press release promoting the plane dismissed plebeian air travel (the kind that paid Boeing's bills) as so much thin gruel: "The BBJ lets our management team eat, sleep, work and even entertain while we travel," the release said. "No matter where we happen to be in the world, it relieves us of the need to check in and out of hotels, visit restaurants and spend time processing through congested airport terminals."

A partner company that helped develop the plane's $250,000 water-saving AquaJet shower also raised eyebrows within the company. It was a startup called Knowledge Training LLC, whose only listed officer was Condit's friend Granville Frazier, his now-wife Geda's former husband. Frazier had retired in March 1997, announcing, to roars, late at his retirement party, "I only regret I had but one wife to give for my company." (Condit and his third wife had separated in January 1997, and the divorce became final in December 1998.) Frazier left the company with a substantial amount of Boeing stock, and some suspected it was at least in part because of his intimate knowledge of Condit's personal life. "It was a golden handshake," said one former manager close to Condit. "Phil knew that Granny knew a lot of shit."

Frazier denies this. "Any rewards I got was due basically and totally to my own abilities, not to anybody giving me anything," he said. The shower venture drew internal opposition and was quietly disbanded.

Late in the summer of 2000, as Condit told it, he came home and confided to Geda, "I think we need to move the corporate headquarters for fundamentally strategic reasons." (His style became more ponderous over the years, and certain words and phrases, like "fundamental" and "the answer is . . ." became frequent tics.) He had hired Ted Hall, a McKinsey and Company consultant, to discuss how to manage the sprawling company, by now a giant in space and defense as well as commercial jets. It was the kind of big-picture planning Condit relished. GE famously had its headquarters in Fairfield, Connecticut, separate from the diverse businesses it owned. As he and Hall talked, Condit became convinced that Boeing needed a similar structure. "Headquarters is supposed to be thinking longer-term: Where are markets going, have we positioned the company correctly, are we developing the right people, what's the compensation structure that we have—the kind of things that are not how-do-you-design-an-airplane stuff," as Condit recalled it later. "How do you avoid getting deeply engaged in the day-to-day activity, and ignoring those strategic things?"

On March 21, 2001, Condit stunned the city where Bill Boeing built his first wooden float planes by saying he would move the headquarters to one of three cities: Chicago, Dallas–Fort Worth, or Denver. It would be "a new, leaner corporate center focused on shareholder value," the statement said. The secret had been so tightly guarded that Boeing hadn't even told Seattle's mayor, Paul Schell. "John, why didn't you call?" the mayor plaintively asked a high-ranking Condit lieutenant. Condit met the press at the Ronald Reagan Building of the International Trade Center in the other Washington—Washington, D.C.

Previous generations of Boeing leaders prided themselves on knowing everything about the aircraft they built: they got deeply engaged in precisely the "how-do-you-design-an-airplane stuff."

The executive that Condit is thought to have edged out in the CEO succession race, Jim Johnson, made a point of leaving the factory through a different door every night so that he could talk to different people on the line. Johnson invited mechanics to have lunch with him once a week without their bosses. (He departed Boeing in 1993 after Condit was named president.)

Condit had lived in a lakefront home, on a houseboat, in a forested mansion, and in the Boeing suite at the Four Seasons through his various marriages. Moving on was nothing new. During the messy disputes since the merger, "Where's Phil?" had been the frequent refrain among executives at the Seattle headquarters about their conflict-averse boss. He spent the equivalent of seventy days a year in the air, much of it visiting Washington, D.C., or the lavish new training center near St. Louis. He told reporters that traveling would be easier from a more centrally located headquarters (again, oddly casting shade on Boeing's main business) and that he'd have a "more global view of opportunities." The move ultimately stemmed from Condit's insecurities—his fear of conflict and his fear that investors wouldn't recognize his attempts to remake Boeing without a dramatic flourish. "As long as we are side-by-side with commercial airplanes, the view always is that's what we're about," he said.

When Boeing set up a sweepstakes pitting cities against one another (much as fellow Seattle behemoth Amazon would do, to great fanfare and controversy, nearly twenty years later), it was a powerful statement of the ascendancy of the corporation. After seven weeks, with each of the contestants promising tens of millions in tax breaks, Condit climbed into his jet and had the pilots file three separate flight plans. Finally, he announced, "We're going to Chicago."

The Boeing World Headquarters would be thirty-six stories above the Chicago River in what used to be called the Morton Thiokol Building—named, ironically, after the infamous maker of the failed O-rings in the *Challenger* explosion. Condit's old office had been in a gritty industrial strip of south Seattle, its windows looking directly onto the field where employees would one day test and fly the 737 MAX. Boeing's new, supposedly "leaner" headquarters had nineteenth-century rugs, an antique French barometer topped with a carved eagle, a glass scepter, and an English Regency gilt mirror among the objets d'art dotting its leather-and-wood executive suites. The white-columned hallway and wooden floors inlaid with oak and mahogany in the Office of the Chairman evoked a colonial gentleman's estate.

Stan Sorscher, the physicist and Speea official, quit Boeing soon after the strike ended to join the engineers' union full time. He kept talking to analysts, trying to understand Boeing's new lodestar of shareholder value. One asked him why Boeing needed so many engineers in coordination meetings (like the huge gatherings that had kept the 777 on track). "In my world," the analyst said, "the next word after coordination is cost." In a conversation with another Wall Streeter, as Sorscher argued against excessive cost cutting, the analyst quickly cut him off. "What you're saying is you're different," he said. "*Everybody* thinks they're different. Nobody is different. This works for everybody. It works for running shoes, ladies' garments, hard drives, cell phones, integrated circuits. And it will work for you, too."

Sorscher thought about it for a minute and answered, "So we'll do the experiment. If you're right, then you and everybody who looks like you will be happy. And if we launch a new airplane program and it doesn't work, we'll all be unhappy."

Boeing's success used to come from piling people and money onto problems until it crushed them—from conquering what the author James Collins called "big, hairy, audacious goals" in the 1994 book *Built to Last*. He and coauthor Jerry Porras selected Boeing among eighteen "visionary companies" worthy of the book's title, with McDonnell Douglas among a group of more conservative also-rans. When *Fortune* interviewed Collins in 2000, he was already starting to rethink the idea. "If in fact there's a reverse takeover, with the McDonnell ethos permeating Boeing, then Boeing is doomed to mediocrity," he said. "There's one thing that made Boeing really great all the way along. They always understood that they were an engineering-driven company, not a financially driven company. If they're no longer honoring that as their central mission, then over time they'll just become another company."

The new ethos, Sorscher came to understand, was primarily about extracting gains from stakeholders, not about working together to create new products. As it sold off plants, Boeing would squeeze its smaller and more vulnerable suppliers for better deals. Pitting cities and states against each other would secure more in tax breaks. Employees would be asked to sacrifice their pensions and benefits. Amassing influence over government would bring defense contracts and more predictable regulation. Keeping all parties off balance and uncertain, with a mysterious Oz thundering behind the curtain in Chicago, was precisely the point.

The battle for Boeing's soul would play out dramatically in the high-stakes decision-making that led to Boeing's next big endeavor, the 787 Dreamliner. At first, Mulally had proposed a futuristic plane called the "sonic cruiser," which would cruise near the speed of sound and shave as much as 20 percent from flying times. Coming so soon after the headquarters move, the idea harkened back to Boeing's innovative past, even if Airbus dismissed the concept as a "paper airplane." (And in fact, the first sketches did have a suspicious lack of finishing touches, such as windows for the passengers in front.)

A week after the new headquarters opened, the September 11 attacks caused a steep downturn in travel. Mulally's commercial airplane business had to cut a third of its workforce. Airbus, its sales team led by a silver-tongued New Yorker named John Leahy, continued gaining ground. The A320 snatched away even rapidly growing low-cost airlines like JetBlue and EasyJet, which departed from Southwest's model of using the 737 as the short-haul workhorse. In 2003, the European plane maker surpassed Boeing for the first time as the largest maker of commercial aircraft in the world, delivering 305 planes to Boeing's 281. "We're number two," Mulally told a gathering of his top executives. "Say it, and let it sink in."

Boeing shifted its attention away from Mulally's proposed cruiser and toward a less futuristic, more conventional plane. The Dreamliner wouldn't be any faster than its predecessors, but it would incorporate advances, like a lighter and stronger carbon-fiber frame, to achieve big gains in fuel efficiency. At the time it wasn't even certain whether Boeing would stay in the commercial airplane business at all, with its center of gravity shifting toward the military. More than half of its $49 billion in sales in 2003 came from selling fighter jets, missiles, and other weapons to governments around the world. "There is the question out there about whether Boeing is headed the way of McDonnell Douglas," Byron Callan, the aerospace analyst with Merrill Lynch, told the *Wall Street Journal*. "Douglas frittered away a pretty solid market position by not taking risks."

The International Association of Machinists, the union representing Boeing's assembly-line workers, hired Merrill Lynch that same year to study the merits of undoing the merger and spinning off the commercial airplane business altogether. The analysis found the airplane unit accounted for less than three dollars of the value in the stock, then trading at thirty-five dollars. (Condit's "five in five" mantra of quadrupling the stock price had long since been shelved.) The union teamed with a private equity group to make a buyout offer that was quietly rejected.

Stonecipher had made good on his retirement plans after hitting Boeing's mandatory retirement age of sixty-five in June 2002. But he continued wielding influence on the board along with John McDonnell. His legacy also lived on at the leadership center near St. Louis, which by now was like an upscale business hotel, with a billiards room, a Baldwin grand piano in the lobby, hiking trails along the river, and a dining room named "Harry's Place" in his honor.

It functioned as a reeducation camp akin to the "Discovery" program that the fired Douglas employees had been subjected to a decade earlier. Thousands of executives took a two-week course there whose highlight was a role-playing game that simulated running a business. Under soft-spoken finance chief Boyd Givan, Boeing had sought to keep cost data out of the hands of rank-and-file engineers, to keep the information from compromising their designs; now the opposite was true. Boeing wanted them all to make decisions with the cold eye of a Jack Welch or a Harry Stonecipher. After finishing the course, engineers were meant to "understand, God, that program has to be produceable, I can't put every bell and whistle on it," said Boeing's vice president of learning, Steve Mercer, the former deputy at Crotonville.

Michael Sears, Stonecipher's protégé, was a frequent guest speaker at the center. Still the chief financial officer, he had also been elevated to the Office of the Chairman with Condit, giving him the inside track to become the next CEO. A Purdue University electrical engineering graduate who'd grown up in St. Louis, Sears made his mark at McDonnell Douglas with a system to track cost savings on the F/A-18 Super Hornet. ("Very functional and very detailed," as a former boss described the system.) Sears was no Boy Scout. People who worked with him say he kept conversations short and affected the same impersonal detachment about the products as Stonecipher. He said he was "a math guy," not an "airplane freak."

When it came to the Dreamliner, Stonecipher and John McDonnell were insisting on very tough math indeed. They told fellow board members that new plane's development costs had to be no more than 40 percent of what Boeing had spent on its wildly successful predecessor, the 777. What's more, they wanted assembly costs held to 60 percent of what it took to build each 777. Considering that it had been nearly a decade since the earlier plane's introduction, this was an aggressively low target. The only way to meet it would be to outsource pieces of the plane, as McDonnell Douglas had done, to its detriment.

Trying to retain at least some of the sonic cruiser's marketing magic, Boeing for the first time started a "name that plane" contest, with the winner to be announced at the Paris Air Show in June 2003. People could vote online for eLiner, Global Cruiser, Stratoclimber, and the eventual winner, Dreamliner. After thirty-five thousand layoffs in two years and constant strife over outsourcing, employees came up with a few of their own. Among those circulating in emails: Bottom Liner, Global Snoozer, Plant-closer, Sub-sonic cruiser, and End-of-the-Liner.

Dissidents inside Boeing latched on to a paper that had been pinballing around its intranet ever since February 2001, when a senior technical fellow at Boeing's Phantom Works unit in Southern California presented it at the leadership center. John Hart-Smith, then sixty, called the paper "Out-Sourced Profits—the Cornerstone of Successful Subcontracting." In fifteen densely worded pages, he laid out from his own experience at Douglas Aircraft how parceling out construction of the DC-10 had impoverished the company while enriching its suppliers. The basic point was that outsourcing is never simple. Design specifications actually had to be more precise, because any omissions would lead to costly disputes involving lawyers. Making sure the work got done right led to additional overhead costs that no one had counted on. Finally, all those extra costs had the perverse effect of making the company doing the outsourcing look less efficient than the ones it awarded business to—a vicious cycle that only encouraged more of the same destructive behavior.

Taking aim at financial metrics like RONA, Hart-Smith said the answer was not merely to dispose of assets. A far better response, he said, "would be to develop and sell *new* products that could be produced profitably with the *same* equipment and personnel." He appended an author's note that amounted to an epic troll, saying the views were his alone and not those of the management: "Conversely," he wrote, "the visible policies of the management are not necessarily those that the author would have recommended, had he been asked."

The debate over the future of Boeing's next product was still unresolved when Stonecipher's protégé Michael Sears gave one of his lectures in the Cockpit early in 2003. He told the assembled managers that they should avoid even the appearance of an ethical conflict. Polishing his résumé to succeed Condit, he was working on a book for John Wiley & Sons called *Soaring Through Turbulence: A New Model for Managers to Succeed in a Changing World*. People shifted in their seats as he preached against any hint of impropriety. One executive raised a hand and asked, perhaps impertinently: Speaking of perception, could he explain a recent hire?

Boeing had just named Darleen Druyun, one of the most powerful acquisition officials in air force history, as the deputy director of its missiles division. The company was still in the midst of a bruising, years-long fight over a $23 billion air force order for one hundred tanker planes, a critical lifeline after the 2001 recession. Critics of the deal, including Senator John McCain, had called the order a backdoor bailout; now Druyun's hiring looked like an example of the revolving door at work. At the air force, Druyun had been so important to McDonnell Douglas's financial success—ever since she'd helped accelerate payments for the C-17 back in the 1990s—that she called herself the plane's "godmother." A giant sign proclaiming THANK YOU, MRS. DRUYUN hung at the Long Beach plant.

Sears brushed aside the question about the ethics of hiring Druyun that day in the Cockpit. But by summer, the stench of over-the-line dealings in the military programs acquired from McDonnell Douglas was out in the open. First came a scandal at the rocket launch business, where it emerged that executives had used thousands of pages of proprietary documents from competitor Lockheed Martin to help win the lion's share of a critical contract. That July, the air force stripped Boeing of $1 billion in deals and barred it from future work while the government initiated a criminal investigation. "I was hired to win . . . and I was going to do whatever it took to do it," a former McDonnell Douglas executive was quoted as saying by a Defense Department special agent who investigated the case.

In November, investigations of Boeing's tanker dealings escalated. It turned out Sears and Druyun had met in Orlando a year earlier to discuss the prospect of Druyun joining Boeing. There,

Sears learned that Druyun had not yet officially recused herself from the tanker negotiations. He sent an email to others in the Office of the Chairman, including Condit, about this "non-meeting" and proceeded to recommend for her a $250,000 annual salary with a $50,000 bonus (though he added an "important dimension"—"could get by with 40K"). Druyun ultimately confessed to criminal investigators that she'd systematically favored Boeing in acquisition deals, the company where, it turned out, her daughter and son-in-law also worked—Sears had helped secure their jobs in 2000. Both were fired, and each executive eventually pleaded guilty to conflict of interest charges and served time in prison. Wiley pulped Sears's book.

In the aftermath of the scandal, the long leash Condit had enjoyed from his board finally gave out. He resigned December 1, 2003, saying he hoped to "put the distractions and controversies of the past year behind us." In a move that was a surprise only to Boeing outsiders, Stonecipher, who had stepped down from the number two role a year previously after reaching mandatory retirement age, came out of retirement to replace him. In the view of Boeing veterans, the McDonnell Douglas takeover of Boeing was now complete.

Two weeks later, a *Business Week* exposé revealed that Condit hadn't fallen quite so nobly on his sword: He'd been fully planning to hang on until the board pressured him to go, in part because of mounting frustration over his strategic missteps. Some on the board also finally raised concerns over his womanizing, and the article for the first time disclosed that a settlement had been paid to the fired former customer relations manager, Laverne Hawthorne, who had pursued a wrongful termination claim after her relationship with Condit. "She immediately went to see him in his office and reminded him of promises he had made to her," read the piece, unusually lurid for *Business Week*. "As Hawthorne recalls it, she looked him in the eye and said: 'One of us in this room has balls, and it certainly isn't you.'"

Stonecipher certainly had no issues in that department. "This was about a company in trouble, and somebody needs to come in who knows how to fix it, and that's me," he told reporters.

The first surprise for any who might have questioned Stonecipher's commitment to the commercial business came in April 2004: the board gave the go-ahead for the Dreamliner, after a $6 billion order from All Nippon Airways. But the project was hamstrung from the start with the returning chief executive's rigid demands on the use of capital. An internal analysis projected Boeing would spend only $5.8 billion on its development, less than half of what the 777 had cost. For the first time in its history, even the wing was to be developed by an outside company, Japan's Mitsubishi Heavy Industries.

Stonecipher had an ever-combative answer for those who claimed he'd taken the cost focus too far. "When people say I changed the culture of Boeing, that was the intent, so that it's run like a business rather than a great engineering firm," he told the *Chicago Tribune* that year. "It is a great engineering firm, but people invest in a company because they want to make money."

As Boeing ramped up work on the Dreamliner in 2005, its R&D spending, at 4.8 percent of commercial sales, was just over half that of Airbus, estimated Morgan Stanley analyst Heidi Wood. Stonecipher sold off giant parts-making operations, including a factory in Wichita that Boeing had owned for seventy-five years and employed seventy-two hundred people. It may have improved the RONA numbers, but it made everyone's jobs harder. Now when they needed a part at the last minute or had an idea for a process improvement, it wasn't a call with a colleague; it was a negotiation with lawyers, procurement-chain executives, human-resources representatives—all the overhead hassles Hart-Smith had warned about in his treatise.

Mulally remained upbeat in public, though some executives claimed they increasingly saw him escaping to a driving range at Jefferson Park in Seattle to smash buckets of golf balls. "In the old days," he reportedly told a colleague in the parking lot one day, "you would go to the board and ask for X amount of money, and they'd counter with Y amount of money, and then you'd settle on a number, and that's what you use to develop the plane. These days, you go to the board, and they say, 'Here's the budget for this airplane, and we'll be taking this piece of it off the top, and you get what's left; don't fuck up.'"

One of the casualties of the efficiency drive was a building in Renton where Boeing had full-scale mockups to show off the interiors of its airplanes. Salespeople jokingly called it the Dirty Pool Room, because it was so supposedly unfair to Airbus. The walls had curved white lines marking, for instance, the less roomy dimensions of an Airbus A340 cabin compared to a 777. While selling that plane back in the 1990s, Mulally had walked British Airways chairman Lord King through one of the mockups, fashioned from plywood, plastic, and actual airline seats. Mulally took the British lord by the shoulders and the arm, pushing him into seats and making a show of ducking under the A340's lower overhead bins before standing up to full height. When they reached the economy cabin, Lord King looked around the rows of seats and said without a hint of irony, "Ah, this is where the passengers sit."

Now the building housing the mockups was to be sold. Klaus Brauer, a silver-haired Boeing sales executive who frequently hosted customers there, kept telling anyone who would listen that getting rid of the mockups was a bad idea. He got a sympathetic hearing from fellow salespeople; the exception, he said, was "people who were on a career track to potentially go to the corporate office." To those in thrall of the metrics, rooms that sat empty most of the time were an enticing target for savings. At his wit's end, Brauer mentioned the fate of the mockups to Ken Dowd, then a vice president at Teague, a Seattle design firm that has advised on the interior of every Boeing commercial aircraft since World War II.

After hearing Brauer out, Dowd went to his Teague colleagues and convinced them to buy the mockups from Boeing. If Boeing wanted to use them, it would pay a fee. It was an unusual arrangement for the boutique firm, not used to fronting large capital expenses for clients, but one the metrics minders at Boeing happily accepted. The mockups were cut up and towed to a ware-house behind a furniture store on West Valley Highway, a sea of big-box retail where garish signs always seemed to be announcing EVERYTHING MUST GO! As Boeing started showing customers what it promised would be the world's most revolutionary modern aircraft, their first impression of it would be this colorless stretch of American suburbia. "It was to me appalling the lack of foresight that we had," Brauer said.

One Sunday, a group of Middle Eastern officials flew into Boeing Field to hear Boeing's pitch for the new aircraft. U.S. marshals escorted the phalanx of limousines into the parking lot, where, outside the furniture store, a thirty-foot inflatable gorilla with a top hat and a cigar was flapping away above their heads. Brauer asked one of the marshals to shoot it.

Stonecipher's return was shorter than anyone expected. During a management retreat at a hotel in Palm Desert in January 2005, Debra Peabody, a forty-eight-year-old executive in Boeing's Washington lobbying office, came over and gave him an unusually long full-body hug as people gathered for an evening cocktail reception. The chemistry was so apparent that at least one of the executives there decided it was time to head back to his room. It's hard to keep a secret in a place where most everybody hates your guts. Someone passed intimate emails between the two to the board, and in March 2005, Stonecipher was fired. His wife of fifty years, Joan Stonecipher, hired the powerful Chicago attorney who'd represented rapper R. Kelly's ex and filed for divorce within days.

Once again veteran Boeing people started dreaming of Mulally, one of their own, getting the top job. He'd always been the one they wanted. Back in the 1990s, the shuttle drivers who overheard everyone's private conversations as they ferried people around Boeing's giant campuses used to say it was only a matter of time before Mulally was running the place.

Mulally never openly campaigned for CEO; he was dismissive of what he saw as the more gauche efforts on behalf of the other main internal candidate, Jim Albaugh, the chief of the defense business. Albaugh was close to Norm Dicks, an influential Washington State congressman who'd been a key tanker backer, and Dicks lobbied for Albaugh with at least two of the board members he knew. "His team is measuring for the drapes in Chicago and we're not doing that," Mulally said of Albaugh at one point.

The board chose neither. It opted instead for one of its own, Jim McNerney, a Jack Welch protégé who was then running the 3M Company. He'd been on Boeing's board since 2001, and, according to one person familiar with the deliberations, he had also been its first choice to replace Condit back in 2003. McNerney had rejected the overtures in part because his contract with 3M ran three years, and he would have lost lucrative stock payments if he'd accepted. This time the board gave him all the incentive he'd need to join Boeing—a pay package worth $52 million that replaced what he was losing at 3M. It was what's known as a "golden hello," and controversial because it guarantees pay before any performance.

"It wasn't even a close call," a former board member said of the decision. The board had duly considered the two Boeing insiders, but hiring McNerney would represent a coup for the scandal-tarred company. He had been one of the most highly regarded American business leaders ever since he'd been one of the three finalists in the much-publicized race to succeed Welch at General Electric. The influential recruiter Gerry Roche at Heidrick & Struggles told people he frequently got requests for a "McNerney type." Within days of McNerney being named 3M chief, its stock had risen almost 20 percent. "The mere mention of his name made everyone richer," as *BusinessWeek* put it.

Boeing veterans grumbled that the board must have thought Mulally, five foot nine and still frequently described as boyish at sixty, just didn't look the part of the stereotypical CEO. McNerney was six foot two, Hollywood handsome, and had the de rigueur head of graying hair. It sounded like shallow gossip, but to the risk-averse Boeing board, appearances were indeed a factor—as was the perception that McNerney would pursue a more shareholder-friendly, predictable, and less expensive strategy.

"There are just some people who look and act like a CEO," the former board member said, drawing on tropes of the typical executive. "Some people say I know an NFL quarterback when I see them. Alan didn't have that look and feel—he's excitable, cheerleadery, high-energy, 'we're going to build that plane.'"

A former high-ranking Boeing executive revealed one more reason the board passed over Mulally: he had been having an affair with a female subordinate, something few would have guessed from his image as a devoted family man who spent nearly every Saturday dining alone with his wife of more than thirty years. After Stonecipher's resignation and the embarrassing revelations about Condit, "the board couldn't take the risk," this person said. "It was a zipper problem." The issue did come up as a "risk factor" at one point in the board's discussions, according to the board source, who said, "I remember there being a fun-loving guy who liked to have a scotch and a glass of wine and liked girls. Even if he was perfect, we liked Jim for the job at the time better." (Mulally didn't reply to requests for comment.)

The Boeing lifer was soon chafing under yet another new boss, having lost out once more on the top prize. Within a year, McNerney began pressing his team to rank-and-yank managers the way he had at GE. Mulally resisted, telling people at a meeting in 2006, "If you hire a team that you think is really good and they're all performing well, why in the hell would you eliminate 10 percent every year?"

One of his deputies, Mike Bair, proved oddly detached in an interview that May as he described how one of Boeing's suppliers had torched an important test part for the Dreamliner after mistakenly leaving a wooden stool in a high-temperature oven. "Let's say we had a campfire," Bair said coolly. At one meeting, Bair walked a roomful of managers, including Mulally, through a color-coded status report illustrating the likelihood that various systems of the airplane would meet expectations. The chart showed mostly green boxes, with a couple of yellows. The uniform positivity, to those versed in the usual travails of new airplane programs, was as disturbing a sign as if they had been uniformly red. Some of the managers in attendance waited for Mulally to pounce, to demand more honesty about what wasn't working. His disengagement showed: he never did.

In September 2006, William Ford Jr. announced that Mulally would replace him at the helm of the Ford Motor Company, becoming the first non–family member to run the iconic automaker. Within a day, movers came to pack up his office and the conference room decorated with framed magazine articles and souvenirs. He said his goodbyes after thirty-seven years from a bare room on a lower floor. Not long after, in a moment whose symbolism was all-too-painfully evident, the WORKING TOGETHER banner on the wall outside his office came down.

For people who thought of Mulally as Boeing's engineering soul, it was hard to watch. "The idealism just went out," a Mulally lieutenant said. "It was no longer about working together, it was about something else—I guess shareholder value."

That November, in a faraway corner of the baroque organization Boeing had assembled to build the Dreamliner, Michael Leon, a technician at Securaplane Technologies in Tucson, Arizona, was working with one of the fifty-pound lithium-ion batteries planned for the new jet. If outsiders had been privy to Securaplane's production schedule, they would have known then to be skeptical of Boeing's promised timelines. The supplier was planning a seven-year design process, with final tests in 2010 or 2011—up to three years *after* the Dreamliner was scheduled to enter into service. It was a period of high turnover and job shuffling at Securaplane, which was using a Japanese-designed battery for shipment to a company in France, which would then supply the unit to Boeing.

Leon had told his bosses he had reservations about the battery. In the midst of his tests, it caught fire and exploded. He and another employee tried dousing the flames with fire extinguishers, but the intense heat forced them to retreat. When firefighters arrived, temperatures reached twelve hundred degrees, and the galvanized metal roof collapsed. The building was a total loss. It was a fiery symbol of a strategy that was also to go down in flames, if anybody thought to look.

6

The Corporate Playbook

Walter James McNerney Jr. was indeed straight from twentieth-century-CEO central casting. His chiseled jaw, hooded eyes, and implacable demeanor called to mind a watchful hawk. It was the same look that had stared down hockey opponents at New Trier Township High School in the tony Chicago suburb of Winnetka, where Jim played center, and on the baseball diamond at Yale, where he was a star pitcher. ("He liked to be in charge," said Peter McNerney, one of three younger brothers.) At Yale, McNerney pledged Delta Kappa Epsilon, one of the oldest fraternities in the country, and was initiated by George W. Bush.

Leadership was practically in his blood. His father, Walter James McNerney Sr., ran the giant insurer Blue Cross and was an early advocate of a single-payer health-care system for elderly Americans, Medicare, enacted in 1965. The senior McNerney went on to advise Richard Nixon on health policy. He led the Task Force on Medicaid that reached a strikingly progressive conclusion in 1970 about coverage for poor Americans: "A sizable unmet need for health service is a disgrace and cannot be tolerated in an affluent society," said the report from the "McNerney task force," as it was known. "We must be prepared as a Nation to spend more money so that all citizens have reasonable access to health care."

By the 1980s, as the Reagan administration preached that government was the problem, not the solution, the elder McNerney pioneered managed care, in which insurers became the dominant middlemen dictating access and prices. He finished his career on the faculty of Northwestern University's Kellogg School of Management, where his lectures somehow made health policy spellbinding. "Because of his drive, brilliance and devotion, many citizens who otherwise would have been left vulnerable or even destitute now have health care coverage," the publisher of *Modern Healthcare* wrote of Walter McNerney.

At home he and his wife, Shirley, who'd attended Vassar College, raised a high-achieving brood of five—four sons and a daughter—who were encouraged to debate the issues of the day, often with business colleagues who dropped in for dinner. "Whatever you do, manage it well," Jim recalled as one piece of advice from his father, a phrasing notable for its expectation of command as much as the commitment to greatness.

After some of the usual rich-kid diversions in his early twenties—he taught sailing on Lake Michigan and worked on a ranch in Colorado—Jim took an insurance job in London. He went back to school for a master's degree in business administration from Harvard University, then joined Procter & Gamble as a brand manager in 1975. (He had the fabric softeners, like Downy and Bounce.) Three years later he left for a stint as a management consultant at McKinsey. In 1982, McNerney finally landed at General Electric, run at that point for little more than a year by a live wire named John Francis Welch Jr.

It was the year *Fortune* magazine first used the term *downsizing* in reference to people. Welch had inherited what he considered a rigid, slow-moving bureaucracy from his predecessor Reginald Jones, a courtly Brit, and immediately set a new course. "Take a look around you," Welch told a meeting of GE corporate planners in 1981, "because you won't be seeing each other anymore." (All but a dozen of two hundred planning positions were eliminated.) At his first meeting with Wall Street analysts at the Pierre Hotel in

New York in December 1981, his speech drew inspiration from Carl von Clausewitz, the nineteenth-century Prussian general known for the concept of "total war." Welch had admired something he read in *Fortune* magazine about the Prussian general: "Strategy was not a lengthy action plan. It was the evolution of a central idea through constantly changing circumstances." He quoted the line to the analysts.

The speech also relied upon the management theorist Peter Drucker, famous for asking the question, "If you weren't already in the business, would you enter it today?" Welch outlined a radical idea for a company that had hundreds of businesses, many of them deeply entwined in local economies: Each one had to be among the number one or number two "leanest, lowest-cost worldwide producers" in their industries, or have some other clear market edge. General Electric had increased its earnings for twenty-six straight quarters and outperformed the stock market over the previous decade, but as Welch told the analysts that day: "We have the commitment and the potential to do better."

Welch's talk, titled "Growing Fast in a Slow-Growth Economy," has often been identified as the birth of the "shareholder value" movement. He never used the phrase. What he was really birthing was the imperial CEO, the notion that a brilliant, Clausewitzian tactician could be entrusted to improvise boldly and impose his will upon economies and nations. GE was an American institution. It had pioneered inventions that dramatically improved living standards: the lightbulb, the X-ray machine, the diesel-electric locomotive, the refrigerator. The people who worked in its factories and labs, in river towns and industrial burgs around the country, thought of themselves as family. Welch was telling investors he wouldn't flinch from the hard decisions to jettison them, whatever the human or political cost. One in four people on the payroll, 118,000 jobs, were gone within five years. "Neutron Jack" had arrived.

—

His arrival was perfectly timed with that of a former GE pitchman, whose presidency unleashed the dramatic shifts in regulation, tax rates, trade, and labor policy that made the ascendance of corporate titans like Welch possible. In the 1950s, Ronald Reagan had hosted the *GE Theater* television drama on CBS, which began every Sunday night with a paean to the company's virtues: "in engineering, in research, in manufacturing skill, in the values that bring a better, more satisfying life." The Hollywood star toured each of the company's 130 U.S. plants and addressed 250,000 employees during an eight-year contract that ended in 1962 (coincidentally, the year he changed his voter registration to the Republican Party). He'd led the Screen Actors Guild through three strikes, making him the only former union leader elected president when he defeated Democrat Jimmy Carter in 1980. But it was an epic showdown with labor that almost immediately defined his presidency.

The week before Welch sketched his vision to financial analysts at the Pierre Hotel, Reagan was hosting the chastened leaders of the AFL-CIO executive council at the White House. The new president's firing of 11,345 striking members of the Professional Air Traffic Controllers Association had shocked the leadership of the country's most powerful white-collar labor union. Federal law barred workers in essential industries from walking out, but many presidents, including Richard Nixon during a postal strike in 1970, had sought compromise over confrontation. Reagan had chosen the opposite.

Four months after the strike began, he had emerged the clear winner. The nation's air traffic barely slowed as managers and scabs replaced the striking controllers. That day in the White House, the AFL-CIO's leaders asked if he would let at least some of them crawl back, defeated, to their old jobs. "Should the military be allowed to strike?" Reagan replied. "Are some laws okay to break and others not?" Days later, Reagan opted to permanently bar them from the FAA for their insubordination.

Labor union membership in the United States had reached a peak of 21 million in 1979. Reagan's tough stance is frequently credited with emboldening a generation of corporate leaders to similarly challenge unions in that decade's wave of downsizing. (George Shultz, Reagan's secretary of state, even claimed the spine he showed impressed the Soviet Union's leaders.) Free trade agreements, meanwhile, lowered tariff rates on imported goods and made it easier for American companies to shift production to lower-cost countries overseas. "Ideally, you'd have every plant you own on a barge," as Welch put it.

While GE rarely suffered strikes during his tenure, it wasn't because he was conciliatory. If any of its businesses had a heavy union membership, they were candidates for an early sale. In a dizzying seven years, GE's workforce went from 70 percent unionized to 35 percent by 1988.

The deregulatory fervor swept through Reagan's federal agencies, with the FAA slashing the number of inspectors early in his administration. It was one of many reductions in federal programs, from college tuition assistance to Medicaid, after one of the largest tax cuts in U.S. history. The tax rate on upper brackets of income fell from 70 percent to 50 percent (and later to 33 percent), causing a 9 percent drop in federal revenue in two years.

At the SEC, run by a former executive from the E.F. Hutton investment bank, the implementation of Rule 10b-18 in November 1982 drew little notice in the press but opened the way to a sustained transfer of wealth. The rule gave companies that purchased shares of their own stock in the open market "safe harbor" from charges of manipulation, as long as they didn't exceed a limit of 25 percent of the daily trading volume. Over the subsequent decades, the University of Massachusetts economist William Lazonick wrote, "stock buybacks have channeled the productivity gains of U.S. business into the hands of the richest households, while the persistent gushers of corporate cash have played a major role in the rise of the financial sector over the once-dominant manufacturing sector." From 1981 to 1983, he calculated, buybacks consumed only 4 percent of net income for the largest U.S. companies. By 1996, it was 27 percent; by 2006, 46 percent; and by 2016, 50 percent. Two generations later, in any prosperous American city, the unequal effects are plain—Teslas, luxury high-rises, avocado toast. And tents.

McNerney's rise at GE paralleled the Reagan revolution, as he ascended through stops including lighting, electrical distribution, and GE Capital. In his first job at GE Information Services in Rockville, Maryland, in the early 1980s, the junior executive crossed paths with Dave Calhoun, then a company auditor. McNerney impressed him as "the one guy in the whole place" who could answer his questions, as Calhoun recalled it later. The business was trying to sell computer equipment to ten different industries; McNerney brought them together with a coherent strategy. His primary skill was reductive.

One task that accelerated McNerney's promotion to a senior position in Hong Kong was firing a fellow manager who had run afoul of Welch over a difference in strategy, according to *At Any Cost,* a 1998 book by a GE beat reporter at the *Wall Street Journal.* "We're taking a different approach to the Asia/Pacific region," McNerney told the manager. "We want more of a sales orientation rather than business development. We're eliminating your position. I'm sorry." A recruiter who knew McNerney found him to be formal and almost robotic, even when they had a long business dinner, at which the airing of at least some personality is expected. "GE screwed him up," the recruiter concluded. "There was Jack Welch and everybody else—those were 'B' players with an 'A' shoe stuck up their ass." By 2000, McNerney was running the aircraft engines unit in Cincinnati—Harry Stonecipher's old stomping grounds— and had been named among three finalists to succeed Welch for what was then the most coveted job in business. "Jack got outlandish performance from the three of us," McNerney said. "I mean, none of us slept for two years. All we did was drive the heck out of GE's three largest businesses."

Fortune had just named Welch "Manager of the Century," and he was enjoying a victory lap. GE's market value had increased from $12 billion to $410 billion over his twenty-year reign. Unprecedented portions went straight back to investors and Welch himself. From 1994 to 2004, GE spent $75 billion, 56 percent of its free cash flow, on stock buybacks and dividends. Welch left with a $417 million severance and still got the company to pay for perks including an $80,000-a-month Manhattan apartment, courtside tickets to New York Knicks games, box seats for both the Boston Red Sox and the New York Yankees, country club fees, and a standby private jet. (The perks were later exposed, to a considerable public outcry, during Welch's divorce from his second wife, sparked by his affair with the editor of *Harvard Business Review* while she was profiling him; he agreed to pay GE for them.)

Welch was hailed at the time for his prowess at developing talent, and he spent a few pages in his memoir—2001's *Straight from the Gut,* for which he got a record $7.1 million advance—reminiscing about how it was done. It amounted to Welch sitting down with GE's human resources chief, Bill Conaty, and poring over binders of senior executives, complete with photographs and miniature biographies. They'd debate about whether somebody was a "top operational leader" or "needs more edge." Or, sometimes, just needed a new picture. "This guy looks half-dead! He can't be any good," Welch remembered joking in March 2001, a typical zinger. One failing was always a career killer: Lack of execution. "Failure to deliver on commitments is, in the end, unacceptable," he wrote.

Just after Thanksgiving in 2000, the year of the contested presidential election, Welch flew into a private aviation hangar in Cincinnati on a bone-chilling night to break the news to McNerney that he'd chosen Jeffrey Immelt to succeed him instead. McNerney, ever composed, said he didn't expect there would be a recount.

Within a week of losing the CEO race, McNerney had his consolation prize: an industrial dinosaur of his own to whip into shape. He got $34 million up front to become chairman and chief executive of 3M, a venerated manufacturer a century old that had some similarities with Boeing. The Minneapolis company was the birthplace of masking tape, Thinsulate, and the Post-it note. It had a culture of innovation that employees treasured. Official policy allowed them to use 15 percent of their time on pet projects, and the tenets of "the 3M Way" included generous funding for independent research. The Post-it note famously emerged after years of trial and error, from an employee who wanted to mark passages in his hymn book.

In just over four years, McNerney doubled the company's annual profits; the stock price rose 30 percent. He did it by going straight at 3M's future, slashing capital expenditures 22 percent in his first full year and 11 percent more to a low of $677 million in 2003. R&D spending was held constant at just over $1 billion from 2001 to 2005, and McNerney cut eight thousand jobs, about 11 percent of the workforce. Many of those laid off were older, higher-paid workers. "We should be developing 30 year olds with General Manager potential," read one email summarizing McNerney's "vision for leadership development" that later turned up in a discrimination suit brought by the Equal Employment Opportunity Commission. Research was evaluated with a new, profit-minded rigor. Steven Boyd, a PhD researcher whose job was eliminated after thirty-two years in 2004, told *BusinessWeek* that after a couple of months on a project, he would have to fill in a "red book" with scores of pages worth of charts and tables, analyzing everything from the potential commercial application, to the size of the market, to possible manufacturing concerns. Critics of the new CEO included the inventor of Post-it notes himself, Art Fry, who said he wouldn't have invented them under McNerney's strictures. "What's remarkable is how fast a culture can be torn apart," he said.

After leaving 3M for the top post at Boeing in 2005, McNerney quickly established an image as a forthright, if stiff, leader. He removed many of the elaborate furnishings and artworks that had adorned Boeing's headquarters during Condit's reign. McNerney won praise from Senator John McCain, the harshest critic of Boeing's shady dealings with the air force, when it settled the ensuing investigations for $615 million—and refused a corporate tax deduction on the payment. At his first annual retreat with managers in

Orlando the following year, McNerney had Boeing's general counsel, Douglas Bain, display a pair of numbers on a screen. "These are not ZIP codes," Bain said, telling the audience they were looking at the federal prison numbers of Sears and Druyun. He ended with four questions: "Do we have a culture of silence? Where was the management throughout this? Is the problem the rank and file? Or is the problem us?"

The answer came soon enough. Four days after Bain's speech, a mechanic at a Boeing maintenance plant in San Antonio approached a lawyer on his staff to report that managers had been overbilling the air force on KC-135 tanker planes for years. He had time sheets, work orders, and emails showing they'd billed for phony work. The Boeing lawyer was hostile and skeptical, according to testimony from the mechanic, Edward Quintana. He filed a whistleblower claim that year alleging fraud under the False Claims Act. Boeing fired him, but the Justice Department later joined the suit, and the company quietly agreed to pay $2 million to settle it.

In the year McNerney took over, Boeing spent $9.2 million on lobbying, with 66 lobbyists. Five years later it spent $18.1 million, with 143, ranking sixth among all American companies. "We used to have a few people in Washington, D.C., and now we have an empire," marveled one former executive. Even the air force refueling tanker, lost in scandal, returned; Boeing won a $35 billion contract.

Another lucrative defense program was Future Combat Systems, run by Dennis Muilenburg. Boeing was tasked with creating a networked system linking mortars, cannons, ground vehicles, and infantry for the U.S. Army. "We are right on cost, right on schedule, and meeting all the performance requirements," Muilenburg told reporters who watched a live-fire demonstration at Maryland's Aberdeen Proving Ground in September 2005. Four years later, Defense secretary Robert Gates killed the program after almost $20 billion had been spent. It was a "toxic" contract in which the industry consortium led by Boeing and a partner, SAIC, had effectively been in charge of overseeing its own performance, *Defense News* reported. "I think this program single-handedly set the Army back a generation in vehicle technology," said Todd Harrison, a defense analyst at the Center for Strategic and International Studies.

If troubled, the military contracts helped cushion the financial blows soon to strike the defining aircraft of McNerney's tenure, the 787 Dreamliner. McNerney had signed off on the unprecedented outsourcing of its design when he was on the Boeing board. Dozens of airlines placed orders, drawn to the undeniable technological leap. As planned, half of the plane's structure was carbon fiber rather than aluminum, reducing weight. It would allow for larger windows and a more comfortable pressure in the cabin, causing fewer of the issues with dry noses and throats after flights. (Carbon fiber doesn't corrode like aluminum, so humidity could be kept higher.) Boeing would also employ rechargeable lithium-ion batteries, giving the Dreamliner more extensive use of electrical power than any other airplane, and saving even more weight by eliminating the need for ducts to bring bleed air back from the engines.

Mike Bair, the Mulally protégé who led the program, talked up the benefits of outsourcing more work, saying that when Boeing had sent specifications to its electronics supplier for the 777, the document was twenty-five hundred pages long. "There wasn't a lot left to the imagination," he said. "We told them exactly what we wanted in excruciating detail," he said. Distressingly, the equivalent specification document for the Dreamliner was just twenty pages.

The issues that Hart-Smith, the outsourcing dissident, had warned about in his paper quickly became apparent. One major supplier didn't even have an engineering department when it won its contract, according to an analysis by Airbus. At a meeting with top executives in 2008, a Boeing engineer complained about sending drawings back to a team in Russia eighteen times before they understood that the smoke detectors needed to be connected to the electrical system.

Managers hadn't thought through another issue: When the vendors sent designs to Customer Services, the department charged with writing manuals telling airlines and maintenance workers how to use their new airplanes, huge sections of them were blank, stamped "proprietary," said Cynthia Cole, the president of the engineers' union at the time. How could Boeing's workers provide instructions if they had no idea themselves how the planes worked?

McNerney finally had to admit defeat in the outsourcing strategy—bringing work back in-house, buying suppliers, and ultimately spending a staggering $50 billion to finish the job. The costs might have bankrupted another company, but Boeing could rely on generous rules known as "program accounting" that allowed it to average the upfront expenses over the plane's decades of expected service. The approach still made some on its finance staff nervous; they considered the projections so unrealistic as to violate the rules. "I used to get calls from inside Boeing and it would go, 'We're all going to jail,'" said Joe Campbell, the Lehman Brothers analyst. "The whole institution broke down in the sense that now they were lying to themselves." (The SEC later opened a probe into a whistleblower's complaint, centering on the projections. No action was taken, and Boeing says it properly accounted for the costs.)

"We lost control," concluded Jim Albaugh, the former defense unit chief who was tasked by McNerney to lead the cleanup. "We gave work to people that did not have, in hindsight, as much experience as we wish they had." He spent his Saturdays leading meetings to get the program back on track. And he convened a group of retired senior engineers—including Boeing legend Joe Sutter—to serve as an informal advisory panel. Asked by a reporter to explain why Boeing had ever considered a plane like the sonic cruiser when it finally ended up with the Dreamliner, the ever-blunt Sutter replied, "It was a real effort, by people who were smoking marijuana."

One more way the company still fell short of the Welchian ideal: its dependence on large, and powerful, labor unions. The engineers, of course, had held their strike in 2000, which emboldened them. But it was the machinists who rankled McNerney, striking in 2005 and then again in 2008. Boeing's machinists—officially, District Lodge

751 of the International Association of Machinists—were practically the last union of manufacturing workers in America with real leverage. The reason was simple: they could, and did, shut Boeing down. A bronze statue outside the union hall in Everett, depicting generations of striking workers—men, women, children—carrying picket signs summed up what seemed to be a doomed relationship. The statue was one of the first things customers saw when driving through the Everett campus, all too frequently while hearing someone at Boeing tell them their airplane would be delivered late because of a strike.

McNerney, from his base in Chicago, told people on his team that he'd learned how to handle unions from Jack Welch. "He was pretty sure that we on the West Coast just couldn't figure it out," said one former executive at Boeing's Seattle jetliner business.

In 2009, the corporate office stunned workers with the announcement of its first jet assembly plant outside the Seattle area. Boeing was moving some Dreamliner assembly to a facility in South Carolina formerly owned by a supplier that made fuselage parts for the plane. The workers there voted to abandon their own union to secure the purchase. This came after the state of Washington, only six years earlier, had awarded Boeing $3.2 billion in tax breaks for the Dreamliner, then the largest state tax incentive ever granted.

Boeing's internal deliberations were revealed in the politically charged legal fight that followed. Albaugh had told the board that the move to South Carolina brought both extra costs and additional risk. They'd have to spend $1.5 billion, train inexperienced workers, and accept lower earnings on the first Dreamliners built there. But Project Gemini, as it was called, would undercut the union's leverage and gain "important political support from a key state." Boeing got more than $800 million in new tax breaks from South Carolina, where Republican Nikki Haley, elected governor in 2010, frequently declared that she wore high heels to kick unions out. Workers would make fourteen dollars an hour there compared to twenty-eight dollars in the Seattle area.

The point person chosen to handle the blowback from the Obama administration illustrated how far the company had come from its roots as a gritty Pacific Northwest family enterprise: J. Michael Luttig, a former federal appellate judge from Texas who had served in the Reagan and George H. W. Bush administrations. Luttig was Republican royalty, groomsman at the wedding of another young lawyer in the Reagan White House, the future U.S. chief justice John Roberts. Luttig helped prepare Clarence Thomas, Sandra Day O'Connor, and David Souter for their Supreme Court confirmation hearings.

After being passed over by George W. Bush for his own appointment to the Supreme Court, he joined Boeing in 2006 as general counsel, one of McNerney's first hires. He'd been wooed by Boeing's lead director, Kenneth Duberstein, the former Reagan chief of staff who'd come over from the McDonnell Douglas board. "Boeing may well be the only company in America for which I would have ever considered leaving the court," Luttig said in his resignation letter to Bush. He also mentioned the need to pay for his children's college education.

Luttig stocked his department with former government lawyers, some of whom had also clerked for him on the federal bench and gone on to work for Supreme Court justices. (An online law journal coined a term for these high-powered ex-clerks, soon studded throughout the ranks of government: "Luttigators.") As an adviser, he tapped Kirkland & Ellis, a Chicago law firm whose attorneys have included such prominent Republicans as William Barr, Brett Kavanaugh, and Ken Starr.

When Obama's National Labor Relations Board ruled in 2011 that the move to the nonunion plant was an illegal retaliation against workers for their strikes, the case became a cause célèbre in conservative media. The Republican-controlled House Oversight Committee held a hearing titled "Unionization Through Regulation: The NLRB's Holding Pattern on Free Enterprise." At a hearing in the Senate, Luttig was impish and dismissive when Senator Tom Harkin questioned the wage cuts Boeing was offering machinists, while paying the lawyer $3.7 million in annual compensation. The previous May, Luttig and his wife had paid $1.8 million for a second home on Kiawah Island in South Carolina. "At this moment, I sense that it's not enough," Luttig answered Harkin, a smirk sneaking across his face.

In the 1960s, Joe Sutter had told the managers who wanted to move his 747 factory for political reasons to stand down—he didn't want anything to get in the way of his sacred plane. Now, the shift to South Carolina was the fulfillment of what the physicist Stan Sorscher had warned about years earlier, the new overlords in Chicago pitting states and workers against each other to gain advantage for themselves. Creating "risk" all the while, in the studiously bland term.

Yet Boeing's incentive structure practically guaranteed it. The compensation of McNerney, Luttig, and other top executives was tied to boosting free cash flow and the net return from assets on hand—the sort of metrics that tend to favor investors over employees and customers. It reflected the shift in priorities at Boeing that had begun under Stonecipher. In 1999, executive compensation had been based on earnings from operations, as well as such intangibles as "customer and employee satisfaction, safety, and diversity." By 2007, the focus was on "optimizing net assets," as the Boeing proxy statement explained. "This is done through more efficient processes, cost containment and minimized inventory, among many other ways."

Such priorities help explain why Boeing waited so long to address the long-deferred question at the center of its product lineup: the 737. The Next Generation models introduced in the 1990s had proven remarkably durable, with orders surpassing seven thousand. What's more, with the initial investments in design and factory tooling long since paid off, the plane was a cash cow: the profit on each one was $12 million. The persistent issue remained: In the biggest, most important part of the aircraft market, the 737 was no longer the premier product. The Airbus A320 was.

And airline customers knew it. Few thought of the 737 as the industry's Apple iPhone; it was more like the Kyocera DuraForce Pro 2, whose defining characteristic was that it was cheaper.

One day in 2010, while Albaugh was hosting a group of consultants, his assistant came in and said Michael O'Leary, the brash chief executive of Ireland's Ryanair, was on the line. Albaugh disappeared for an hour. When he came back, he looked ashen. "Are you okay?" he was asked. "I don't know," Albaugh replied. O'Leary had just offered to buy three hundred 737s—for 20 percent less than Boeing's cost to make them. When Albaugh demurred, O'Leary snapped, "That's too damn bad," and hung up.

"This is like the Wild West—we don't do this on the military side!" Albaugh said. "We talk it over for years and years before somebody buys something." (Ryanair would later buy 175 of Boeing's 737NGs for $15.6 billion, paying what analysts estimated was as little as $40 million apiece for planes then listing at $89.1 million.)

Boeing—the epitome of American engineering excellence—was going downmarket. It even started selling bare-bones versions, offering as options equipment that Airbus sold as standard. A backup fire extinguisher in the cargo hold, for instance, cost extra. This was permissible because a backup wasn't mandated by the FAA. (In places including Japan, however, regulators did require it, mindful of incidents in which the primary system had failed.) In another fateful example, Boeing charged $80,000 for an angle-of-attack indicator—the seemingly peripheral cockpit gauge whose absence would figure in the doomed Lion Air and Ethiopian flights, neither of which was equipped with the optional equipment.

Customers often came back to Airbus and told them Boeing's offer was lower priced, and its salespeople would have to pore through the details to see what was missing, said John Leahy, the New York native who ran sales at Airbus for thirty years. It reached the point that Airbus estimated a bare-bones A320 had $2.5 million to $3 million more in standard equipment than a 737. That logic was one of the things that caused trouble for Boeing, Leahy said: "'Let's make everything an optional extra, let's strip the airplane down; we can't do extra training, we don't want to make the airplane too expensive, we're in a price war.'"

If the Dreamliner had been delivered as planned in 2008, Boeing would have had the cash and engineering resources to have been well along, in 2010, in the development of a replacement for the 737. That had been its plan as far back as 2002, when Mulally had assigned a team to investigate potential future planes in a project code-named for national parks. "Y1" in the Yellowstone project would have been a new single-aisle aircraft to supplant the then-thirty-year-old 737. With delays on the Dreamliner, however, those plans had long since been shelved.

At Airbus, by contrast, momentum was growing to make another technological leap in the 737's competitor, the A320. The impetus wasn't any innovation from Boeing but a Canadian plane maker called Bombardier. The Montreal-based company had started in snowmobiles, like the Ski-Doo, before branching into business jets and small commuter planes. Bombardier and the Canadian government had poured billions of dollars into a 130-seat plane called the C Series. Airbus executives considered it a real threat, even as they dismissed the new plane publicly. They judged that it might start with a few small orders and then catch on, much as the A320 had crept up on Boeing decades earlier.

The cockpit featured sidestick controllers, just like the Airbus planes, and had touch screens with an electronic checklist. The cabin was wider than those of other planes its size. The overhead luggage bins were also bigger and swiveled to make accessing them easier. It was a plane completely optimized to steal market share from the two dominant manufacturers on North American domestic flights. Short hops would no longer take place hunched over, in terror of having your (slightly oversized) bag seized at the gate.

Airbus executives started debating whether to update the A320 in 2010. In December of that year, it began offering airlines a new design called the A320neo, for "new engine option." The new plane would, as the name suggested, feature larger, more fuel-efficient engines. Airbus anticipated a 15 percent cost advantage over the 737, once the plane entered service later in the decade. Another design under consideration would have pressed the advantage still further, with even bigger engines, according to one high-ranking former Airbus executive. The fear was that if they chose that option, Boeing might launch an all-new plane that would leap-frog the A320neo. "It was to some extent a compromise that said 'Let's not make the engine bypass any bigger than is sensible, and certainly not enough that it puts the competition in a direction we don't want to go,'" the executive said.

Some leaders at Airbus still worried the plan would leave them vulnerable to a new Boeing plane. Leahy assured them that if he snatched away an all-Boeing operator as planned, their U.S. rival would have no choice but to respond with its own derivative. Had Boeing instead surprised him by launching an all-new plane, "I probably would have been in serious trouble," Leahy said.

His instinct was right. After the Dreamliner fiasco, Boeing had no appetite for further spending. Albaugh told colleagues in the commercial airplane business at a meeting in January 2011 there was no need for concern over the A320neo—Airbus would prob-ably go over budget building its plane, and Boeing could simply build a better one later in the decade. "I don't think we need to get too spun up over the fact that they're making some sales," he said.

By the Paris Air Show in June, however, Airbus had won more than one thousand orders. Even worse for Boeing that summer, Airbus executives began talking to American Airlines about buying the new version of the A320. This would be no small loss: the giant carrier, based in Fort Worth, Texas, was one of three in the United States that had signed exclusive deals to buy only from Boeing back in the 1990s. Those deals had been ripped up, as a concession to European regulators, in the wake of the merger with McDonnell Douglas. Nonetheless, American hadn't bought an Airbus plane since. The airline was such an important customer that Boeing had sales staff who lived full-time in Dallas–Fort Worth.

The Airbus team courted American's CEO, Gerard Arpey, and its president, Tom Horton, over frequent lunches at the Mansion on Turtle Creek in Dallas, a boutique hotel where they didn't think they'd be spotted. Moving to the Ritz-Carlton during a stretch of hundred-degree days lasting nearly two weeks that July, they reached agreement on an order for hundreds of planes. Arpey called

Albaugh to let him know the carrier was ready to buy Airbus aircraft; what could Boeing do for them?

Albaugh kept his cool and said he'd get back to American with an offer of his own. Privately, though, he was furious that his Dallas residents hadn't picked up any intelligence about the talks and unenthusiastic about making a public U-turn in strategy.

Within a week, Boeing made a counterproposal for a hypothetical 737 outfitted with more powerful engines, a model so new it didn't yet have a name. The world would come to know it as the 737 MAX 8.

Just like the original 737, the design was quick and dirty. Over the decades, the 737's engines had gone from cigar-shaped, to ovoids squished on the bottom, to soda cans clipped in front of the wings. Now, to fit even bigger turbofans onto the same basic low-slung fuselage, Boeing would mount them still farther forward of the wings, and raise the nose gear about eight inches. This would change the plane's center of gravity, not to mention the view from the cockpit for pilots, potentially forcing them to undertake additional training, always costly for airlines. But pressure was mounting; with the A320 winning seemingly every sales campaign that summer, Wall Street analysts were writing about the 737's lost edge. Ryanair's O'Leary called the Boeing strategy "confused."

The Boeing team assured American it would work the technical details out during development. The carrier would get the planes about a year behind the projected Airbus model. After taking in the proposal, Arpey informed Boeing that American had made its decision: it would split the order between the two plane makers.

Though still a sale, it touched a raw nerve at Boeing, where it was perceived as a defection. Boeing tended to view North and South America as its natural territory, and it went to greater lengths to defend it, using levers such as politics, pricing, and trade policy. A small but telling example: One year the Airbus A350 jetliner was among the nominees for the prestigious Collier trophy, awarded by the National Aeronautic Association. Airbus sent a midranking engineer to make its case for the plane, which had been partly designed in the United States. Two of the highest-paid Boeing executives, lawyer Michael Luttig and Government Operations chief Tim Keating, appeared unannounced at the D.C.-area hotel where the nominating speeches were taking place to give a long presentation about why the A350 shouldn't count as an American product eligible for the award. (It didn't win.)

If a mere trophy merited shock and awe, the American Airlines defection sparked an even fiercer reaction. One tense meeting at American's headquarters involved a half dozen executives from Boeing, lawyers among them, according to two people familiar with the events. They warned of consequences up to a lawsuit as Boeing sought to enforce its rights under the terms of their contract. Boeing had, of course, agreed with European authorities not to enforce its 1996 exclusive deal with American, which they said disadvantaged Airbus. But the European ruling lasted only ten years, and the carrier had later signed a side letter that essentially resurrected the deal and entitled it to similar discounts, according to the people involved.

The argument had a chance of working on Arpey, who prided himself on his integrity; when he eventually left American just before it declared bankruptcy, he took no severance pay for himself. But he was determined to split the order, and he telephoned McNerney with a warning that summer: if he didn't call off the attack dogs, Boeing would get nothing.

McNerney relented. On July 20, 2011, American said it would place a $38 billion order for 460 aircraft—200 of the redesigned 737 and 260 of the A320neo. It was far from the exclusive deal to which Boeing had felt entitled, but it spared Boeing the huge financial setback, not to mention the black eye, that a complete loss of one of its bedrock customers would have represented. That month, Albaugh went to the Dallas–Fort Worth Airport and smiled in the American Airlines Executive Club lounge beside Airbus chief Tom Enders, both men holding replicas of planes in the airline's livery. Albaugh predicted "quite a number of orders for whatever we call this re-engined 737."

A month later, it was formally christened the MAX. That left only the matter of building yet one more derivative—forty-seven years after Joe Sutter had first imagined the plane by pulling out a pair of scissors, snipping the engines from the tail, and tucking them under the wing.

Many Wall Street analysts reacted with relief; the program would cost $2.5 billion, compared with $20 billion for a full-blown replacement. But a few called the decision a missed opportunity to disrupt Airbus with a new plane (a prospect that Airbus sales chief Leahy, at least privately, had considered job threatening). "Instead, we have status quo at best," wrote RBC Capital's Robert Stallard of the more conservative plan.

Describing how Boeing had stood up to the A320neo threat in his letter to stockholders in February 2012, McNerney sounded, in his emphasis on the bottom line, something like John McDonnell: "With development costs and risks far below an all-new airplane, the 737 MAX will provide customers the capabilities they want, at a price they are willing to pay, on a shorter, more certain timeline. This approach is an all-around winner for Boeing, too. We maintain our qualitative advantage over competitors in the segment, we free up resources to invest in other growth products, and we reduce our business risk for the next decade."

Later that year, a presentation to the board about the new plane summed up the approach with a catchier tagline: "Stingy with a purpose."

Ironically, one of the management theorists who had inspired Boeing's reinvention—Harvard Business School's Clay Christensen, author of the influential piece about "skating to where the money will be"—had started having second thoughts about pushing business leaders to use rigorous financial metrics that encouraged conserving capital. With interest rates at historic lows, capital was now abundant. In a 2014 article called "The Capitalist's Dilemma," Christensen wrote that companies needed more "market-creating" innovations, not "efficiency" innovations, whose benefits lasted only a year or two and cost jobs. "Much as it pains us to say it, a lot of the blame for the capitalist's dilemma rests with our great schools of business, including our own," he wrote. "We've advanced success metrics that are at best superficial and at worst harmful."

In McNerney's single-minded emphasis on cost savings, there was something else that went unmentioned in his letter to stockholders: Safety. For five years of his tenure—from 2010 through 2014—the word was nowhere to be found in the company's annual proxy statements. As one board member who served during those years put it, "Safety was just a given."

7

The Forrest Gumps

Richard Reed started doing the Forrest Gump impression after one more bad meeting with Boeing. There he was, a staff engineer at the FAA, in his Costco dress shirt, matched up with some necktie-wearing Boeing VP. The guys from Boeing (almost invariably guys) had their jobs because they were good at negotiating. Reed had his because he knew cockpit display systems. He'd been recruited into the FAA's Boeing Aviation Safety Oversight Office in 2011 against his better judgment, as a favor to a manager who was having a hard time finding engineers willing to sacrifice their professional pride and join an office many saw as an embodiment of Boeing's takeover of the agency. Everyone called it "the Basoo," as if it were a musical instrument, because what else would you say? That you worked for the Boeing safety office? The first organizational charts sent around about this new system—mandated by Congress—had the headshot of the FAA manager in charge underneath his counterparts at Boeing. The implication was clear enough: the regulators were there *in service* of Boeing, not to police them.

The office was supposed to supervise more than a thousand Boeing engineers who had been deputized by the agency to vet designs and ensure they met the FARs, or Federal Aviation Regulations, the compendium of rules specifying the steps to prove the airworthiness of a commercial aircraft, drafted in dozens and dozens of meticulously detailed paragraphs. (For instance: "any removable screw, nut, or pin" needs "two separate locking devices" if it is critical to flight.) Joe Sutter and other engineers at Boeing wrote the first set of jetliner regulations, known as SR 422, themselves because no one in government had designed a jet before.

Ever since, the agency had relied on deputies employed by the aircraft manufacturers to ensure safety, but the new system adopted in 2009 obliterated many of the safeguards. It used to be that the agency chose each of its deputies, as a way of filtering out people lacking in technical chops or who were too cozy with the plane maker's management. There was a dotted-line reporting relationship to a manager at the FAA, as well as at Boeing. Now the representatives would be selected by Boeing and report to a manager at Boeing. The FAA would have only vague "organizational" supervision under a plan that was supposed to make the agency more "risk based" and efficient. The implicit message was clear: the FAA's primary responsibility was to hasten the production and sale of American airplanes, not to burden plane makers with red tape.

Reed had been typical of the profile among FAA engineers when he joined in 2007: Already in his fifties, he was old enough to know his field cold, cynical about the fit-for-purpose ways of a corporate bureaucracy, but not yet ready to retire. He'd worked for various aerospace suppliers and even done a three-year stint at Boeing itself, but left soon after the engineers' strike in 2000. Others in the office had also worked for Boeing; some seemed to enjoy sticking it to their old employer, raising obstacles wherever they could. Mostly, though, they were the kind of literal, technical-oriented Boy Scouts who had toiled away on spreadsheets in Boeing's engineering cubicles—which was precisely how those Boeing VPs continued to treat them, summarily shutting down discussions. ("It's compliant to the regulations," they'd tersely argue.)

So it was after one of these meetings that the scene from *Forrest Gump* came to Reed's mind, the one where Tom Hanks, playing the dim-witted Gump in boot camp, assembles a rifle in seconds and calls out, "Done!" When the drill sergeant asks Gump why he completed the task so quickly, he answers dully, "You told me to, drill sergeant." Reed started telling colleagues in a Gump voice what he would say if he was ever hauled in front of Congress to explain why a Boeing plane had been waved briskly through certification: "You told me to, Congressman."

This shift in the balance of power between Boeing and the FAA was the culmination of a decades-long war for influence, one embedded in the very nature of a place sometimes derided as "the tombstone agency" because it only seemed to act swiftly when people were dead.

The FAA owed its existence, in fact, to a crash. On June 30, 1956, two passenger planes—a Trans World Airlines Super Constellation L-1049 and a United Air Lines DC-7—collided twenty-one thousand feet over the Grand Canyon, killing 128 people and scattering wreckage across two buttes. Hikers still come across glinting metal fragments of seat-belt buckles or aircraft skin. It was the worst accident in aviation history to that point and prompted Congress to create the FAA as an independent agency in 1958, replacing a predecessor that had been housed in the Department of Commerce. (Employees began moving into their new headquarters building on November 22, 1963, the day of John F. Kennedy's assassination.)

The new agency had a mandate to ensure safety and better control the national airspace, but the language of its founding act made clear that it wouldn't stray far from its commercial roots: the FAA was also to ensure "the promotion, encouragement, and development of civil aeronautics." Crucially, a separate body that investigated accidents and made safety recommendations—now known as the National Transportation Safety Board—had no authority to impose its findings. That was left to the FAA, which has long been torn between its dual mandates of encouraging growth and maintaining safety. In part citing cost, the agency declined to impose NTSB guidance on radar, runway lighting, deicing protocols, and cargo-bay smoke detectors, among other issues to have emerged in the 1970s and 1980s. The NTSB, somewhat degradingly, releases a

"Most Wanted List" of safety improvements, to gain at least some leverage. (Among those the FAA still hasn't addressed: a recommendation for cockpit recorders capable of recording images as well as voice, to speed accident investigations.)

Mike Collins joined the agency's Aircraft Certification Service in Seattle in 1989. Similar to the way Sorscher viewed his supervisors at Boeing in those days, Collins found his FAA bosses admirably willing to dig deep into the weeds of technical debates. His manager—and his manager's manager—were experts in their fields. If he had an issue with a design proposed by Boeing, they typically backed him up in bringing it to the attention of one of the FAA's deputies at the manufacturer. Then they all worked together to try to find a way for the design to meet the minimum standard. "There was a direct relationship that was built on knowledge and trust," said Collins, who retired in 2018.

After TWA Flight 800 exploded and crashed into the Atlantic Ocean off Long Island in July 1996, Collins participated in the NTSB-led investigation as it zeroed in on the possibility of a spark igniting vapors in the 747's center fuel tank. The only wires entering the tank were extremely low voltage; they were supposed to be spark-proof. Two years later, with Boeing still suggesting in court documents that a bomb or missile might have brought down the plane, Collins watched in a lab at the Everett plant as engineers snaked more than a hundred feet of wires like the 747's. The room was like a bank vault, shielded from any outside electrical signals. They turned out the lights and switched on a relay to simulate a tiny short-circuit in a chafed wire. A spark jumped, the culprit in Flight 800's detonation exposed. It led to mandates Collins helped write to inspect the wires, shield or separate them, and add sensors or surge protectors in thousands of commercial aircraft.

Though safety developments like these emerged, the 1990s largely brought a renewed business mindset to the FAA, as the Clinton administration's triangulating zeal for a reinvention of government mingled with the Republican-led drive to diminish it. Five months after sweeping the 1994 midterm elections with promises of lower taxes and less regulation, House speaker Newt Gingrich, in a nationally televised address from the congressional floor, held up an ancient vacuum tube used in the FAA's control towers to symbolize waste and inefficiency. The Georgia Republican declared plans to "totally remake the federal government, to change the very way it thinks, the way it does business, the way it treats its citizens." That year, Thomas McSweeny, director of the certification office where Collins worked, was asked how he saw the FAA's role in light of its already substantial delegation of work to private manufacturers. "I don't know, I've thought about that," he told the *Seattle Times*. "We ought to start with asking ourselves if we should even exist."

Congress passed a transportation funding bill that included changes in the way FAA employees were compensated, a personnel reform also backed by the Clinton administration. Starting in 1996, pay increases were tied to a raft of performance-based measures. These included goals for safety, but also metrics like efficiency and modernization. The "superior contribution increase," for example, allowed managers "to identify the highest contributing employees in the areas of collaboration, customer service, and impact on organizational success." As a result, an FAA employee's support for a plane maker (and its bottom line) could be rewarded with an additional bump of as much as 1.8 percent in base pay. The agency's overall budget, though, was held flat throughout the decade. From 1996 to 2012, when another Republican-led austerity drive imposed automatic spending cuts known as sequestration, the agency's workforce fell 4 percent (excluding air traffic controllers, whose numbers were unchanged).

McSweeny, later to become a Boeing lobbyist, began soliciting advice from industry working groups on how to cut the onerous costs of certifying airplanes for flight. One of them, led by Webster Heath, Boeing's senior manager of technical affairs, sent its recommendations to McSweeny in October 1998, asking for the "earliest possible issuance" of a new rule transferring more authority to the manufacturers themselves. Plane makers wanted license, in other words, to deputize and police themselves.

—

The influence war between government and corporation played out in sterile conference rooms, in places like the Hyatt Regency Crystal City at Reagan National Airport, where one of the industry working groups met in February 2001, a month after George W. Bush's inauguration following the contested presidential election. The meetings of the Aviation Rulemaking Advisory Committee were open to anybody from the public, at least anybody who carefully monitored the *Federal Register* for the dates and times. The chairman of the group was Albert Prest, a vice president at the Air Transport Association. He opened with a lighthearted comment about the novelty of having a gavel, then ran through a roll call. There were a few trade union representatives, but it was mostly executives from Boeing, Airbus, Pratt & Whitney, the Helicopter Association International, and others from the industry. Then Tom O'Mara spoke.

"I'm here because my only child died at Sioux City, Iowa, in 1989, when a DC-10 crashed," he said. "One hundred eleven died, one hundred eighty-nine lived. Heather was twenty-four years old. She was a graduate of Tulane Law School, a member of the New Jersey Bar, and a captain in the U.S. Army JAG Corps, serving at Fort Collins, Colorado, at the time of her death. She was found on the tarmac."

O'Mara, balding and round-chinned, paused in his prepared speech for a moment. He said he'd been "a corporate guy" like most of them before the crash, a sales manager for the *Wall Street Journal*. But soon after the crash he saw the newspaper's headline referring to "the Achilles heel" of the DC-10. He said it was the first time he'd considered that regulators might let a safety problem linger because of a cold cost-benefit analysis. "Pretty naive, wasn't I?"

As he'd learned, ever since that first crash of a Turkish Air DC-10 at Orly, when the cargo door popped open and hydraulic lines under the floor snapped, regulators had known how vulnerable those lines were. In the accident that killed his daughter, a blown engine spewed fragments that severed all three lines and left United Airlines captain Al Haynes without controls to steer the jet. He lined up for an emergency landing by alternating thrust on the two working engines. But the right wingtip hit the runway first, igniting fuel, and then the plane careened over and broke into pieces. If a safety valve for the hydraulic lines had been mandated fifteen years earlier—"a $10,000 item back then," O'Mara said—the flight controls would not have been lost.

For the families of crash victims, he told the group, that knowledge was just as painful as losing them. "The first mugging is the crash," he said. "The second mugging is discovering that their loved ones didn't have to die."

People applauded, and Prest from the Air Transport Association thanked him. Then he motioned for the next speaker, a consultant from a firm called Information Overload Corporation. His presentation, in this context, was more like a third mugging. The consultant went directly into his own prepared remarks about how data should guide all of the advisory committee's decisions—in his case the data in question was an industry-funded study showing no correlation between cabin air quality and flight attendants' health. After the grieving father's emotional speech, it was a jarring juxtaposition. "By focusing on performance-based outcomes rather than design end points, participants are given a greater latitude in utilizing qualitative and quantitative information in reaching a defendable solution," he said. "This allows for more creative, cost-effective and measurable deliverables."

Prest called last on the Association of Flight Attendants' representative, Christopher Witkowski, who wasted little time addressing the elephant in the room. "It's our belief that Congress and the American people have lost oversight of the deep workings of this major rule making committee," he said. "It's dominated by industry representatives whose goals may sometimes be at odds with the public interest."

President Bush's choice to run the FAA would be someone deeply familiar with the backstage workings at the agency. Marion Blakey had run a public affairs consulting firm in Washington. Her biggest clients were transportation companies. She helped plan their

PR campaigns, write white papers, and set up "Astroturf" organizations to give corporate messaging the appearance of grassroots support. A native of Gadsden, Alabama, Blakey had attended the Johns Hopkins University School of Advanced International Studies before working as a communications specialist at the National Endowment for the Humanities, the Education Department, and the White House during the Reagan administration.

In her first major speech as FAA administrator, at the Aero Club in Washington in February 2003, Blakey announced what she called the "customer service initiative." It was a breathtaking shift in emphasis. She said the FAA needed to be more responsive to its customers—by which she meant manufacturers and airlines, not the flying public. She expressed sympathy for the inconsistent answers and long waits they sometimes experienced—as if the country's top aviation authority was some kind of corporate call center—without mentioning the funding shortfalls that had starved it of resources.

That year happened to be the centennial of the Wright brothers' first flight in 1903, and she titled her speech "The Spirit of December 14th." As she pointed out, this wasn't the date of their historic twelve-second flight, but three days *earlier,* when Wilbur stalled the Flyer and crashed it into the dunes. "I want to bring to the FAA such a spirit of readjustment, for the willingness to correct, to recalibrate, is the real secret of aviation," Blakey said. The message seemed to be that the industry should get points for trying. Then she all but encouraged corporate managers to second-guess the agency's decisions and tattle on inspectors who tried to hold them up. "We're going to let them know that they have the right to ask for review on any inspector's decision on any call that's made in the certification process—that they can 'buck it up' to first-line supervisors, field office managers, regional division managers, or even to Washington if necessary—with no fear of retribution," she said. "Information on how to do this—names, titles, and phone numbers—will be prominently displayed on the Web and in all our regional and field offices."

Blakey still stressed the importance of safety, but the message was awkwardly mingled with business buzzwords. "One of these goals, our stock price—if you will—is the lowest possible accident rate, first and foremost," she said. "Second comes our ability to smoothly manage demand." And to accomplish those goals, "We are committed to a dynamic, results-oriented plan that we're going to pulse regularly, measure quarterly, and adapt as necessary real-time," she said. "In short, we will run the FAA more like a business."

Bush signed an aviation funding bill that December, and in it Congress mandated changes in supervision that had been percolating in the industry working groups. The FAA described its new approach to aviation oversight as "a means to provide more effective certification services to its customers"—a term Blakey was now encouraging in all of the agency's communications instead of the more customary "applicants." (A "customer feedback" link even appeared in the signature line of staff emails.)

The formal rule was adopted in 2005. General Electric, one of the largest makers of jet engines and thus a key beneficiary of the loosened oversight, said in its comments that "it was particularly satisfying to see that the FAA had left intact the spirit of the recommendations" developed in the working groups.

Among the critics of the new mandate was Jim Hall, the former chairman of the NTSB who had pursued the investigations into rudder defects on early 737 models and the explosion of TWA Flight 800. "The primary reason we've been able to build such a safe system is the structure we've had in place for years," he said. "The ultimate responsible party for safety is the government, and this new FAA policy essentially is trying to transfer that responsibility. It may work in the short term, but in the long term the public will see that what we have is a less safe system."

The customer service initiative had predictable results. Southwest Airlines, annoyed by one inspector's aggressiveness and emboldened by its newfound clout, complained to the inspector's superior. (*The customer is always right.*) Upset, the inspector brought his own concerns about a culture of coziness to federal agents and, eventually, to a congressional committee. He documented how the carrier tried to pick and choose its inspectors, who sometimes looked the other way while it skipped mandated safety checks. "There is nothing in place to support the inspectors that are intimidated by the FAA management and by the airline because they do their job," Bobby Boutris, the inspector at Southwest, testified in 2008. "In the performance of my duties, I have been asked by Southwest Airlines management to make a violation go away. In addition, I have been threatened by Southwest Airlines management that they could have me removed from the certificate"—denied the authority to certify planes—"by picking up the phone."

Southwest had flown dozens of jets on tens of thousands of flights without inspecting them as required. When it finally did, it found cracks in a half dozen of the planes, including one crack that was four inches long. (Corrosion and cracking had also caused an Aloha Airlines 737 to rupture midflight in 1988, killing a flight attendant.) In part because of the congressional scrutiny, the FAA proposed a $10.2 million fine on Southwest that year. It was the largest fine it had ever levied on an airline—but it amounted to the loss of about one-third of a single day of operations for the airline, which had $11 billion in revenue that year.

By then Blakey was gone. She'd been hired in 2007 to run the Aerospace Industries Association, the industry's main lobbying group, before finishing her career at Rolls-Royce North America. McSweeny left that same year, telling staff in an email that he'd been debating whether to join Boeing for the previous year and a half before making the leap. It struck some who read it as a potential admission of a conflict of interest. In an interview with a trade publication, he had a direct answer for why he took the job as director of international safety and regulatory affairs: Boeing offered more money and he wouldn't have to leave Washington.

One of the most enthusiastic backers of shifting the FAA's burden of safety inspection onto airplane makers was Ali Bahrami, who ran the Transport Airplane Directorate based near Seattle and set up the forty-person BASOO to oversee work with Boeing. Inside the FAA's largest and most important office, a cultural war was under way that had some parallels to the one at Boeing.

Bahrami had worked for ten years as an engineer at McDonnell Douglas early in his career before joining the FAA's Los Angeles office and then moving to the Seattle area. Staffers say he and others who had worked in Los Angeles, such as Dorenda Baker, another certification official, started moving up the ranks. They did it by pursuing the FAA's new business mantra with gusto. "From top down the managers are all essentially groomed and promoted based on this metric of satisfying the customer—they call it 'stakeholder needs,'" said a current engineer in the office. "Essentially if you want to move up you are pretty much pressured to delegate even more"—to hand over more of the responsibility of oversight to manufacturers.

Bahrami even told staffers at one point that part of his bonus depended on Boeing meeting its schedules, said one former senior engineer who worked for him in Seattle. People in other offices had the impression their managers had similar targets. "I've heard cash incentives," said Marc Ronell, an FAA software engineer in the Boston Aircraft Certification Office in Burlington, Massachusetts. In 2012, for instance, managers in the office overrode their own specialists' concerns at the last minute to approve the Sikorsky S-76D helicopter—a decision Ronell was told had to do with their financial incentives.

The goals set for managers in the agency's formal business plans reflected the shift. Though the plans continued to stress safety as the first priority, other priorities crept in over time. These included measures related to encouraging the use of manufacturer "delegates," or for approving work by certain dates. In fiscal 2007, one goal assigned to Dorenda Baker, then deputy director of aircraft certification, read: "Certify the GEnx 1B [a General Electric engine] on the Boeing 787 by September 30, 2007."

(The FAA declined to make anyone available for comment and didn't respond to questions about the performance incentives.)

Almost immediately, Boeing began wielding the authority it had gained in this new system, which had the comically opaque name of Organization Designation Authorization. Now that the company was in charge of choosing its own deputies, it began putting more junior employees into the roles, often recent college graduates. Ronell and others believed it was because they'd be more willing to listen to their managers, less likely to dig in their heels than senior staff. "It's basically asking companies to oversee themselves," he said.

In a more subtle shift, the deputies were no longer called "designated engineering representatives." They became known as "authorized representatives" or the even more neutered term "unit member." Some simply called themselves "Boeing authorized representatives."

At one point, Boeing managers asked for input from the FAA engineering staff on a particular staff appointment. Giving the lie to their efforts at consultation, they ended up choosing the person who had received the *most* objections from the FAA, according to a report prepared by a group of the agency's unions. Boeing also promoted another person whose FAA evaluations had shown "a consistent lack of integrity, unsound judgment, and an uncooperative attitude towards FAA," the 2017 report said.

Conversations that used to take place at the specialist level became tense negotiations with higher-ranking executives in the Boeing regulatory unit. Steve Foss, a former FAA test pilot, watched as Boeing executives buttonholed his supervisors in parking lots after meetings. "It was push, push, push, shove, shove, shove, to get the airplane into the customer's hands," he said. When the specialists raised technical issues, they'd be told to stand down—often by Bahrami, the official in Seattle most responsible for ensuring the safety of Boeing airplanes. One senior manager who disagreed with the new approach remembers Bahrami frequently assuring staffers they should trust Boeing. "They know the systems, they know the rules," Bahrami would say. After this person raised his concerns privately, Bahrami gave the impression the manager's career depended on going along: "I'm trying to help you," Bahrami said. The fragmentation of responsibilities left Ken Schroer, the FAA program manager who'd had such a warm feeling about collaboration with

Boeing on the 777, struggling to get clear answers; it was often difficult to tell who was telling who what. He retired in part because of his frustration.

Early on, one of the FAA's engineers, Steve Oshiro, asked his counterparts at Boeing why the plane's design didn't include an enclosure around the new lithium-ion batteries, according to three people familiar with the conversation. Fires are considered one of the very worst hazards on airplanes, and lithium-ion batteries are notorious for erupting in flames, as the Arizona building collapse in 2006 well attested. Boeing had agreed to "special conditions" precluding the possibility. Oshiro thought Boeing should design a steel box that vented outside the airplane to help avert such a disaster. He was told not to worry about it. The review of the battery was delegated to one of Boeing's deputies, who decided the fire risk was remote enough that an enclosure wasn't needed.

Disagreements over delegation split the staff, and in 2012 the Transportation Department Inspector General's office was called in to investigate complaints that Bahrami had relaxed oversight too much. One of the complaints came via an anonymous fax. The inspector spoke to fifteen employees; seven said they'd been retaliated against for trying to raise concerns about Boeing designs. The investigator, Ronald Engler, said in a memo to the FAA's audit office that it was clear Bahrami and the FAA's headquarters "had not always supported . . . efforts to hold Boeing accountable" and "this has created a negative working atmosphere." ("There was nothing there," Bahrami later said of the probe.)

Some in the office had a negative opinion of Bahrami for reasons other than his views on delegation. They suspected him of having an affair with his executive assistant, at the time married to an FAA inspector herself. She'd earned promotions while working for Bahrami, and then one weekend, someone spotted the two together in a vacation getaway spot, miles from Seattle. Concerns about the relationship were reported to a human resources manager, John Barrett, according to people familiar with the events. Some staffers overheard him discussing the issue with other managers, including John Hickey, the agency's number two safety official. Barrett told them not to repeat what they'd heard, and ultimately no action was taken, according to the people. Bahrami and his wife, Mary, divorced in 2010, and he later married the assistant who also divorced her husband. She now works at the Transportation Security Administration.

"It speaks to the guy's character, and it speaks to the FAA management culture that they covered it up and hid it," said one staffer. (The FAA and Bahrami didn't respond to questions about the matter.)

What happened next with the Dreamliner, given the volatile material it employed and the hands-off approach to supervision, could only be seen as inevitable. On January 7, 2013, firefighters at Boston's Logan International Airport extinguished a blaze sparked by overheating lithium-ion batteries in a 787 Dreamliner parked there. No one was hurt. A few days later Ray LaHood, the former Republican congressman from Illinois then serving as Obama's transportation secretary, appeared with the FAA administrator and the head of Boeing's commercial airplane business at a press conference in Washington. They said they'd review the incident but assured people the plane was safe.

A week later, on the evening of January 15, Boeing CEO Jim McNerney was just setting out some fish to bake at his house, a many-gabled French country-style château in the Chicago suburb of Lake Forest, when his phone started vibrating with messages about another battery fire. Passengers had to descend on the emergency slides of an All Nippon Airways Dreamliner after the captain smelled smoke in the cockpit and diverted midflight to the nearest runway in Japan. A flurry of phone calls followed, but to little effect. The next morning, despite the dramatic events, both Boeing and the FAA agreed the plane should keep flying. The agency's administrator, Michael Huerta, spoke to LaHood and told him the staff was reluctant to ground the plane. Data still suggested battery fires were a rare event; it was possibly just a fluke that two happened in such close proximity.

LaHood decided to trust his gut instead. "Michael, it's my call, I'm doing it," he told him. He ordered the FAA to ground the Dreamliner, the first time the agency had done so for a Boeing jetliner and its only grounding of any model since the McDonnell Douglas DC-10, when a federal judge ordered it after the Chicago crash in 1979. LaHood called McNerney, and the CEO started raising objections. "I know you're not happy," LaHood replied in his prairie-flat midwestern accent. "And you know what, I'm not happy about the fact that there's smoke and fire in these planes!" He said the Dreamliners could fly again when he got a "100 percent guarantee" they were safe.

It took three months to design the fix—an enclosure like the one the FAA engineer had asked about years earlier. In April, Bahrami and other managers were called to testify at an NTSB hearing that laid bare the scope of the agency's reliance on Boeing for airplane safety supervision. The employees entrusted to do the FAA's job had tested for a potential short circuit in the battery simply by driving a nail through it. Most troubling to the agency's specialists was that it wasn't even a particularly complicated engineering problem; it was resolved almost as soon as it was raised.

It was the kind of sloppy mistake Boeing would make again, to much more disastrous effect. Lithium-ion batteries were known to catch fire, as had by then been observed in a range of products large and small. "This wasn't rocket science," said one FAA engineer. He suggested Boeing's authorized representative in this case reached the most convenient answer instead of pushing for more thorough testing. "You're behind schedule, over weight, and over cost," he said. "What's your career going to look like if you go to a manager and tell them to put in a box that's going to add weight, etc.?" Documents submitted to the FAA had put the odds of a failure of their battery at one in 10 million flight hours. Instead it happened twice in 52,000. The NTSB faulted Boeing for inadequate testing and the FAA for inadequate supervision.

Congress, however, was more forgiving. At a hearing in the

House of Representatives that June, the main concern of the congressmen who had pushed for expanded outsourcing of safety supervision was not to reemphasize the importance of passenger security but to make sure the fires wouldn't derail further plans to delegate oversight.

Roger Williams, a Texas Republican, asked an FAA official a couple of perfunctory questions. "Would you feel comfortable flying on a Boeing 787?" (Yes, came the answer.) "Do we need to get more involved?" (No.) "Less government is the best government," he concluded.

At another hearing that October, Jimmy Duncan, a Tennessee Republican, told attendees including a vice president from the Aerospace Industries Association that the FAA in effect needed a swift kick. "They should be handling these certifications much, much faster," he said. Apparently unaware of the shift in manager incentives already in place, Duncan added, "In fact, I think if they started giving out some bonuses to move some things faster, they probably would see a lot of this backlog wiped out pretty quickly."

He got no argument there. "Our members have a keen interest in efficiency of the FAA certification activities, because those activities govern our ability to bring new and innovative products to the market," said Ali Bahrami, the official in the hot seat. He'd just started a $300,000-a-year job at the lobbying group.

8

The Countdown Clock

Long before he helped design the controls of the 737 MAX, Rick Ludtke flew a black-and-orange Pitts Special biplane in aerobatic tournaments. His father, also a pilot, advised that if the ancient plane broke up in midair, Ludtke should "fly the biggest piece home." Ludtke's passions for flying and tinkering led him to start a business restoring vintage airplanes and then, in 1996, to join Boeing, where he worked on flight test aircraft as a mechanic before rising to engineering roles, earning two U.S. patents for cockpit alerts. In 2011, he started at Boeing's Flight Deck Design Center. For an airplane buff, it should have been a dream job. The center develops cockpits for all of Boeing's planes, from the MAX to the not-yet-in-service 777X.

But Ludtke's career spanned a different era at Boeing. Buffs weren't as welcome as they once were; they got in the way.

After his trial by fire on the Dreamliner, Boeing's watchful hawk, Jim McNerney, could have communicated several lessons. The need to strengthen the safety culture. Rethink the total war on costs. Show some humility. Instead, McNerney only increased the intensity. The drive for efficiency was ratcheted up to the degree that workers were running scared throughout the development of the 737's latest overhaul, the MAX.

Sorscher, the Speea union official and PhD physicist, was still keeping up his dialogue with analysts. At the time many of them kept asking a version of the same question: "Why does Boeing hate Speea?" The company's giant plant in South Carolina had finally given it the leverage it needed to challenge organized labor head-on. A Speea strike would no longer necessarily hobble the company; a threat from corporate to move work outside of the Pacific Northwest had real teeth. Boeing started doing exactly that, and also sought pension reductions, even as plane orders rolled in and earnings soared.

During the MAX's development, Boeing shipped more than thirty-nine hundred jobs out of the Puget Sound area. Product support for 737s shifted from Seattle to former McDonnell Douglas offices in Southern California, puzzling some airlines that complained that new staffers knew little about their planes. Boeing closed an advanced research unit in Seattle and sent the work to Missouri and Alabama, two less union-friendly states. The pilots who worked on the MAX came under pressure, too, as some jobs in their unit shifted to Florida and other states. "We've made choices there to go to more affordable areas within the business to again drive productivity and profitability," Greg Smith, Boeing's chief financial officer, told analysts in July 2013.

The union saw it as a way of lessening the power of their bargaining unit. In part thanks to its threats and the leverage it now held, Boeing secured long-term contracts with both the machinists and the engineers. In July 2014, McNerney, approaching sixty-five, was asked on a conference call if he planned to retire that year. He was feeling confident enough to joke, "The heart will still be beating, the employees will still be cowering."

They were. Boeing had introduced a new employee-ranking system that, according to Speea, made it more likely that experienced workers would be laid off. For engineers in their forties, the chances of a layoff doubled; in their fifties, it tripled. (It echoed the strategy McNerney had used to pare the workforce at 3M, which the Equal Employment Opportunity Commission determined was unlawful—3M in 2011 paid $3 million to settle an EEOC lawsuit from hundreds of people over forty-five laid off while McNerney was running it.) "We no longer think that we're hiring people forever," the Boeing CEO told the publication at his alma mater, the Harvard Business School, in 2013. "We understand that we are not going to get fiercely loyal people who will never leave like we did in the 1950s."

On his first call with analysts after the Dreamliner was flying again in July 2013, six months after its grounding, McNerney quickly dispensed with updates about the plane. Its safety went without question, he implied. His voice got really animated, though, talking about something else: the need to squeeze suppliers. "There is a chance to increase volume significantly while helping us work flow, cash, and margins," he said, using *work* as a verb, in the finance shorthand he frequently employed. "We are determined and committed, and the reason we are is that we are facing a 'more for less' world."

McNerney's phrase—"more for less"—became the company's driving theme as it embarked on the MAX, a sharp contrast to "Working Together," the motto Phil Condit had advanced in the early 1990s during the successful creation of the 777. The implications were clear: More performance, lower cost. More range, less fuel burn. But also: more work, fewer people. And ultimately: more risk, catastrophic return.

Boeing had always encouraged spirited debate in its development programs. Big commercial jets, after all, were defined by a founding partner of Perkins Coie, the law firm that had long defended it from product liability claims, as "a bundle of compromises, arrived at by exchanging expert views." On the 737-600, one of the Next Generation models introduced in the 1990s, Paul Russell, the product safety executive, stood up to argue with colleagues who were thinking about making a change to the fuel tank that might have created a single-point failure. "How much blood do you want on the seat covers?" he demanded of people in the room. (The design was changed.)

Just like its much-hailed predecessors, the MAX involved thousands of people spread across offices at Boeing and suppliers around the world, making tens of thousands of individual decisions. Boeing had computer software called DOORS that was supposed to keep everyone around the world updated instantly on the status of each change. It was like an Excel spreadsheet on steroids, with cells that turned red and also sent an update to the finance staff when critical project milestones were breached.

But the MAX's chaotic reporting lines betrayed the dysfunction that would one day become obvious to all. After one early design meeting, Pete Parsons, an executive in the commercial airplane unit with a mouthful of a title (director of program management best practices and program management functional excellence), declared the plans "the best I've seen." He told Boeing's internal newsletter that he was especially impressed with the "clear communications" and "high level of collaboration."

In practice, people tended to communicate the way they do in offices everywhere—with emails, instant messages, and phone calls. Whoever yelled loudest got what they wanted, said one person who worked directly with the engineers who coded the MAX software. When it came to fulfilling the FAA's requirements, he said, the regulator was just one more constituency to satisfy. And not a particularly forceful one. In dealing with the agency's specialists, Boeing's engineers came up with what was called "the drawer full of paper" technique. "If you can just inundate them with information it makes them go away," he said.

Jim Albaugh, then the commercial airplane chief, laid out the marching orders for the MAX in December 2011: "We're going to make this the simplest re-engine possible. We're only going to touch the part of the airplane impacted by the engine and a couple of other improvements."

The program's managers made sure everyone got the message, installing what they called a "countdown clock" in a conference room where meetings about the program took place—a reminder of "the value of a day," as the MAX's general manager, Keith Leverkuhn, later put it. The clock marked the time left to achieve major milestones culminating in the plane's first flight.

The program's chief engineer, Michael Teal, reported to

Leverkuhn, but none of the fifteen hundred engineers who worked on the plane reported directly to him. They answered to business-unit leaders, something that would have astonished the forceful Joe Sutter in an earlier age at Boeing.

The 737 by then accounted for about a third of the entire company's profit, but it was still the redheaded stepchild, not something you spent money on. "It's a pig with lipstick, just a simple old airplane," said one former Boeing pilot. The resources and people devoted to the program reflected that; it got the "B" team. Many of the others working on it, like Ludtke, squeezed in their work on the MAX alongside other more pressing projects. "The 737 was something of a backwater," said Peter Lemme, a former flight controls engineer.

What's more, low-cost Southwest Airlines, the biggest customer, had no desire to push the envelope. It wanted its ten thousand pilots to be able to step into the new plane without any additional training, which would save it huge costs as well as logistical headaches. Early in the program, Boeing managers told the flight controls team that under no circumstances were they to make any changes that would require pilots switching from the previous 737 to the MAX to step into a simulator. The reason: Boeing had promised Southwest $1 million per airplane if simulator training was required—and the carrier by 2019 had ordered 246. That was all the incentive Boeing needed.

Simulators are engineering marvels in themselves. Picture a squat pod raised ten feet in the air and mounted on spider legs that let the whole contraption move up, down, left, right, forward, and back. To meet regulatory requirements, the pilots sitting inside must be shown a realistic representation of what they'd see outside a real cockpit, so images are projected onto a curved mirror. Many simulators use cinema-quality sound to create a cacophony of alerts and warnings. Each machine costs as much as $15 million, and training costs hundreds of dollars an hour, because each session involves three highly paid professionals. There is the pilot being evaluated, a second "seat dummy" acting as copilot, and the instructor. If the training takes days, there are also travel, hotel, and meal expenses—real money for an airline with thousands of pilots.

Paying for pilots, maintenance, and cabin crews, plus all of the training needed to operate aircraft safely, comes to 20 percent of an airline's operating budget—more than is spent on fuel. It was in the aircraft manufacturer's and the airline's short-term financial interests, then, to keep the burden of simulation training to a minimum.

As he worked to design its controls, Ludtke was already getting a bad feeling about the MAX. "It's such a kludge of an airplane," he said. "These pilots today really rely on automation. And this airplane did not have much." The mandate to avoid simulator training struck him as a perversion of the normal give-and-take, the bundle of compromises, in any airplane program. "What was weird about the MAX was that some of those normal conflicts were broken down," he said. "It was easier for the program leaders to drive their wishes into the design teams. They just didn't have people that understood that you need to say 'no.'"

The industry was in the midst of the greatest order boom of the jet age, as the combination of millions of wealthier new travelers in Asia and cheap money in the form of low interest rates prompted airlines to order planes at a frantic pace. From 2010 to 2020, carriers took delivery of single-aisle jets worth $442.2 billion—36 percent of all such planes manufactured in the previous half century, according to Richard Aboulafia, the Teal Group consultant.

At a meeting in 2012, Reed, the FAA engineer who had so reluctantly joined the Boeing Aviation Safety Oversight Office, questioned Boeing managers about the plan to leave the cockpit of the new MAX largely unchanged. It would make the 737 the last big commercial jet flying without an electronic crew alerting system—like the one Boeing had pioneered on the 757 and 767 fully thirty years earlier. "I was saying, 'Guys, make the break, put a modern flight deck in this airplane,'" Reed recalls. He pointed out that many of the older pilots who grew up with 737s were retiring. Younger pilots had often started in commuter planes made by Embraer in Brazil or Bombardier in Canada, with far more advanced cockpits.

Even the newest military planes had checklists that appeared on touch screens. If a hydraulic pump failed, a message would pop up showing specific actions the pilot should take. On the 737, a light showing "low hydraulic pressure" might illuminate with no further explanation. Pilots would have to rely on memory or turn to their paper handbook.

"Training issue," the Boeing executive responded to Reed, in rejecting such changes. If Boeing had been building a brand-new plane, it would have been required to have the electronic checklist. But because the MAX was being examined as an amendment to the original type certificate awarded in 1967, managers could pursue an exception. The MAX was actually the thirteenth version of the plane, counting all the variants along the way—the official application would call it an update of the 737-100, 737-200, 737-200C, 737-300, 737-400, 737-500, 737-600, 737-700, 737-700C, 737-800, 737-900, and 737-900ER.

Even the numbering system had reached its limits. With no one apparently eager for a "737-1000," this latest version was officially known as the 737-8, because its closest cousin was the 737-800. For marketing, Boeing called it the 737 MAX 8—the word MAX chosen because it "optimizes everything we and our customers have learned."

Over the next two years, the team led by Michael Teal worked on "how to structure our cost story" to win a vital exception to the regulation requiring the electronic checklist, whose installation, they determined, would have "cascading effects" on the other systems in the plane. They would also need "buy-in" from the Boeing deputies representing the FAA, as the memos circulating then put it.

The proposal they sent to the agency suggested it would cost more than $10 billion to switch to an electronic checklist, in return for, they argued, a negligible improvement in safety. Managers at the FAA agreed. Boeing had optimized its relationship with them.

Early testing revealed a fateful problem with the MAX. In a wind tunnel with a scale model of the plane about the size of an eagle, engineers noticed that it had a tendency to pitch up during tight, high-speed turns—a result of the bigger engines that were to be mounted to the front of the wings rather than beneath them. Ray Craig, then the chief 737 pilot, took a closer look in a simulator. The pitch-up took place in a part of the flight envelope where few commercial jetliners ever ventured. It was theoretically possible, though, that pilots might make such a turn when they were responding to sudden turbulence or some other upset. If the problem weren't fixed, it could lead to a stall.

Boeing's engineers considered using tiny vanes on the wings to change the aerodynamics, but they weren't satisfied the result would be effective. Another solution would have been to make modifications to the tail—the thing Ed Wells and other Boeing engineers, faced with another difficult aerodynamic problem on the 707, had agreed to do all those years ago in that icy meeting with test pilot Tex Johnston. But that would have been expensive, involving changes that would ripple out to other parts of the plane, and potentially jeopardize the all-important schedule.

So they settled on a solution that would, in such an event, use software to automatically push down the plane's nose. It would move the horizontal stabilizer, the small wing at the back of the plane. Boeing had already designed a similar piece of software for the refueling tanker it was developing for the air force. The tanker version was called the Maneuvering Characteristics Augmentation System, or MCAS. Boeing used the same name for the software on the MAX.

To many of the engineers aware of it at the time, the software seemed unobjectionable. It kicked in based on readings from two alerts, ensuring redundancy—an accelerometer measuring g-forces on the plane and the angle-of-attack vane mounted on the nose.

Chief pilot Craig, for one, didn't like the solution; he preferred a hardware fix. But the benefit of software was simple enough: it was cheaper. The MAX program was already under cost pressure. Managers talked frequently about how any change would have to "buy its way onto the airplane"—suggesting that even safety-related improvements took a back seat to cost.

On the previous version of the 737, before Boeing's financial revolution had taken root, test pilots weren't made to record all the hours they spent evaluating it. For the MAX, managers asked for detailed accounting. Test pilots, for instance, were charged against the cost of the program at hourly rates of $216, similar to the cost of senior leadership. At a budget meeting in 2012, managers took a pencil to the planned test flights even before they had begun, asking for a reduction of three thousand work hours for flight test support and eight thousand hours for use of an engineering flight simulator. It was an inversion of one of Joe Sutter's axioms, which counseled people to expect and plan for surprises.

Though software was convenient, a concern was that the FAA would treat it as a new feature that would jeopardize what employees began referring to as a "program directive": no simulator training. Keith Leverkuhn, the MAX program manager, tracked the training issue as one of a half dozen "risks" that he updated superiors about regularly.

Boeing's engineers wondered if they should even refer to the existence of MCAS at all. They decided in June 2013 to use the name internally but externally to refer to it as just a tweak of the existing electronic flight controls, reducing the chance that anyone would ask questions about it. "If we emphasize MCAS is a new function there may be a greater certification and training impact," said a memo that month, summarizing their discussion. An ancillary benefit was less work for everyone. As the memo noted, if everyone agreed it was just part of the same old system, no one would have to design any training or update the manual.

There was one more consideration in their planning. Boeing had chosen an unproven supplier to build the simulator for the MAX, the lowest bidder, and those simulators likely weren't going to be ready in time for the MAX's entry into service. Simulator training, then, wasn't just a costly line item to be kept to a minimum. It could prove an obstacle to getting the entire program finished on time if the FAA ruled that pilots had to get into simulators before flying the new plane.

It was one compromise too many, and someone needed to say so—to stand up and make a "blood on the seat covers" declaration. No such objection came. The FAA's deputies at Boeing signed off on the software solution to thwart potential stalls.

Ludtke and other flight controls engineers, though, weren't willing to give up on the idea of modernizing the MAX's vintage system of crew alerts. One of the most vocal was Curtis Ewbank, a graduate of Embry-Riddle Aeronautical University then in his late twenties who had only been at Boeing a few years. Ewbank had a bushy black beard that made it look as though he'd walked out of an 1800s logging camp. But in his zeal, he fit in with Boeing's engineering Boy Scouts. A rocket he had helped develop at Embry-Riddle set an altitude record for a student-built vehicle in 2007 when it soared 199,580 feet from a NASA launch pad.

In 2014, Ewbank was among a group of flight controls experts who started raising questions about how erroneous information from the plane's sensors might compromise the MAX's safety. Sensors like the angle-of-attack vanes or the pitot tubes, which measure airspeed, sit outside the plane. They're vulnerable to bird strikes, damage from jetway equipment, or other obstructions. FAA records showed more than two hundred instances of malfunctioning AoA vanes alone since 2004, some of which had set off cockpit alerts. Ewbank and the others urged implementation of a backup system called "synthetic airspeed" already in use on the Dreamliner— essentially a computer program to compare values of all the sensors. If an illogical reading came from any of them—such as the AoA vanes linked to the new MCAS software—it would be deactivated.

In rejecting the safety enhancement, managers twice cited concerns about the "cost and potential (pilot) training impact."

"People have to die before Boeing will change things," Ewbank was told by his manager.

When Ewbank and the others raised the idea a third time in a meeting with the MAX's chief engineer, Michael Teal, he cited the same objections as he killed the proposal. Keith Leverkuhn, Teal's boss and the MAX program manager, later said he never even heard about the idea.

The developers of Boeing's not-yet-built airplanes divide up the work almost as if they're sitting inside an imaginary version of it. One team has the flaps and slats, another propulsion, and so on. This is in part because the work depends on knowing exactly how a change made in one area affects another. Picture the basement of a hundred-year-old house, knob-and-tube wiring snaking through the joists, water pipes (some lead, some copper) running up the walls, all a reflection of compromises made over the decades. Boeing's 737 was like that, too, except its parts numbered six hundred thousand.

Ludtke's group, called Flight Crew Operations, was supposed to represent the pilots sitting in the cockpit. He estimated that the group's head count fell by half, from thirty to fifteen or so, during the MAX's development. Some were laid off or took buyout offers, while others grabbed better opportunities. His young colleague Ewbank quit in 2015, despairing of the shortcuts that managers kept pushing for.

Many of those who departed were experts in human factors, trained to spot flaws in how people interact with the machine that engineers might miss. (As a joke in the field goes, "Dogs have fleas, and engineers have human factors.") One person who left was a PhD—"the kind of talent you can't afford to lose," Ludtke said. "They were targeting the highly paid, highly experienced engineers." It was the same kind of lucrative purge McNerney had overseen at 3M, which ended in his successor determining that the belt-tightening had come at the expense of innovation.

Overall, Boeing's workforce fell 7 percent in 2015, while making many more planes. The climate didn't reward people willing to buck managers, said Mark Rabin, who worked in a flight test group that supported the MAX. He was let go that year after a seventeen-year Boeing career. "It was pretty intense low morale because of all the layoffs—constant, grinding layoffs, year after year," he said. "So you really watched your step and were careful about what you said."

Once Rabin made a joke about how the executives got a fancy holiday dinner at a golf club and all the engineers got was a potluck. His manager pulled him aside and told him to be more diplomatic. Another time, at an all-hands meeting, one of the executives droned on for some time before handing the floor to a young female engineer. "Hey, wake up!" she said when she began her presentation. Not long after that, she got a layoff notice. Talk in the "pews," as Boeing engineers called the aisles where they worked, was that it was because she had offended the droning executive. Some engineers warily eyed a floor where young programmers from the India-based outsourcing firm HCL were based. The contract workers in the United States with H-1B visas earned half of what the Boeing engineers made. In India it was even less, as little as nine dollars an hour. (They worked on flight test verification software, but not specifically MCAS.)

The shift of Dreamliner production to South Carolina had come with its own drawbacks. The state might have been cheap, but the people Boeing hired—at half the hourly wage of those in Seattle—had little experience building airplanes. William Hobek, a quality manager there, filed suit in federal court claiming he'd been fired after reporting defects up the chain of command. When he complained, a supervisor replied, "Bill, you know we can't find all defects," according to the suit. Hobek called over an inspector, who quickly found forty problems. Other employees described defective manufacturing, debris left on planes—wrenches, metal slivers, even a ladder—and pressure not to come clean about it. Al Jazeera sent a hidden camera into the plant in 2014 and caught some employees on tape saying they'd never fly on the planes because of shoddy workmanship.

In May of that year, McNerney and the successor he groomed, Dennis Muilenburg, by now his vice chairman, had what amounted to a ceremonial handoff at the annual investor conference in Seattle's

Fairmont Olympic Hotel. The "more-for-less world," as McNerney put it, meant no more "moonshots" like the original 707, or the ambitious if flawed Dreamliner program. Muilenburg, whose goal in college had been to be the world's greatest airplane designer, had discovered a new inspiration. "In the past, we may have said our best engineers are working on the new thing," he said. "Now, we want our best engineers working on innovative reuse."

The strategy was finally starting to make real money. In a 2015 filing detailing the performance bonus plan for executives over the previous three years, Boeing estimated that its cumulative "economic profit" was $8.3 billion, compared with a target of $5.7 billion. For the higher-ups, that meant a maximum award of twice their targeted bonus. The rank and file weren't as lucky. The average bonus for salaried nonmanagement staff for 2014 was $4,500.

While they pressured the engineers for savings, Boeing enriched shareholders, spending $41.5 billion on stock buybacks from 2013 to 2018—enough capital to develop several all-new aircraft, had they chosen to. Almost 80 percent of the free cash during that period went to buybacks. McNerney himself made $231 million from 2001 to 2016, with a retirement package that wasn't Welch-sized but in the neighborhood: at least $58.5 million. For his part, Muilenburg made $106 million from 2011 to 2018.

Some saw cause for concern in all this enrichment. The Teal Group analyst Richard Aboulafia wrote a 2015 article in *Forbes* arguing that building a commercial jet wasn't the kind of manufacturing that responded to the usual corporate playbook, those strategies that Boeing leaders since Harry Stonecipher had executed, with investors reaping the greatest benefit. It depended instead on knowledgeable workers and continuous learning.

In just a few years, his headline would read as prophecy: "Boeing Will Pay High Price for McNerney's Mistake of Treating Aviation Like It Was Any Other Industry."

Mondays at 6:30 a.m., if he wasn't traveling, Dennis Muilenburg joined a handful of colleagues for Bible study. Seated on hard chairs in the cafeteria of Boeing's defense division in St. Louis, which he ran from 2009 to 2013, they took turns reading photocopied passages of scripture and excerpts from books like *God in the Marketplace* and *Doing Business by the Good Book*. The curriculum was composed by a group called Biblical Business Training, and the idea was to draw on lessons from the Bible to manage workplace struggles: How do you avoid the urge to say something harsh or untruthful? How does faith make you impenetrable? Why was the belt—his truth—the vital piece of Paul's armor?

A product of the Midwest like so many of his executive forebears at Boeing, Muilenburg grew up in Sioux Center, Iowa, Dutch Calvinist country that even today has the feel of Holland in the 1800s. Storefronts have signs in Dutch, and in some parts of town, Reformed churches turn up on every other street corner. Muilenburg's father, Dwaine, had the kind of all-consuming faith for which the Reformed tradition is known; he "read to his children from the Bible at lunchtime and then from a children's Bible storybook in the evening," as his obituary published at the Memorial Funeral Home of Sioux Center noted. The family had a farm where they grew corn, soybeans, and alfalfa, and raised livestock including cattle and pigs. Dennis, one of four siblings, milked the cows in the morning as one of his daily chores.

This part of northwest Iowa was and is one of the most conservative in the country; in 1980, Ronald Reagan won 76 percent of the Sioux County vote, and in 2020, Donald Trump won 81 percent. It was at Sioux Center's Dordt University, where Dennis's brother Harlan was the grounds supervisor, that Trump, speaking to fifteen hundred people during his first presidential campaign, mused, "I could stand in the middle of Fifth Avenue and shoot somebody, and I wouldn't lose any voters."

At Sioux Center High School, Muilenburg was a standout, and not just for math. He was one of the best artists Ted De Hoogh, one of his teachers, ever taught. This was especially so with pencil sketches; his drawings had a great command of light, shading, and texture. For years Dennis's depiction of the high school's facade adorned the booklets handed out at the graduation ceremony.

But his work for De Hoogh was sometimes more experimental. A quirky, Dalí-style drawing showed the toaster in the Muilenburg family kitchen, a slice popping out of one slot and a hand emerging to remove it from the other. Another depicted the biblical story of Daniel in the lion's den, all the lions perched around him licking their chops.

In college at Iowa State in the early 1980s, Muilenburg, then a young aerospace engineering major, impressed one of his room-mates, Steve Haveman, when he and a couple of friends invented a way to project drawings—or diagrams or flowcharts—onto the wall with a slide projector. It was like a rudimentary PowerPoint. First they would pry the photos out of the cardboard slides. Then they would take a sheet of clear plastic, letter on it with a fine-tipped pen, and pop it back into the cardboard. Muilenburg was a few years older, and Haveman, then a freshman, admired how goal oriented and confident he was, even scoring an internship at prestigious Boeing. Their apartment, shared among four guys in their late teens and early twenties, was no frat house; a wild night for them was playing tennis after ten p.m.

That summer internship at Boeing, when he climbed into his '82 Monte Carlo and drove across the country, was the first time Muilenburg had seen the ocean. Boeing was then led by the crusty T. Wilson. It was the very summer in which Wilson issued his remarkable mea culpa for the 747 crash in Japan, after the jet plowed into a mountain ridge because of a bad repair job at Boeing.

After graduating from Iowa State in 1986, Muilenburg returned to Boeing for a full-time job. He played pickup basketball in a company gym with other young employees, married a veterinarian, and earned a master's degree in aeronautics and astronautics from the University of Washington in Seattle. When his career ascent required a cross-country move to Washington, D.C., he and his wife, Becky, did it with one young son, three dogs, and four cats.

While Muilenburg participated in research for a high-speed civil transport, most of his career was spent on military projects: the F-22, the 767 AWACS, the 747 Airborne Laser, the EX surveillance platform, the Advanced Tactical Fighter, and "a number of proprietary programs," as his résumé put it. They were the kind of predictable programs (and predictable revenue) that Mr. Mac and his progeny, part of Boeing's DNA since the merger, had always preferred. The outcome depended on lobbying, politics, and closed-door maneuvering as much as standout engineering.

Muilenburg's first prominent role was as director of Weapon Systems for the Joint Strike Fighter, a $200 billion contract that Boeing ultimately lost to Lockheed Martin. His ambition was apparent even in a restrained *Nova* television documentary about the contest that appeared on PBS in 2003. "When I daydream, I see it hovering; I see it taking off from airfields; I see it operating around a ship," he said of his proposed jet. "And sometimes I even see it shooting down the Lockheed airplane."

By the mid-2000s, Muilenburg's picture was on the wall of the "visibility" room, a conference room at the Chicago headquarters displaying headshots of the most promising executives. After running Global Services and then Boeing Defense, Space & Security, he was McNerney's apprentice for a year as vice chairman before becoming chief executive in July 2015, midway through the development of the MAX.

With his blond crewcut, steel-blue eyes, and rake-thin build, Muilenburg had the look, as one newspaper profile put it, of a 1960s astronaut. A Boeing lifer and a trained aeronautical engineer, he presented himself as every bit the Boy Scout. But as chief executive, he only picked up where McNerney left off in driving for efficiencies. In his own supplier squeeze, he asked for cuts of another 10 percent, on top of McNerney's previous 15 percent. Long before, Boeing had been known as "the Lazy B" for its technocratic culture of second-guessing. Now the jokes were about keeping up with Muilenburg's energy. In St. Louis, he'd end meetings in a ground-floor conference room by inviting people to walk or run eight flights back upstairs with him. An avid cyclist, he led pelotons of employees during site visits and boasted of getting in more than one hundred miles a week. People called him "a machine," one that seemed fueled by the half dozen cans of Diet Mountain Dew he chugged in the course of a day.

Many of the employees felt like machines, too. A former manager of fuel systems on the 737, Adam Dickson, says the sales team would sell planes for delivery four years out at prices the company couldn't yet hit from an engineering standpoint—creating immense pressure to drive down costs. "How long do you want to keep polishing that apple?" was a phrase the Boeing managers sometimes used with engineers who wanted to keep testing. The message: the product is fine, let's keep things moving. In 2016, Boeing started asking for specific time and cost reductions as part of managers' performance evaluations, and by 2018, Dickson said, his superiors warned "very directly and [in] threatening ways" that pay was at risk if the targets weren't met. "It was engineering that would have to bend," he said.

"Idea's [*sic*] are measured in dollars," as a manager put it in another engineer's annual evaluation.

What's worse, it appeared to Dickson that the FAA was complicit in the effort. Increasingly, he said, airplanes came with an "IOU," as managers at both the FAA and Boeing agreed to table disagreements about technical issues in order to avoid delays. "That culture is new, and that culture is toxic," he said. "It's putting profits ahead of real compliance."

Collins, the FAA engineer who'd been so impressed with his managers' knowledge early in his career, could see the change, too. Boeing was in the midst of assembling the first MAX in mid-2015 when the agency's senior management overruled thirteen of its own engineers, one of its pilots, and at least four other managers on what the specialists felt was yet another flaw: the lack of shielding around its rudder cables. They wanted design changes that would prevent shrapnel from an engine blowout shredding the cables—a situation like the one that brought down the DC-10 in Sioux City in 1989. Boeing executives argued the changes were impractical. But Airbus had had a similar issue on the A320neo, and it did make modifications.

In a similar case that frustrated Collins, who'd written painstaking fuel-tank safety rules after the TWA Flight 800 crash, an FAA manager told Boeing it didn't need to put a fast-acting circuit breaker on MAX fuel pump wires carrying high voltage. Inexplicably, the agency did require the safety feature on its European competitor, Airbus.

Boeing surveyed the FAA deputies the next year, and almost four in every ten said they had encountered situations of "undue influence" like those Dickson had been so concerned about.

The countdown clock kept ticking.

9

Human Factors

Among the Boeing pilots, it would have been hard to guess that the most famous of them to emerge from the MAX's development would be Mark Forkner. In the pecking order of Boeing's pilots—who knew their pecking order implicitly—Forkner's group came in about dead last.

First came the test pilots, the Chuck Yeagers and Tex Johnstons who executed the daring maneuvers and talked to the press about it in leather bomber jackets afterward. They might nose the plane into a stall, or drag its tail along the runway like a hot-rodder on a motorcycle—the "velocity minimum unstick" test to determine takeoff speeds. The test pilots were sometimes known as the "McChord mafia" because many of them had flown for the air force at the nearby Lewis McChord Joint Base.

Next came the production pilots, who tested each of the planes that came off the production line. After that were the trainers, who flew with Boeing's airline customers or worked with them in simulators.

Finally there was Forkner's group, called Flight Technical and Safety. They wrote the manuals. They weren't even in the same division of the company as the test pilots, in part because Boeing had decided two decades previously that customer training was a business that should make money. Forkner's group reported to Boeing Global Services in Plano, Texas, which had been tasked in 2016 with an ambitious target from Muilenburg: increasing revenue to $50 billion within five or ten years, from just under $15 billion.

Despite his lowly status, Forkner was technically McChord mafia. He was a former air force pilot who had flown C-17 cargo planes and then worked at Alaska Airlines before doing a stint at the FAA in the air-traffic management unit. His wife worked there, too, as a manager in an office that oversees airports. They lived in a $1.3 million house with a pool on the Sammamish Plateau outside of Seattle, the same woodsy climes where Phil Condit used to bring managers to hear poems about the corporate soul. Forkner was a guy's guy in a cadre that still had some secret-society elements about it. Some of the pilots were rumored to be members of the Quiet Birdmen, or QB, an all-male aviator group dating to World War I. (First rule of QB: Don't talk about QB.) In some ways, the fraternity hadn't changed all that much from the days of the proudly copulating Tex Johnston. "I just like airplanes, football, chicks, and vodka, not in that order," Forkner wrote in one email.

Colleagues considered him hardworking and dedicated, if hotheaded at times. One person who served with him in the air force called him a "Pickett's charge kind of guy," referring to a self-defeating infantry assault ordered by Confederate general Robert E. Lee at Gettysburg. In documents later handed to congressional investigators, Forkner was frequently found blasting emails off until midnight or later (unfortunately, often while also sipping Grey Goose, which loosened his tongue). He usually wore a Seattle Seahawks jersey at work. Forkner was such a fan that he went to both Super Bowls the football team played in, just about every home game—even road playoff games. In an airport once, he spotted Ethan Pocic, a college lineman the Seahawks had recently drafted, and Forkner went military officer on him, barking, "You have one job, and that is to protect Russell Wilson, understood?" The six-foot-seven-inch Pocic meekly replied, "Yes, sir." After that the other pilots would say "there's your boy" whenever the lineman showed up in a game on television.

By the time the MAX entered development, Boeing's attempts were well under way to turn the unglamorous but all-important business of customer training into a profit center of its own. Many pilots were unnerved by a dispute with Boeing over its hiring of outside contractors. It was enough to prompt some who normally opposed unions—pilots are a notoriously independent bunch—to vote for representation by Speea, the union of engineers. The effort wasn't popular with everyone, including Forkner, who joined in a drive to decertify the union.

The tensions had started all the way back in 1997, when Boeing formed its training venture with the Warren Buffett–owned company FlightSafety. After buying out its partner in 2002, Boeing rebranded the training unit as Alteon—some pilots grumbled it sounded like a health-care company—before renaming it Boeing Training & Flight Services in 2009.

Alteon chief Sherry Carbary, later president of Boeing China, warned, as many in the industry then did, about the reckoning looming ahead, with the wave of new planes coming at the same time as an influx of relatively inexperienced pilots. She said it demanded a response that was hard to imagine in practice: shorter training times, lower costs—and better quality. One of the unit's innovations was a points-based system for its airline customers akin to the airlines' frequent-flier programs. Instead of providing expensive simulator time for a set number of crews, as it previously had, it offered points that could be used for a combination of training for pilots, maintenance technicians, or flight attendants. "It's like swapping fries for boiled potatoes," she told the trade publication *FlightGlobal* in 2007.

Carbary wasn't a pilot, and she struck some of them as standoffish. She rarely joined the pilots in the cafeteria for meals and avoided eye contact in the elevator. In regular Thursday meetings, she encouraged the pilots to give her good news, not bad news—an inversion of Mulally's old rule about not hiding problems.

The industry's rapid growth badly stretched its ability to recruit and train people to fly all the planes it was selling, and in at least some corners of Boeing, pilots well knew how much these customers struggled with basic proficiency. After a visit to an airline in Africa, a Boeing trainer reported to his boss that he'd be writing up a short report: "Should not fly airplanes." A carrier in Russia, S7, was considered dangerous enough that some Boeing instructors refused to fly on it unless they were at the controls. Most admitted privately that for young pilots, so accustomed to having computers tell them what to do, their 737 was a difficult beast. One high-ranking Boeing executive told people that if he were flying in Asia, he would prefer to be on an Airbus.

Many of Boeing's instructors wanted to offer more intensive training, but were told the company had other priorities. "We felt like shortcuts were being taken and that the quality of training was being sacrificed," said Charlie Clayton, a former Boeing trainer. The airlines, too, had "a vested interest in getting pilots out and flying as quickly as they can, as cheaply as they can." Another instructor, Mike Coker, said he used to tell managers, "You're giving us too many guys"—more pilots than they could reasonably train. Tensions boiled over with a plan to use contractors, often retired airline pilots, to fly with crews for initial training rather than Boeing staffers.

In 2012 the trainers and manual writers voted four to one to join Speea, expanding the ranks of unionized pilots. Managers made it known that the vote wouldn't help their chances at promotion, especially to one of the plum test-piloting jobs. "We're not going to have a union here," one of the chief test pilots declared at one meeting. Others talked about how they didn't want the union to "infect" the rest of the piloting corps.

The next year, in the middle of negotiations for a new contract for several dozen pilots, managers delivered a bombshell: they were moving simulators to Miami from the Longacres building near Seattle, the one Peter Morton inaugurated with an orchestral work for the 777's introduction all those years ago. Boeing said it was what customers wanted. In Miami, and in cities such as Singapore and London, amid the historic wave of orders, the plane maker relied on hired help known as "purchased service pilots," or PSPs. (Boeing's longtime pilots came up with their own acronym for them—DBCs, short for "dirtbag contractors.") The outsourcing to freelancers meant that training wasn't always consistent. A former American Airlines pilot would train other pilots the way he was trained; a United pilot might have a different style.

The Miami center didn't please all of Boeing's airline customers. Some objected to instruction from contractors instead of full-fledged Boeing pilots. The building was shopworn, too, with one room where trainers had to shout to be heard over an air-conditioning unit. A simulator acted up so much the pilots called it "Christine," from the Stephen King horror movie. Airbus had its own training center not far away in Miami, and pilots thought it was far more comfortable, with a full dining room and an airy, modern lobby. The Boeing center had a vending machine with snacks and coffee for purchase.

It was a natural outcome of the profit imperatives that had been placed on training in the 2000s, and the very risk that Peter Morton had warned about back in the 1990s. There was indeed a lucrative market for aviation training, worth $3.5 billion a year by 2014. In order to succeed, Boeing had to keep its overhead low and avoid offering too much free training—exactly what less established airlines like Lion Air needed.

One longtime airline pilot who had joined Boeing's training operation in the past decade after twenty-five years of flying was dispirited by his experience at a company he had idolized. He remembered thinking he could throw away his résumé after he got the job, having finally reached the pinnacle of aviation in his last stop before retirement. But his department—the Flight Technical and Safety group where Forkner worked—withered, as many of its pilots left out of frustration. Instead of flying, they spent their days answering emails in offices, pressed to meet unrealistic schedules, with little opportunity for advancement to the (nonunion) test pilot roles. This former airline pilot left, too, after a few years in which the department shrank to eighteen from about thirty-five. Eight of those pilots had assisted with accident investigations; by the end, two were left in that role.

Instead of replacing them with full-timers, Boeing managers just hired more of the "dirtbag" contractors from Cambridge Communications, a pilot recruitment company based in the Isle of Man—an effort led by one of Forkner's bosses, Carl Davis. Boeing didn't have to pay their health care or pensions, reducing the "burden rate" managers kept talking about.

"You never got the impression that this is *the* manufacturer, as good as it gets," the former airline pilot said. "It was a mess."

In practice, the turmoil left the aircraft's cockpit designers alienated from instructors. It was teachers who regularly saw how the typical pilot responded to unusual situations, but the division between their ranks meant it was difficult for such information to trickle back to the people most empowered to do something about it. "When we were all at the Longacres facility and the simulators were downstairs, there was an extreme amount of crosstalk," said Coker, one of the former instructors. The manual writers and the engineers, he added, could "sit in a simulator session and watch how somebody handled the procedure and see where the flaws were. Much harder to do when you had to go to Miami, or tell somebody over the phone."

Eventually, a use was found for the big empty bay where the simulators had been, where an orchestra had once played the first movement of *The Miracle*. The Boeing security department used it as a kennel to train sniffer dogs.

Forkner, often with Ludtke and other flight-deck engineers in tow, frequently hosted the FAA's chief of 737 training requirements, Stacey Klein, at the company's engineering simulator, in the Systems Integration Laboratory near Boeing Field. The building's long, sterile corridors gave it the feel of a hospital. Behind an innocuous-looking door marked 737 MAX CAB, the engineering flight-deck simulator—everyone called it the e-cab for short—stood in the center of a vast room. The contraption looked like a giant metal Matchbox toy airplane, cut in half. It was mounted atop a platform, with cables and wires snaking underneath. Inside the mockup was a faithful re-creation of the MAX cockpit, with a curved mirror in front and a high-definition screen to project a realistic scenario to pilots. MAX program manager Keith Leverkuhn, in a video recorded in 2015, said the careful reconstruction would make the plane "right at first flight."

Klein, the FAA training official, had little engineering background, per se. She had previously worked for six years as an instructor pilot at a regional carrier called Skyway Airlines. People from Boeing viewed her as in over her head. "With all the inexperience present, we should be able to gang up on them and steer it the direction we want," a Boeing official wrote before one meeting. The Boeing team repeatedly reminded Klein they wanted to ensure that pilots didn't need simulator training for the MAX, which was near the end of its development. One presentation in May 2015 was so arcane that Forkner likened the FAA officials in attendance to "dogs watching TV." He confessed to a colleague that he didn't really understand it himself. "Curves, slopes, graphs, blah blah blah, stuff non-engineers and test pilots can't really understand, other than the lines all line up between max and NG, which is supposed to prove they fly the same."

Incredibly, Boeing's sales team had already started telling airlines—long before receiving any official blessing—that the plane wouldn't require simulator training. When someone wrote that same month to ask Klein's Aircraft Evaluation Group if what Boeing was saying was true, the AEG replied that it wasn't—in fact, there had been "very contentious" discussions with Boeing, and reason to believe that computer-based training would be "insufficient."

With Klein refusing to tip her hand, Forkner got nervous enough that he mentioned the standoff to chief engineer Michael Teal, who called a meeting with one of her bosses, a manager at the BASOO named John Piccola. Teal told Piccola he wanted to make sure everyone was "aligned." He got an agreement that no one would be making any "new interpretations of existing regulations."

It was one more reminder that Boeing was in charge, and the Forrest Gumps at the FAA should do as they were told.

—

Finally, a finished MAX—not just the mockup—was ready for testing. On an overcast Friday in January 2016, thousands of employees gathered outside the 737 factory in a Seattle suburb for the MAX's first flight. Thousands more watched a live feed at their desks. Two of Boeing's ace test pilots sat at the controls. One of them, Craig Bomben, was a navy veteran who'd also flown experimental planes for NASA. The other, Ed Wilson, was an ex–U.S. Air Force fighter jock. As the pilots fired up the first engine, the hulking plane rolled forward several feet—they'd forgotten to set the parking brake. Later, after the uneventful flight landed to cheers, there was some teasing of the crack duo in the cockpit for missing one of the steps in the preflight checklist.

For pilots in the know, it pointed at the differences among their ranks. Bomben, the chief Boeing test pilot, had graduated from the so-called Top Gun navy aviator school near San Diego. He was a fan of Fox News host Bill O'Reilly, once writing in to tell him, "O'Reilly, your talking points on national security was [sic] the most brilliant piece of journalism I've seen in a long time." Before joining Boeing, he flew modified F-15 fighter jets as a research pilot at NASA's Dryden Flight Research Center in Edwards, California. In one 2006 test, the nose of the plane jerked upward in a sign that the stabilator, the small wing controlling up-and-down motion, had jammed. "It's not something a pilot ever wants to feel," as Bomben described it to *Popular Mechanics*. "You can lose your stabilator a bunch of ways—computer failure, stuck actuator, missile up the tailpipe—but when you lose it, you're out of Schlitz. You're not going to fly the airplane home." But, as the magazine explained, it was just a test; within one-eightieth of a second, an on-board neural network under development at Dryden had detected the malfunction.

Unlike many of the pilots he now managed, Bomben had never worked for an airline. He tested planes to their physical limits, but it was in the daily routine—*don't forget to set the parking brake*—where those who flew them as line pilots came to understand their own limitations. Once, one of the Boeing trainers arranged for Bomben to sit in with some Alaska Airlines pilots on their usual milk run, making multiple takeoffs and landings in a few hours. "He came back and said, 'Wow, that is work!'" the trainer recalled.

Ribbing aside, the successful first flight of the MAX meant that managers could finally exhale. It was Boeing's centennial year, and in his statement marking the event, Ray Conner, head of the commercial airplane business, said the successful flight "carries us across the threshold of a new century of innovation." At Seattle's Museum of History & Industry, on the lake where Bill Boeing flew his first model, the soaring exhibit hall that summer would feature hanging airplanes and a continuously running loop of employees extolling the virtues of one of the oldest, and perhaps most fabled, companies the city had produced.

A month after the first flight, the program's chief engineer, Michael Teal, got a surprise call from Mike Delaney, a onetime McDonnell Douglas engineer who was now the vice president of engineering. "Congratulations!" Delaney said. Teal would be getting additional restricted stock to thank him for reaching the first-flight milestone. In the conference room near Teal's office, the countdown clock had finally ticked to its last second.

From Boeing Field, now with less fanfare, the test pilots led by Bomben and Wilson took the MAX up day after day. They tested stalls, climbs, turns. In the back, the plane was loaded with a handful of engineers, a mountain of computer test equipment, and giant barrels of water where the seats should have been. On repeated flights, they filled and unfilled the barrels to examine different weight and loading conditions—the barrels representing a fully loaded jetliner of people. Only a month after that congratulatory call to Teal, the pilots had something to report.

The same propensity to pitch up at high speeds, the quirk of design that had led to the adoption of MCAS, was also present during some tests of low-speed stalls. Regulation required the control stick to give steadily increasing forces in such an event, signaling to pilots the onset of a stall; instead it got mushy, less reactive.

The pilots told Teal the plane wasn't "certifiable" in that condition, meaning it wouldn't pass muster with the FAA.

By the end of that March, the engineers and test pilots had arrived at a solution. Again—all but unavoidably at this late stage— the answer would be the software. They would expand MCAS to cover low speeds as well as high. It had the benefit, once more, of being cheap. "All changes are minimal / low collateral damage, therefore no additional flight testing," one memo said. The same day Leverkuhn and Teal approved the plan, Forkner emailed the FAA's Klein for permission to delete MCAS from the flight manual because it "only operates WAY outside of the normal operating envelope." Still focused on his mission of minimizing training, he possibly didn't even know about the software changes. Klein certainly didn't; she agreed.

By this time, many of the engineers who had worked on the MAX early in its design had moved on to other projects. Ewbank and others with expertise in human factors were gone. Many of those who remained (the pilots thought of them as interchangeable units from the University of Washington, making $90,000 a year) lacked the clout to make a "blood on the seat covers" declaration, had they wanted to.

Chief engineer Teal assigned a small team to implement the change. To his boss Leverkuhn, he called it a "flight squawk"— a routine glitch, in Boeing-speak.

And it would have been, in an earlier era. But those working on the new software appeared not to understand the ripple effects of the change. Just as a car traveling at low speed requires larger movements of the steering wheel to turn, the stabilizer needed to move at a greater angle to alter a slow-moving jet's trajectory. Teal's team reprogrammed the MCAS software to make it capable of adjusting the stabilizer 2.5 degrees in low-speed conditions, instead of the previous limit of 0.6 degrees.

Critically, at low speed, this meant that a second sensor necessary to ensure redundancy—the accelerometer measuring g-forces at high speeds—was no longer applicable. The software would now fire on the basis of a single sensor, the angle-of-attack vane. And it would do so at low speeds, which usually meant when a plane was most vulnerable: at takeoff or landing. No one appears to have fully considered the human factors—how a failure in the single sensor would make the plane appear to go haywire at a time when pilots were already busy and dangerously close to the ground.

Test pilots like Craig Bomben were used to planes going haywire; it was their job. So the chief pilot climbed into the simulator and investigated a simple scenario to test the new software—a failure of one AoA vane and the loss of another, leading to a "runaway stabilizer." The team of engineers, with time now running short to finish the MAX, reasoned that if the software failed, for any reason, it would set off the trim wheel between the two pilots in the cockpit. The wheel is black with a white stripe and makes a clacking noise when it moves. They thought pilots would notice it and hit the cutout switch, turning off the stabilizer motor. The test pilots had no problem doing this procedure in four seconds. But they didn't simulate what would actually be happening in the cockpit in such an event—the cacophony of alerts and the "stick shaker" that would be thudding in a pilot's grasp.

One of the engineers emailed a colleague and asked, "What happens when we have faulty AOA or Mach number?"—a bad angle-of-attack vane or an unreliable airspeed reading. The colleague replied, "If they are faulty then MCAS shuts down immediately."

That wasn't true, as it turned out. In its simplicity, the software was like an old-fashioned toy buzzer. It would fire for ten seconds whenever the vane suggested a high angle of attack, then reset. If the situation persisted (as with a faulty AoA vane it very well could), MCAS would fire again.

By June, as testing of fault scenarios continued, the test pilots themselves had noticed the issues this caused: the plane was trimming itself due to repeated MCAS activations. "Is this considered a safety or cert issue?" an engineer asked, meaning the impact on certification from the FAA. A colleague responded no. "I don't think this is safety, other then [sic] the pilot could fight the MCAS input and over time find themselves in a large mistrim." The fatal flaw was there, tantalizingly close, if the team had been encouraged to slow down and run all their concerns to ground. Still Boeing trusted the pilots, in the heat of the moment, to react as needed.

Leverkuhn, the MAX program manager, didn't investigate the details. He later described the brief summary he gave to his own boss, the jetliner division chief Ray Conner: "There had been an issue that had been discovered during flight testing and . . . a solution was available."

Even if they weren't saying so to their own bosses, some at Boeing began expressing doubts about the trajectory of the company to which many had given their entire working lives. Steve Taylor, one of the managers in the pilot training operation, was the son of Dick Taylor, a famed engineer and test pilot who pioneered twin-engine planes like the 777. The Seattle Museum of History & Industry interviewed the younger Taylor as part of its centennial exhibit in 2016, and he volunteered some frustrations about how Boeing had changed since he started there in 1986. "We're not leading the market with the technical innovation that we might have been," he said. Moreover, letting Alan Mulally go—"an incredible leader that people naturally gravitate to"—was a big mistake: "He brought technical excellence to Ford."

That May, Suzanna Darcy-Henneman, another training manager, sat down to record her own contribution to the hagiographic audio clips that would run on a loop at the museum all summer. She was a Boeing veteran who had once completed a flight from Seattle to Bangkok in a 777, Boeing's "Camelot" aircraft, in world-record time. The pilot was happy to say politic things about her career at Boeing. But there was something she had to get off her chest—as long as it didn't appear in the museum's archives until long after the exhibit had closed. "Okay, Sean," she told the interviewer, "this is the part you get to publish in July of 2017." She talked about the merger with McDonnell Douglas, the resulting obsession with costs, her fights with finance people. The company, she said, was something like a pilot who had pulled too hard on the stick and now had to push it back in the other direction.

"It was all about the bottom line and the feeling that you were just a cog in that, and that people didn't matter," she said. "In the jobs I had—it was all about people, whether it was in production flight test, experimental flight test, in the training team. Does your finance person very clearly understand what it takes to run your piece of the business?"

The Pacific Northwest summer, when not shrouded in wildfire smoke, is glorious. Endless temperate days, a mild breeze off the ocean, and the famous snow-capped Mount Rainier "out," in the local parlance—in clear view from highways or office towers or airplanes. That August of 2016, MAX program manager Keith Leverkuhn, his engineering chief Michael Teal, and the boss who'd awarded Teal his stock, Michael Delaney, all teed off in the Boeing Classic Korean Air Pro-Am golf tournament at TPC Snoqualmie Ridge, a private course in the foothills of the Cascade Range outside Seattle. Bernhard Langer collected the glass trophy and donned the traditional brown leather flight jacket for the winner.

For the Boeing family, it was also a month of mourning. Joe Sutter, the blunt-spoken lead designer of the 747, who had once described his chief contribution as making sure that everyone on the team understood how their own small piece of the plane affected the whole, died at age ninety-five. Ray Conner, the head of Boeing's commercial airplane business, called him "an inspiration—not just to those at Boeing, but to the entire aerospace industry."

On August 15, 2016, Boeing's engineers loaded the software package containing the latest MCAS revision—the "black label" version, signifying it was ready for production—onto the 737 MAX 8's flight control computer. The MAX ultimately completed 297 certification flights, some with Boeing pilots at the controls and others with FAA pilots. They simulated stalls and near-stalls. They triggered deliberate failures of various systems, to see how the plane and the pilots would react. They even flew it into some of the steep banking turns that caused the MCAS software to kick in, deflecting the stabilizer to its new maximum angle of 2.5 degrees.

No more squawks.

The next day, Klein gave word that the FAA planned to approve the training that Boeing had lobbied for through Mark Forkner. Pilots who had flown the 737 Next Generation could complete their training for the MAX in a few hours on an iPad. Marketing slides soon went out showing a pilot sitting with a tablet. One salesperson wrote Forkner to congratulate him and his team, advising them to get "really DRUNK . . . Call me if you bros need cabs tonight!!"

Finally, in November 2016, Boeing's engineers handed over the system safety assessment of the MCAS software to the FAA. The document didn't include anything about the new angle of the stabilizer, or the software changes made to MCAS in the final "black label" version. That version was known as Revision E. The FAA's specialists, the Forrest Gumps, were shown analysis based on an earlier iteration of the software, Revision C. They got their bewildering "drawer full of paper," as one of the engineers had put it. But it was the wrong drawer.

Rick Ludtke, the controls designer, didn't have much time to join in the festivities when the MAX won official certification the following March; he was laid off. "I was getting too expensive," he said. Employees were still finding bugs in the manual in April of that year, when the MAX started rolling out of assembly lines. "Oh I'm sure it'll get better when Boeing engineers design a whole new one. Wait? Who is left to do such a thing?" one worker wrote in an email later turned up by investigators. "No one!" came the reply.

Eventually one more mistake would be discovered: An alert showing a discrepancy between the two angle-of-attack vanes wasn't lighting up on a majority of the MAX planes Boeing had started delivering. The alert was mistakenly tied to an optional indicator showing the raw angle-of-attack data, which most airlines (including Southwest and Lion Air) hadn't paid for. Boeing's engineers decided to defer a fix until the next software update—in 2020.

For the time being, after fulfilling his assignment that fall of 2016, Forkner, chief of the MAX manual writers, felt relaxed enough to send a note to an old friend he'd worked with at the FAA. "Things are calming down a bit for my airplane cert, at least for now," he wrote. The only things left were validating the simulator for the MAX and a bit of traveling, or, as he put it: "Jedi-mind tricking regulators into accepting the training that I got accepted by FAA etc."

By November, though, he was seeing the plane in a different light. Sitting in a hotel room in Miami with a Grey Goose, he vented to his deputy, a former Ryanair pilot named Patrik Gustavsson, about the plane's "egregious" performance in the simulator. No one had told him that MCAS, originally intended to prevent stalls at high speed, could now possibly fire at speeds as low as 150 miles per hour. "I'm levelling off at like 4000 ft, 230 knots and the plane is trimming itself like craxy [sic]," he wrote. "I'm like, WHAT?"

Gustavsson's first reaction was the sheer frustration of the fed-up office worker. "Oh great," he replied—now they had to update the description in the manual. But Forkner appeared to have deeper concerns. He wrote that it meant he had "lied (unknowingly) to the regulator" about the system's authority over the stabilizer, its ability to flummox a pilot. "Why are we just now hearing about this?" Forkner asked.

"I don't know, the test pilots have kept us out of the loop," Gustavsson replied.

"They're all so damn busy, and getting pressure from the program," Forkner said.

They couldn't have known it at the time, but they were remarking on the 737 MAX's fatal flaw, the feature that, two years later, would contribute to two crashes and 346 deaths.

For all his alarm, Forkner, a Pickett's charge guy to the end, stuck to his mission. In a conversation with Klein later that month, he didn't mention any of his private concerns to her. Later he reminded her that they'd agreed to delete MCAS from the manual. And when Lion Air, receiving its first MAX planes the next year, asked for simulator instruction, he didn't respond charitably. "Idiots!" he wrote, before orchestrating a few days of conference calls to convince the airline it was unnecessary. Recounting his intervention later to a colleague, he wrote, "I save this company a sick amount of $$$$."

More weight had been heaped onto the back of the 737 MAX—and the people charged with its creation and sale—than it could bear. Something was bound to break.

10

Crash

The captain, Bhavye Suneja, had the flu. First officer Harvino had been rousted at four a.m. with the unexpected assignment to fly the MAX. Still, as passengers filed in behind them and stowed their bags that day in October 2018, the Lion Air pilots had every reason to take comfort in the plane's modern appearance. Compared to the earlier 737 that both had flown extensively, the cabin was blissfully quiet, even during the five minutes it took for each of the big new engines to warm up. Their seats were cushier. Four large color screens arrayed in front of them made altitude and speed readouts easier to see—nothing like the old analog dials that Boeing designers once called the "steam gauges."

Suneja was coughing every other minute this morning, but in better health he was a sunny, life-of-the-party kind of guy. He loved to cook pizza or biryani for friends. Machines were another passion: on road trips, Suneja was always the one behind the wheel. He was looking forward to exactly that, planning to fly home to New Delhi from Jakarta, and then drive through the highlands near Nepal the next week with his wife of two years, Garima. Airlines were a family affair for the Sunejas. His mother was a manager at Air India, and his younger sister aspired to become a pilot. After flight school in California, Suneja had joined Lion Air in 2011, the same year the airline placed what was then the biggest single order in Boeing's history, the $22 billion MAX purchase that founder Rusdi Kirana sealed with a handshake from President Obama.

Kirana's own story was one of remarkable ascent. He had started out as a distributor of Brother typewriters before opening a travel agency in Jakarta with his brother; in the early days, he would hold up a name board at Soekarno-Hatta to pick up arriving passengers. They eventually cobbled together $900,000 and leased an ancient 737-200 as well as a woeful Russian-made competitor, the Yakovlev Yak-42. From such humbling beginnings, Lion Air was born in 2000.

By 2015, Kirana was a billionaire. With his jet-black hair and neatly trimmed black mustache, frequently attired in jeans and an untucked shirt, Kirana, then fifty-two, retained a youthful appearance. Even after he'd made his fortune, he sometimes sounded regretful about his chosen profession. He once mused that "only stupid people" start airlines. "If I had money," he said, "I would buy plantations or do mining or property or restaurants."

Lion Air would go on to order hundreds of A320neos from Airbus in addition to the MAX. It controlled half the domestic market in Indonesia, a nation of 250 million people living on seventeen thousand islands stretching three thousand miles from east to west—with a majority of that population yet to take its first flight. With such untapped markets at its disposal, it was no wonder Boeing's Muilenburg, who became CEO that same year, frequently talked about how the aerospace industry had reached some kind of cycle-busting new normal.

If Lion Air's growth resembled that of Southwest Airlines, its safety record didn't. For almost a decade, until June 2016, the airline had been banned from European Union airspace, along with most other Indonesian airlines, because of concerns about maintenance and training practices in the country. One Lion Air flight overshot a runway at Indonesia'a Solo Airport in 2004, killing twenty-five people. Another undershot a runway in Bali in 2013 and landed in the water, splitting the fuselage; all 108 aboard miraculously survived.

Airbus had taken a different approach to training from Boeing's, after signing its own deal with Lion Air in 2014. It based instructors with the carrier full-time, providing courses and simulators for the jointly owned Angkasa Aviation Academy in Jakarta. Other employees worked from a Lion Air maintenance hangar. "Airbus helps us to be better," Kirana said.

The support from Boeing was more haphazard. In the 1970s and 1980s, it had stationed people at maintenance hangars, too, so they could watch over what airlines were doing with their planes and offer advice, according to John Goglia, a mechanic at United and USAir for thirty years who was an NTSB board member from 1995 to 2004. More recently, he said, Boeing had relied on field service representatives covering multiple airlines, often stretched thin across thousands of miles. "It just faded away over time—there's a Boeing rep around there someplace, but you have to call," he said.

Thanks to the lobbying Forkner and his colleagues had done, pilots like Suneja or Harvino, who'd already flown the 737 Next Generation, didn't need to step into any simulator to fly the MAX. (Cost to the airlines in lost crew salary: "Zero," as a Boeing employee wrote in one email.) But Boeing still needed to help develop a MAX simulator for pilots newly qualifying on the type. More than a year after the plane itself had entered service, the employees in Flight Technical and Safety were still trying to work out the bugs—all the while assuring various global regulators that the plans were on track. "The lies, the damned lies," one person wrote, despairing that a pilot had been asked to sign one certification document "clearly based on a lie." There had been audio problems with the devices, software glitches, old data, leaking air lines. In instant messages, the employees commiserated over Boeing's cost-motivated decision to award the simulator contract to the low bidder, a unit of Textron called Tru Simulation + Training based in Goose Creek, South Carolina. "I'll be shocked if the FAA passes this turd," one wrote in a message later turned over to congressional investigators.

Confronting multiple problems, and with regulators again asking questions, at least one employee expressed remorse for his role in hurrying the simulator toward completion. "I still haven't been forgiven by God for the covering up I did last year," the employee said in an instant message. In another exchange, someone wrote, "Would you put your family on a MAX simulator trained aircraft? I wouldn't." "No," came the reply. Dozens of the planes had already entered commercial service, and dozens more were entering the fleet each month as Boeing ramped up the production rate.

One person deeply involved in the development who wasn't around for the aftermath: Mark Forkner. Southwest was just getting its first MAX deliveries, and few of the airline's pilots could claim to know the planes or the simulators better than he did. Forkner took a job there as a first officer and moved his family to the company's home base in Dallas. In his late forties by then, he told friends he didn't see how he would have made it to retirement at Boeing, once seen as the pinnacle of aviation.

Others were just as disillusioned. "Everybody has it in their head meeting schedule is most important because that's what Leadership pressures and manages," one person wrote. He was a manager himself. He'd participated in a "Go/No Go meeting" that, he said, became known internally as the "Go/Go meeting" because saying "no" wasn't an option. Yet as he pointed out, "We haven't even fully checked the requirements Tru is supposed to be meeting." The manager lamented how "the lowest ranking and most unproven supplier" had won the simulator contract, "solely based on bottom dollar."

Then he put his finger on the forces that had been building for years, decades even, and would soon destroy lives and reputations: "It's systemic. It's culture. It's the fact that we have a senior leadership team that understand very little about the business and yet are driving us to certain objectives. Its [sic] lots of individual groups that aren't working closely and being accountable. . . . Sometimes you have to let things fail big so that everyone can identify a problem."

At the factory on Lake Washington near Seattle where the 737s were made, that's exactly what Ed Pierson feared he was seeing. Pierson had been a navy officer for thirty years, commanding a squadron before joining Boeing in 2008. After working in the flight test unit under Bomben, he'd become a senior manager in 737 assembly. He was dismayed to find operations in disarray as people scrambled to meet Muilenburg's target of raising the production rate from forty-seven to fifty-two planes a month by June 2018, and to fifty-seven in 2019. Half-finished planes stacked up in assembly bays, on a lakefront tarmac, and across a bridge to the runway. The overtime rate doubled, and jobs behind schedule spiked to ten times the normal amount.

Instead of slowing things down, managers only heaped on more pressure. At town hall meetings, some 737 managers asked underlings pointed questions about the delays, in front of a hundred or more of their peers. Boeing tracks quality defects in a computerized database, and Pierson saw that reports of issues—malfunctioning equipment, missing inspections, incorrect parts—had risen 30 percent.

He decided to go outside the chain of command. Pierson wrote to the general manager of the 737 factory, Scott Campbell, telling him, "Frankly right now all my internal warning bells are going off. For the first time in my life, I'm sorry to say that I'm hesitant about putting my family on a Boeing airplane." Campbell assured him in his response that safety and quality came first. A month later, with conditions only worsening, Pierson asked for an in-person meeting. He laid out all of the evidence that quality was suffering and asked Campbell to shut down the line. "We can't do that. I can't do that," Campbell said. Pierson replied that he had seen operations in the military shut down over less substantial safety issues. Campbell answered tersely, "The military isn't a profit-making organization."

At profit making, Boeing now excelled. Two decades after Harry Stonecipher had berated its proud engineers as hobbyists who didn't know how to run a business, Boeing had become a Wall Street darling. It had reported a 67 percent jump in 2017 earnings, to $8.2 billion from $4.9 billion the previous year, and its operating margin—the amount of sales left after expenses—had climbed to a once-unthinkable 11 percent. The stock price had responded, tripling in the three years of Muilenburg's tenure. Early in 2018, the price exceeded $300, a stunning milestone for a company long in the shadow of GE. After Wall Street's skepticism of Condit, the slights of the Stonecipher era, and the stumbles under McNerney, Boeing was finally the industrial titan against which all others were measured. GE's own recipe had failed, the financial crisis exposing the shortcomings of its in-house bank; the stock collapsed that year to less than ten dollars.

Not long after Boeing reported record earnings, cash flow, and commercial deliveries for 2017, Boeing's finance staff gathered at the JW Marriott on Adams Street in Chicago for their annual off-site meeting. CFO Greg Smith told staff the stock could hit $800 or $900 if Boeing continued pushing for efficiency and redirecting cash into dividends and buybacks.

The plodding Lazy B was no more. In interviews, Muilenburg declared that Boeing's ambition was to be nothing less than a model of profitability—in short, something like what GE used to be. "Our aspiration is no longer to be just the best in aerospace—we have to be a global industrial champion," he told one outlet. To the chagrin of some on his staff who saw it as tempting fate, he also claimed the boom-and-bust cycles of airline travel were a thing of the past, with one hundred million passengers in Asia taking their first flight every year. On CNBC, at the Economic Club of Washington, or at shareholder meetings, Muilenburg's appearances had an assured, if practiced, crispness. Audiences loved to hear somebody who looked like John Glenn talk about the future of spaceflight. Muilenburg, still in his early fifties, often said he expected the United States to send humans to Mars on a Boeing rocket within a decade, while he was still helming the company.

Corporate hubris often reveals itself through extreme sports. Just before Enron crashed, Jeffrey Skilling, the chief executive, boasted to a reporter about how it wasn't a vacation unless he busted up a mountain bike or two. That spring of 2018, Muilenburg talked about how he handed out jerseys to Boeing employees on site visits and took them for impromptu cycle races, part of his now-140-mile-a-week pace. "Can anybody go faster than you?" the interviewer at the Economic Club asked. "Some try," Muilenburg answered.

With Wall Street, the FAA, and the nascent Trump administration all on his team, the wind at Boeing's back was like nothing it had ever seen. The new associate administrator for safety at the FAA was none other than Ali Bahrami, who had set up the BASOO in Seattle, and who'd so upset the specialists working under him for his seemingly close ties to Boeing. After leaving the FAA for an industry lobbying job, he had then taken a pay cut to rejoin the agency in July 2017. He told air cargo operators at a conference in a Washington, D.C., suburb a month later that he was especially excited about working *with* the industry, rather than against it, to address safety issues. Over the previous two years, Bahrami proudly said, enforcement actions had dropped 70 percent. "We used to measure success by how high our stack of hate mail was," he said. "That's no longer the case." On a call that year with analysts, Muilenburg complimented the government for its "focus on deregulation" and the "streamlined" certification process that had helped bring the MAX to market.

After lobbying from Boeing and others, the bill authorizing funding for the FAA the next year went further than ever before in handing control to the manufacturers, disempowering the agency created to oversee them. The FAA was stripped of some of its most fundamental authority—to decide, for instance, whether a manufacturer like Boeing was qualified to certify its own work. Under the new law, delegation to private industry was considered the default. If regulators had doubts about a system—the Dreamliner's batteries, say, or the MAX's flight controls—they first had to make a formal case for why they should retake certification control from airplane makers.

In their blind compliance the proud specialists at the FAA were no longer like Forrest Gump, as BASOO engineer Richard Reed had grimly joked. They were more like Barney Fife, neutered deputies walking around with guns unloaded and a single bullet in their breast pockets.

The new law also nudged agency officials even closer to having their pay determined by the very people they were supposed to supervise. It created a working group of mostly aerospace executives to weigh in on FAA compensation. That was only slightly watered down from an earlier version of the bill that would have given them input on individual employees' pay, former agency official Peggy Gilligan told the *New York Times:* "It appeared they were looking to influence the individuals' pay outcome in some way, and for the FAA employees to know that potential pay impact."

The agency, in other words, had become a rubber stamp. After starting with a system in which Boeing's deputies reported to managers at the FAA, it was now in many respects the opposite: the government officials had to answer to Boeing. That organizational chart showing the headshot of the FAA manager underneath his counterpart at Boeing turned out to be exactly accurate. To Marc Ronell, the certification employee who'd heard talk of managers getting cash bonuses for approving a helicopter design on time, it appeared the handover of his authority was complete. "It's basically putting the regulatory decisions into the hands of those who are being regulated," he said.

Despite some initial awkwardness, Muilenburg and President Trump turned out to be kindred spirits, an unlikely relationship somewhat emblematic of the larger contradictions in a religious right that looked past the president's moral failings in exchange for welcome policies. The crass showman and the Bible-studying businessman found common cause in regulation, taxes, and a trade war aimed at forcing the planes made by Canada's Bombardier—and their more advanced technology—out of the U.S. market.

Trump had picked Boeing for one of his early calling-on-the-carpet rituals in December 2016, blasting the "out-of-control" costs on a 747 *Air Force One* contract. Within hours, Muilenburg was on the phone, explaining the plane's specifications. He flattered Trump by handing the self-professed great dealmaker his deal, offering what he told reporters was a discount to pull two used Boeing jumbos out of desert storage and reconfigure them as presidential transports. After that, Trump came to treat Boeing as a kind of corporate Bill Rancic—the Season 1 *Apprentice* winner Trump couldn't stop plugging. "Is Boeing here? Boeing?" the president called out at a meeting of business leaders in Tokyo in 2017, before gushing to the head of Boeing's Japan operations, "Oh, look at my guy. Stand up. Boy, have I made him. . . . Fantastic. Great job you're doing. And I do love the F-18 also."

A month into his presidency, Trump made one of his first corporate visits to the Boeing plant in South Carolina that had been a cause célèbre for conservative media. At the White House, he surprised Finland's then president during a joint press conference with a declaration that the country had agreed to purchase F-18s made by Boeing in St. Louis. President Sauli Niinistö later called the remark a "duck," Finnish for joke, and said the country hadn't made up its mind. Trump let Muilenburg listen in on a call he had with competitor Lockheed Martin to discuss a rival fighter, the F-35, and appointed a former Boeing executive, Pat Shanahan, to a Pentagon post as deputy defense secretary in charge of acquisitions.

As international competition heated up in the market for commercial jets, in part because of the unlikely advent of a dangerous rival from Canada, Boeing leveraged its relationship with the federal government. It had long been nervous about the potential for the new C Series planes from Montreal's Bombardier to cut into the 737's market, and with good reason: in 2016 one of the flagship U.S. carriers, Delta, ordered seventy-five of them. But the plane's development costs had stretched Bombardier's finances, and it wanted a buyer to take over the program.

By one high-ranking executive's account, Boeing lawyer Michael Luttig, who considered himself a master tactician, devised a strategy intended to swallow the 737 competitor on generous terms: In initial negotiations with the company, Boeing would extract some concessions. Then Luttig would file a trade complaint against the Canadian government over development subsidies it had kicked in. With the jet shut out of the U.S. market, Boeing would then use that leverage to squeeze even more concessions and ultimately take the plane for nothing—in fact, probably with massive sweeteners attached.

After weeks of high-level talks that the Canadians believed were making progress, one of the chief lawyer's "Luttigators" called Canada's ambassador to the United States on a Saturday in August 2017, abruptly halting the conversation. The Trump Commerce Department duly responded to Boeing's complaint against Bombardier with proposed tariffs of almost 300 percent. The lawyer appeared to be winning his game of three-dimensional chess.

That October, according to the executive apprised of the events, Luttig was updating Boeing board members about the strategy when their phones started buzzing with alerts: Airbus, they learned, would be taking a majority stake in the Canadian airplane program. It would sidestep the U.S. duties by building the planes at a factory in Mobile, Alabama, rather than in Canada.

Setbacks for Boeing followed in quick succession. The U.S. International Trade Commission rejected Boeing's complaint, four to zero. Delta placed an additional order—but for one hundred Airbus jets, not the MAX. The Canadian government canceled a $5 billion order from Boeing for F-18 fighters. It amounted to more inklings of the plane maker's hubris. But Boeing simply turned to negotiations with another maker of small aircraft, Brazil's Embraer, and agreed to buy most of the company for $3.8 billion. Nothing, it seemed, could stop the mighty Boeing.

In August 2018, Muilenburg and Jennifer Lowe, a vice president in Boeing Government Operations who had helped plan the ceremony for Reagan's funeral in a previous job as a Republican congressional staffer, were at Trump National Golf Club in Bedminster, New Jersey. They had the prime seats next to Trump and his wife, Melania, at a dinner for business leaders. "We're going to build a record number of airplanes this year thanks to the policies of this administration," Muilenburg said. Trump cut in, "Boeing is doing very well. I think Boeing has to like me a lot. Right? You're doing very well. Yeah, I think everybody, frankly, in this room likes me. We'll keep it that way."

A month later, Muilenburg was onstage again, this time at First

Baptist Church—near the gated mansion on two acres he'd once owned in the St. Louis suburb of Edwardsville—for its "Leadership Luncheon" series. "Surprises happen a lot in this business," he said to the crowd, his fellow congregants for years while he rose through the ranks at Boeing. He told them he'd learned from failures—naming one that was rather unmemorable, the shutdown of a new air-traffic management venture. The host asked how he managed to work so much while also practicing his faith. "I ought to be the same person, the same leader, the same man, whether I'm at work or at home," Muilenburg answered. "My faith is an important part of how we operate."

On September 24, he gave his most public endorsement yet of Biblical Business Training, the St. Louis nonprofit whose curriculum had formed the basis for those early-morning study sessions in the cafeteria. (The leader of the local branch was a Boeing training executive who'd helped recruit Muilenburg as chairman of the national organization.) The group's stated purpose was to "equip and empower God's people in the workplace."

The piece Muilenburg published that day, titled "Pursuing God's Mission," opened with Luke 12:48: "From everyone who has been given much, much will be demanded; and from the one who has been entrusted with so much, much more will be asked." Muilenburg went on to say that "the growing crisis of character of leadership in the workplace" was what made it so important to bring together small groups for faith-based discussions. "We need to understand how the Bible applies to what we do every day," he said.

In front of cameras at Luke Air Force Base in Glendale, Arizona, the next month, Muilenburg joined Trump around a table once more. This time it was for a conversation with military contractors and Patrick Shanahan, the former Boeing executive who was then deputy defense secretary. Shanahan's mug shot had been on the wall of the "visibility room" at Chicago headquarters. He was widely thought to have been the runner-up for Muilenburg's job. Gesturing to Shanahan, Trump pronounced him a smart buyer of equipment for the Pentagon before turning to Muilenburg: "What do you think, Dennis, is he okay?" Muilenburg quickly answered, "He's tough. He's good."

For a few minutes they had a stilted conversation about the importance of investing in aerospace and education—Muilenburg once again thanking Trump for "your policies around tax reform and regulatory reform"—before the president, now addressing the reporters in the room, broke in. "I don't know if you know what's happening," he said. "People are coming over from Honduras. They have like 5,000 people. Honduras and Guatemala, El Salvador. Some of these people are hard criminals. Hardened criminals." It was a month before the 2018 midterm election, and misinformation fueled by Trump on Twitter and then picked up by Fox News had turned footage of a protest march by Central American migrants into a supposed "caravan" of asylum seekers heading for the United States. "They broke through in Guatemala," he said. "These are some bad people coming through. These aren't babies, these aren't little angels coming into our country, going to work for Boeing." When a reporter asked for evidence they were criminals, Trump's tone got derisive: "Oh please—don't be a baby. Take a look." (The reporter was a woman.) Muilenburg and Shanahan, both data-driven engineers with masters' degrees, listened mutely.

On October 22, Boeing collected the Robert W. Campbell Award for leadership in safety from the National Safety Council, then led by the former NTSB chairwoman who had investigated the Dreamliner battery fires. On October 24, just days before a single fateful vane on an Indonesian plane would malfunction and go undetected, Boeing reported that third-quarter free cash flow jumped 37 percent to $4.1 billion, more than double analyst estimates, sparking a 3 percent jump in its share price. "The cash is the cash, you can't deny it," said Ken Herbert, an analyst with Canaccord Genuity.

The first drop was like falling into a deep hole. Then came the screams, everyone praying to God. This was not the deadly flight but another, luckier Lion Air flight. Minutes after the 737 MAX departed Bali for Jakarta, just after nine p.m. on Sunday, October 28, 2018, the software that Boeing had pressed regulators to delete from the manual had kicked in. As the plane seesawed up and down over the next ten minutes, Surprianto Sudarto, seated in the second row, saw flight attendants and pilots going in and out of the cockpit carrying what looked like dictionaries. "Is that the instruction book or what?" he thought to himself. At least one person vomited.

Unknown to pilots, at the base in Bali mechanics had replaced a faulty angle-of-attack vane on the almost brand-new jet with a used one from a repair shop in Florida. The vanes, sitting like nostrils on either side of the plane's nose, are designed to detect how steeply the craft is flying into oncoming winds. A protruding part of the vane rotates in response to the airflow. It's attached to what looks like a system of gears inside—actually small electrical transformers called resolvers that read the angle in comparison to a static reference and then feed that information into the plane's computer. A test is supposed to be performed before installation to make sure the resolvers are properly calibrated. No one at the shop or the maintenance base noticed that the resolvers on this particular vane were misaligned by 21 degrees.

It was sloppy—one of the links in the "chain of errors" often said to accumulate in aviation accidents, the heartbreaking clarity coming only in hindsight. But the sloppiness had started at Boeing, in the early compromises of the plane's design, and then in the loose ends left dangling in the final days of development. The MCAS software was designed to only take input from a single sensor, alternating from one side to the other after each flight. The bad sensor happened to be the one feeding into the captain's controls, so when the Lion Air jet took off, it set off a thumping "stick shaker" that made the control wheel vibrate in his hands, triggered altitude and airspeed warnings, and, most perilously, commanded the plane's nose down.

By chance, this crew had an advantage that pilots Suneja and Harvino would not when they stepped into the very same plane, only hours later. A third, off-duty pilot was sitting in the jump seat between the two at the controls, hitching a ride. In the commotion he noticed the trim wheel between them moving. That suggested to him the proper checklist, among the dozens in the handbook—the one for a runaway stabilizer. The captain flipped a switch to turn off the stabilizer motor, just as Boeing engineers had reasoned a pilot would. For the rest of the flight, he had to turn the wheel himself, a remarkably rustic thing to ask of a pilot of a large commercial aircraft in the twenty-first century. The control column also kept vibrating in his hand; there was no mechanism in the MAX to shut off the stick shaker if the data were faulty. But the crew managed to land safely in Jakarta ninety minutes later.

Back on the ground, the captain documented what had happened in the logbook, and Lion Air's mechanics got to work clearing the plane for the next flight. The captain's note included the alerts he'd seen—ALT DISAGREE, IAS DISAGREE, and FEEL DIFF PRESS (indicating bad altitude, airspeed, and hydraulic pressure). He and the mechanics never saw the alert that would have pinpointed the problem—AOA DISAGREE, suggesting a discrepancy between the left and right angle-of-attack vanes. The reason: Lion Air hadn't paid for it. They had purchased a bare-bones MAX plane, with no such indicator. Moreover, Boeing had never disclosed the potential issue to customers.

So the Lion Air maintenance team never knew to replace the bad vane. They turned off the power, followed the procedures for the other alerts, and, without any other reason to hold it back, the plane was allowed to depart the next morning. A quirk of the software, however, meant that after a power-down, the bad sensor would again feed into the captain's controls on the left side. Suneja and Harvino would be unwitting guinea pigs, this time without a third pilot to guide them. The IOU that Boeing's engineers had left dangling in the hastily completed software finally came due.

At eight a.m. in Jakarta on October 29, 2018, Fenlix, who went by a single name as is common in Indonesia, was driving to a meeting and had just pulled over for coffee when he got a text from an old friend: a Lion Air jet had just gone down in the Java Sea. Fenlix knew that his brother, thirty-one-year-old Verian, was on the plane, bound for their hometown with Andrea Manfredi, a former pro cyclist from Italy. Verian had his own bicycle shop and Manfredi was a supplier. They were headed for a vacation after wrapping up business. Fenlix tapped out a text. "Bro?" he wrote.

Within hours of the crash, the Indonesian Diving Rescue Team was in the water, retrieving crumpled cell phones, ID cards, bags, and photos. Winches started pulling up larger pieces of debris, and the divers began hunting for the flight data recorder and cockpit voice recorder. The pilot Suneja's father went to Kramat Jati Police Hospital in East Jakarta, sitting mutely as a gloved orderly swabbed the fleshy skin inside his cheek to obtain a DNA sample to identify his son's remains. During the search, one more name was added to the death toll: diver Syachrul Anto, forty-eight, drowned.

In Seattle, John Hamilton, Boeing Commercial Airplanes vice president of engineering, convened pilots and flight controls experts to discuss what had gone wrong. The shocking accident involving a nearly new plane had sent the company's shares down 7 percent that Monday. It wasn't a long discussion, as Hamilton described it later to congressional investigators. "We quickly identified that this MCAS activation could have been a scenario," he said. "And, once the flight data recorder came up later in the week . . . we started working on a software change immediately."

With its spotty safety record, Lion Air took most of the heat for the crash. A week after the accident, grieving family members crowded into a sweaty auditorium for a meeting led by Indonesia's transport minister. They spotted Lion Air founder Kirana in the crowd and demanded he identify himself. He stood and bowed his head, a gesture they took as either contrition or shame.

At the FAA's Boeing Aviation Safety Oversight Office in Seattle, engineers began scouring their files for information about the software in question and discovered what looked like incomplete and inaccurate work by the deputies entrusted to oversee safety at Boeing. The system safety assessment for MCAS had been turned over

to the agency just five months before the plane was officially certified, which, given the voluminous paperwork involved, suggested
a suspiciously hasty approval. The Boeing deputy who'd vetted the
software design had categorized the risk of a failure as relatively
minor. But the documents on file reflected the software's earlier
design (Revision C), not the more powerful version later added in
flight tests (Revision E). They showed the stabilizer had the capacity to adjust a plane's ascent or descent by only 0.6 degrees—in its
final form, it had been given the authority to make adjustments at
four times that angle. "When they changed the design it drastically
changed the potential criticality of the MCAS feature," one FAA
specialist said. "And that was not communicated to the FAA engineers who find compliance. In fact they didn't even know about it."

Boeing's Safety Review Board, a formal gathering of engineers
and pilots to go over recent safety incidents, discussed the Lion
Air crash in early November. Among themselves, they had quickly
acknowledged some of the software's flaws. Their expectation that a
pilot could safely untangle the chaos of confusing alerts and inter-
vene to turn off the stabilizer had been challenged.

But even within the fraternity, there's an omertà in aviation
accidents, and it applied here. Partly this is for self-protection: if
someone writes openly about a flaw, it exposes the manufacturer to
additional liability for having known about the issues in advance. In
the wrangling over the Boeing rudder design blamed for two crashes
back in the 1990s, litigation had eventually turned up a memo
titled "We Have a Problem," in which engineers acknowledged—
even before a second crash—that a rudder valve had the potential
to jam. Some pilots had seen the anguish it caused colleagues who
were asked to explain themselves years later, and they became more
careful about what they put in writing.

There was another reason for the reluctance to push back against
Boeing's stated assumptions—one that involved race, not cost. The
empathy that Boeing's aviators might have had for a pilot who
looked like them wasn't being extended to Suneja and Harvino.
Conversations at Boeing kept focusing on how Harvino, once he
took over the controls, hadn't been able to trim the plane with the

thumb switch. Boeing's pilots, predominantly older white men, had long had private jokes about the incompetent crews they ran into overseas. "Too dumb to spell 737," went a frequent refrain of one pilot. Another trainer would ask rhetorically if "Chung Fo Ho" could handle a certain procedure.

The Safety Review Board concluded that Boeing should issue an alert directing pilots in such a situation to the right checklist— the one for arresting a runaway stabilizer that the luckier Lion Air flight had relied upon. The FAA went along with the recommendation on November 7, issuing an emergency airworthiness directive "prompted by analysis performed by the manufacturer." The bulletin told pilots and airlines that if an erroneous input is received from the angle-of-attack sensor, "there is a potential for repeated nose-down trim commands of the horizontal stabilizer" and, in the anodyne language of aviation, "possible impact with terrain." It still made no mention of the MCAS software responsible for the malfunction.

In plain language, the directive was saying that Boeing's brand-new airplane, supposedly a marvel of modern technology, could crash itself into the ground based on bad data from one tiny sensor. It sounded like the kind of single-point failure commercial aircraft weren't supposed to have. And as Boeing began privately talking more with airlines about MCAS, elaborating on how the flight control software worked, the pilot grapevine started jumping.

What most alarmed pilots was that this new feature overturned decades of Boeing design philosophy, the thing the manufacturer had always claimed set it apart from Airbus. "If it ain't Boeing I ain't going," pilots would say, proud of the fact that a computer would never take the plane out of their hands. Now the colossus of American aviation was casually telling them it had done exactly that.

MCAS had been shoehorned into the controls to address a quirk of physical design, and reacting to the new software asked a lot of pilots. They would have to notice, within seconds, the stabilizer running away, then start working the right checklist with robotic efficiency. There are dozens of them in the Quick Reference Handbook, the inch-thick guide to emergency situations (itself adapted from the even thicker Flight Crew Operations Manual, running more than a thousand pages). Pilots have to analyze the many varieties of mechanical ailments the way a doctor might parse physical ones. A half dozen separate procedures, for instance, cover anomalies involving the flaps, each of which presents slightly differently in flight.

What's more, if MCAS fired and the pilots simply tried to pull back on the control column to push the nose back up—the natural instinct—it wouldn't respond. The software had been given the authority, not them. Adding MCAS to the flight controls also led to a change in the switches under their thumbs, and few of the MAX's early pilots were even aware of it. Earlier models had two switches—one to turn off all electric power to the stabilizer and another to disable only automatic trim, the tiny adjustments that kept the plane's shifting center of gravity in tune with the air flow.

The MAX had a single cutout switch. If pilots flipped it, as directed in an emergency, they'd no longer be able to adjust the electric trim with the button under their thumbs. They'd have no choice but to use the manual trim wheel, the one that the deadheading third pilot had noticed was moving on its own the night before the Lion Air crash. That wasn't easy. Pilots trained on moving the wheel in refresher courses once a year, but some went their whole careers without ever using it in flight. It was especially rare to have to deal with conditions so jarring in the midst of a takeoff or a landing, the most critical moments of any flight. Boeing had reports of the stick shaker activating at or shortly after takeoff only thirty times between 2001 and 2018, during which hundreds of millions of flights had taken place. Of those instances, twenty-seven were on 737s.

Pilots that November began registering their concerns in the anonymous Aviation Safety Reporting System maintained by NASA. "I think it is unconscionable that a manufacturer, the FAA, and the airlines would have pilots flying an airplane without adequately training, or even providing available resources and sufficient documentation to understand the highly complex systems that differentiate this aircraft from prior models," one wrote. "The fact that this airplane requires such jury rigging to fly is a red flag. Now we know the systems employed are error prone—even if the pilots aren't sure what those systems are, what redundancies are in place, and failure modes. I am left to wonder: what else don't I know?"

Another captain called the MAX flight manual "inadequate and almost criminally insufficient."

The *Wall Street Journal* on November 13 said Boeing had "withheld information about potential hazards" of the new system, citing pilots, safety experts, and midlevel FAA staffers. The report got the attention of Boeing's board members. Arthur Collins, former CEO of Medtronic, attached the story in an email to Muilenburg and said crisply, "I am sure you have already read . . . and will brief the board." Muilenburg had conversations with both Ken Duberstein, the former Reagan chief of staff who'd been the longtime lead director after coming over from the McDonnell Douglas board, and Dave Calhoun, who had only recently transitioned into the lead role, according to records unearthed in a later suit by shareholders.

That day, Muilenburg, in a gray suit with a crisp white shirt and a purple tie, went on Fox Business. "New questions this morning for Boeing," intoned host Maria Bartiromo, who called the *Journal* story "very concerning." Muilenburg immediately launched into the first point of his mental script, sounding, as usual, a little too rehearsed. "Well, Maria, I think it's important that we all express our sympathies for the loss of Lion Air 610 and certainly our thoughts go to the families affected," he said. "We've been very engaged with the investigative authorities throughout," he continued, finally concluding, "The bottom line here is the 737 MAX is safe. Safety is a core value for us at Boeing."

She asked what happened, and he essentially blamed the pilots. The airplane "has the ability to handle" a bad sensor like the one suspected in the Indonesian crash, he said. Boeing, he stressed, had already issued a bulletin pointing pilots to "existing flight procedures." Over footage of rescue boats picking wreckage out of the water, Bartiromo asked him if he regretted not telling pilots more about the system. "No, again, we provide all the information that's needed to safely fly our airplanes," he answered, hewing to the

script again. Bartiromo pressed: But was that information available
to the pilots? "Yeah, that's part of the training manual, it's an existing procedure," he said. "Oh, I see," she said, apparently mollified.

MCAS, of course, wasn't in the manual—not unless you counted
the glossary, which defined the term but didn't explain what it did.
(The definition was likely a vestige of an earlier draft, before Mark
Forkner convinced the FAA to delete a fuller description.)

The next morning Muilenburg climbed into Boeing's Challenger
jet and landed at a new regional airport in Iowa a little over a mile
from the farm where he grew up, the guest of honor at a ribbon cutting. He was still dealing with the blowback from the *Journal* story,
and assured Duberstein that day, in a businesslike email "closing the
loop" on what he called "the Lion Air matter," that he would send
a formal update to the board. "Press is terrible," Duberstein replied,
taking a staccato, man-of-the-world tone. "Very tough. Lots of
negative chatter I'm picking up. Not pleasant." Muilenburg told
him the FAA had put out a "helpful" statement clarifying it wasn't
doing a probe of its own, and that Tim Keating, who ran Government Operations in Washington, was "engaged on [the] political
side too." The pilot unions, he told Duberstein, just wanted to stir
up doubt so that the MAX might be classified as a new airplane
type requiring "more pay" to fly. "On it, and working all angles,"
Muilenburg concluded. His intentions were the opposite, but the
email, in six crisp sentences, crystallized the captured regulators, the
outsized political influence, and anti-union rhetoric that had made
Boeing blind to its own faults.

A crash in a foreign country wasn't on the minds of the crowd
of white-haired burghers who greeted Muilenburg for the ribbon
cutting back home in Iowa. He had on a gray suit and purple tie
exactly as the day before, and they applauded at the inside joke as he
recalled how the prime tract of land they were on used to be called
"million-dollar corner"—and, "well, it's now more than a million
dollars!" His mother, two of his siblings, friends, and neighbors all
came to see the local boy turned business celebrity. Mingling with
them afterward, Muilenburg smiled so much, it was like a wedding.
"Hey roomie," he greeted Steve Haveman, his old college room-

mate. Ted De Hoogh, the teacher who had so admired Muilenburg's artwork at Sioux Center High School, mentioned that his own son was a pilot for Delta. "Oh, that's great!" Muilenburg replied. At the event's conclusion it took him just a few steps to reach the Challenger parked in everyone's view on the tarmac, a bag-toting assistant trailing behind him. After a wave from the top of its short flight of stairs, he was off. Muilenburg's mother, Alyda, stood with a reporter from the *Sioux County Journal* and watched the sleek plane bank over the old family farm. "I am so proud," she said.

Agents on the ground in Indonesia were already working to limit the damages for Boeing and Lion Air. It was one more protective angle, one so routine Muilenburg hadn't mentioned it in his brief email. An Ibis hotel in Jakarta had become a makeshift crisis center. Dazed relatives turned up every day that month to glean what information they could, some still holding out irrational hope for a miracle. The plane had plunged so fast that parts of it lodged beneath the seafloor and were never recovered. Divers put the remains they did find into forty-nine rubber bags that were sent to a police laboratory, where forensic investigators sought to match the remains through fingerprints, dental records, and DNA. The first victim identified, Jannatun Cintya Dewi, a twenty-four-year-old woman who had worked at the Ministry of Energy and Mineral Resources, was laid to rest in a brown-wood casket stamped with a bar code.

On November 5, Rini Soegiyono took her newly orphaned nieces, then eleven and seven, to one of the rooms in the Ibis to meet with a psychologist. Her sister, Niar Soegiyono, and brother-in-law, Andri Wiranofa, had both been on the MAX. Only the previous summer, Niar had treated her sister Rini and the girls to a Celine Dion concert in Jakarta. Andri was a high-ranking state prosecutor, and Niar orchestrated an enriching routine for their daughters familiar to any busy parent: martial arts, piano lessons, Bible camp. Now the girls were crying for hours at a time. That same day, Rini got a call from a notary who invited her to an office on the third floor of the hotel to sign some documents.

The notary was there along with two officials from Lion Air, and they showed her a release form that she'd need to sign to claim 1.3 billion rupiah, or $91,600. "I was not in a state to sign anything," Rini said. A petroleum engineer who also happened to be fluent in English, she scanned an appendix that listed eight pages of companies grouped into two columns, more than four hundred names in all—including Boeing, Lion Air, and a who's who of the world's major aerospace suppliers. All were to be released from liability in any global court in exchange for the money. She asked if she could take the document home and study it; they told her it couldn't leave the room. Rini left without signing it. That evening, someone from the forensics lab called to say her sister's remains had been identified.

It was hard to imagine that a low-fare airline had mobilized such a well-coordinated legal response just a few days after the crash; solving the puzzle of who did became a consuming passion for Rini and the lawyers she eventually hired.

Michael Indrajana, an Indonesian American lawyer living in northern California, had started hearing about the crash from family and friends as soon as it happened. Indrajana, then thirty-five, was an intellectual property attorney and litigator who represented Silicon Valley startups. Born in San Francisco, his family had moved back to Indonesia when he was a baby and he'd lived there until his teens. After high school in Davis, California, he studied applied computational physics at the University of California's Davis campus and earned a law degree from the University of the Pacific's McGeorge School of Law. He was a tech whiz, fond of building custom computers and tinkering with the innards of Xbox game consoles; when a law professor assigned a paper on the legality of installing a "mod chip" to copy games, the professor awarded him the highest marks and commented that it sounded like he did it in real life.

A week after the crash, Indrajana met his mentor and co-counsel, Sanjiv Singh, at a coffee shop near a Best Buy to help transfer files from a balky laptop to a new one for a case they were working on together. Before starting a solo practice, Singh had worked at the powerful New York firm Skadden Arps. He was almost comically pedigreed, in fact. Still just forty-six, he'd finished his undergraduate studies at Harvard University, earned a law degree from UCLA—and then also become a licensed doctor after completing a medical degree at UCSF and a residency in internal medicine at Stanford University. (The latter path was inspired by a why-not vote of confidence from his father, an eminent UCLA cardiologist, after Singh mused about it during dinner at a Chinese restaurant.)

At the coffee shop, Singh and Indrajana started talking about the Lion Air crash and the airworthiness directive the FAA had only recently issued, describing the software glitch that could push the nose down. The directive was so pedestrian on its face, its neutral wording like an iPhone bug notice, but so paradoxically earth-shattering. At the same time, Indrajana told Singh there was lots of chatter on WhatsApp among his old friends, cousins, and schoolmates in Indonesia. Some asked for his help in advising the victims' families. On instinct, despite all the reporting about pilot error and shoddy maintenance, Singh told Indrajana he wanted to sue Boeing.

That night, Indrajana broke the news to his wife and three-year-old son that he'd be flying to Indonesia a month earlier than their planned visit for the holidays, and within forty-eight hours he was in his brother's guest room in Jakarta.

He soon began hearing about loosely identified, official-looking people milling around the crisis center talking to families. Relatives had the impression they worked for the airline, or maybe the government. Some of them, he would learn, were actually local lawyers working on behalf of the insurer for both Boeing and Lion Air, and they were trying to convince family members to sign forms like the one Rini saw.

"Oh my God, this is insane," one relative wrote in a WhatsApp chat thread, describing how he'd been brought into the room and told he couldn't consult anyone about the form. It felt like a CIA interrogation. A camera was mounted on a tripod in a corner of the room, a table with folding metal legs in the center. Indrajana heard about other families ushered into the room who couldn't even read—they were verbally told what the agreement said and urged to sign it. In the United States, additional disclosures would have been required to avoid violating state and federal laws against fraud and negligent misrepresentation. Indrajana and Singh were experienced lawyers but new to what Singh called "the Wild West" of aviation accidents in non-Western countries. Indrajana, raised in Indonesia, saw it as a cynical and ultimately racist deception that would never have happened after a crash on U.S. soil. He called Singh one day and told him, "I think we've got something here that goes beyond the crash itself."

Global Aerospace Underwriting Managers Limited, based in London, is one of the world's biggest aviation insurers, tracing its roots to a group of bowler-hatted bankers in the famed insurance markets of the City, who formed a pool in 1924 to back the emerging airplane industry. Over time many of the major airlines and manufacturers came to be insured by Global Aerospace, which typically spreads the risks among other insurers through its pool. Germany's Munich Re and a unit of Warren Buffett's Berkshire Hathaway are the company's controlling shareholders, according to the most recent corporate disclosure. Crucially for the victims in Indonesia, Global Aerospace was the lead insurer for both Boeing and Lion Air.

There was a standard procedure for crashes like this one, and the insurer executed it. The people working on its behalf in the crisis center helped convince the families of as many as seventy of the victims to sign the settlement offer. Even by Indonesian standards, the amount was a pittance when considered as compensation for the wrongful death of a loved one—not even four times a typical Jakarta professional's salary of $25,000. Still, for families that had just lost their main breadwinner and had bills coming due, the money wasn't easy to pass up. "We wanted the psychological pressure to stop," Dedi Sukendar, a relative of one of the victims who signed the release in order for the dead man's two children to stay in school, later told the *New York Times*.

The settlement also listed Global Aerospace among the hundreds of companies that, in return for the money, were to be released from liability. Left unexplained was that the amount was almost exactly what a 2011 Indonesian law already mandated a responsible party pay for loss of life in an aviation accident, or that the amount was supposed to be a *minimum*, without limiting relatives' right to sue. (The insurer and Boeing have declined to answer specific questions about the matter.)

A similar strategy had been pursued after two previous crashes of 737s in Indonesia. One of the planes, flown by Mandala Air, went down in a residential neighborhood in 2005, killing 149 people. Another, flown by Adam Air, crashed in 2007 after the pilots became preoccupied while troubleshooting the inertial navigation system; 102 died. After those crashes, Allison Kendrick, a lawyer for Perkins Coie who became Boeing's chief counsel for product liability in 2010, worked with lawyers for the insurer who had documented the collection of similar releases from the victims' family members. Kendrick then presented them to American courts as justification for the families' subsequent cases to be dismissed from the United States, relegated instead to far less expensive jurisdictions overseas.

The agents who protected Boeing's interests were just starting their work when Indrajana spotted what was happening at the Lion Air crisis center. As he and his co-counsel Singh gathered information and prepared their lawsuits against Boeing, they fought a second battle to keep families from signing the releases. Rini, too, spread the word on the WhatsApp chat thread—but heard that some families felt they had little choice. Some had borrowed money just to make the trip to the Jakarta crisis center. "The underbelly of aviation is the disenfranchisement of people of color globally— they're being treated like absolute pawns," Singh said.

Every commercial aircraft crash is unique, frequently involving multiple nationalities and corporate entities around the world. International treaties dating back a century set strict formulas for the recovery of damages unless misconduct is proven, which is why the determination of venue is so important. Singh saw the strategy

to limit Boeing's liability, to that point hugely successful, as one reason the significance of such crashes seemed lost on the company's
leadership. "It's the same mistakes, the same arrogance, the same
notion that they could just push things through on their timeline,
their agenda, and they could just finesse the process," Singh said.

By late November, the story was already fading from worldwide
headlines. There were only two people aboard the doomed plane
who weren't from Indonesia—the pilot Suneja, a citizen of India,
and Andrea Manfredi, the former pro cyclist from Italy. The *New
York Times,* among others, began digging into Lion Air's spotty
safety record. "Interviews with dozens of Lion Air's management
personnel and flight and ground crew members, as well as Indonesian investigators and airline analysts, paint a picture of a carrier
so obsessed with growth that it has failed to build a proper safety
culture," the *Times* report concluded November 23. That month
Cowen analyst Cai von Rumohr summed up the mood on Wall
Street, which was more willing to see the crash as an unfortunate
aberration. "Because the MAX is a derivative aircraft, we doubt that
this is a difficult-to-correct technical issue."

Muilenburg held a briefing for board members just before
Thanksgiving; attendance was optional. In a memo to employees, he reassured them, "We're going to learn from this accident
and continue to improve our safety record." Again, he pressed the
questionable idea that Boeing had been completely up front with
customers. "You may have seen media reports that we intention-
ally withheld information about airplane functionality," he said.
"That's simply untrue. The relevant function is described in the
Flight Crew Operations Manual, and we routinely engage customers about how to operate our airplanes safely."

Some pilots weren't so willing to let the matter drop. In Shanghai
that fall, a couple of Boeing trainers ran into a pilot from American
Airlines, who laid into them for "the lives that we cost" in Indonesia, as one of the pilots later described the uncomfortable encoun-
ter. "Hey, hold on," the Boeing pilot responded, cautioning him

to wait for more evidence. Back in Seattle, he joined a half dozen fellow Boeing trainers for a briefing about how the MCAS software worked from Patrik Gustavsson, the former Ryanair pilot who had traded frustrated messages with Forkner two years earlier. Gustavsson was now the chief 737 technical pilot. When Gustavsson told them the software fired based on a single angle-of-attack vane and that it would continue firing even after a bad reading, "we were universally shocked," this person said. The group consisted of trainers who'd been left "out of the loop," as Gustavsson himself had put it. They instantly recognized the flaw in its design. "The pilot's fighting the jet the entire time," as one person there put it.

One of Boeing's engineers had said virtually the same thing during the testing of MCAS, but his email had an unhurried, innocuous tone—you could sense the coffee and air-conditioning. To these pilots, the stakes were immediately clear. The situation was life-threatening.

Boeing sent Mike Sinnett, a vice president who had also led the response to the Dreamliner battery fires, and Craig Bomben, the chief test pilot who'd been at the MAX's controls since the first flight, to clear the air with pilots from major U.S. customers. On November 27, they visited the American Airlines pilots' union in Fort Worth, Texas. Dan Carey, president of the union, had agreed with staffers beforehand that if what they heard sounded insincere, he'd record the conversation. The Boeing executives had only been talking for a few minutes when Carey discreetly turned his phone's recorder on (legal in Texas, where only one party's consent is required).

Sinnett has a mellow, almost stultifying voice, and as the recording started he was saying, "One of the things that we see in the press is that 'Boeing put a system on the airplane and didn't tell anybody about it.'" (The air quotes were apparent.) "It's just a little bit of software," he went on. Failures like the one in Indonesia were fully accounted for in the design and certification, the engineer explained. It was wrong for the press to call it a "single-point failure," he said, because "the function and the trained pilot work side by side and are part of the system"—an assertion that brought the first of several challenges from a pilot with a West Texas drawl.

"I'm sorry, did you say *trained* pilot?" interrupted American captain Michael Michaelis, who had gone by the call sign "Taz" as an F-16 pilot in the U.S. Air Force and had the physical appearance of a compact bulldog.

"Yes, yes," Sinnett answered. He started to continue his presentation, but the pilots didn't let him talk much longer before jumping in again. There was the obvious fact that Boeing hadn't trained the pilots on MCAS—as Michaelis pointed out, "These guys didn't even know the damn system was on the airplane." And if it malfunctioned, the pilots said, it would be hard for a pilot in the heat of the moment to diagnose the problem amid all the conflicting alerts.

"We struggle with this," Sinnett acknowledged. Then he raised an issue that some of the pilots took as a subtle dig at their "airmanship," a term used among fliers to describe their natural facility for piloting—and by extension, their manhood. If there's a runaway stabilizer, Sinnett asked them, why does the reason matter? Can't a pilot in such a situation just run the checklist? The American Air fliers knew instinctively that an AoA malfunction like the one on the Lion Air jet would take time to diagnose. "This particular one is masked by so many other distractions," union spokesman Dennis Tajer answered. "Exactly," Michaelis agreed.

The plane was still new to the pilots, and few had flown it much yet or done more than the cursory iPad training. Michaelis fumed about the fact that, from the accounts he'd read, the software had kept whacking the nose of the plane down. "You're touching my stick, you know?" Boeing "would've had a real shitstorm," he continued, if the same failure had happened on a MAX flight out of Miami and American had dropped a plane into Biscayne Bay. "Somebody at the corporate level made the decision that this isn't important to brief our pilots on," he said.

Michaelis asked if any alert would tell them when the sensors had failed. "On your airplane, yes," Sinnett answered. Without mentioning that Boeing had botched the software implementation on other planes, he explained that American had purchased the optional angle-of-attack indicator, which Lion Air had not. Had it been Michaelis's plane, a little flag notice would have popped up alerting him to disagreement between the AoA vanes, and mechanics would have fixed the sensor on the ground. "So you would not have taken the airplane," he said.

The pilots kept raising scenarios for Sinnett, and they ended up almost talking among themselves. One pilot wondered why he only got forty minutes of training on the MAX when the displays were so different. Another pointed out that American still didn't have a MAX simulator.

Sinnett finally summoned the words to match their intensity. "You've got to understand that our commitment to safety is as great as yours," he said. "It really is. And the worst thing that can ever happen is a tragedy like this. And the even worse thing would be another one. So we have to do all the things we can to make sure that this never happens again."

He said Boeing was working hard on an MCAS update to tame the system. "Not a year, but a couple—maybe six weeks–ish," he said.

The next day, Indonesian authorities released the results of their preliminary investigation. Their report suggested the pilots had been confused by the automated software, while also pointing out the mistakes made by the maintenance crew. Boeing put out its own statement, which highlighted the maintenance mistakes as the beginning of the chain of errors.

Which of the two narratives prevailed was easy enough to glean from stock quotes. Within days, Boeing shares had risen to $360, higher even than *before* the crash. Muilenburg's confident assurances were holding, despite the skepticism of the people who actually flew the planes and the fury of the victims' families. "The trust in the machine is shaky now," Suneja's mother, the Air India manager, said on CNN. "Someone should have questioned this."

Lion Air founder Rusdi Kirana got on the phone with Muilenburg, retinues listening. He dropped multiple f-bombs and accused

Boeing of betraying one of its best customers. He went public, too, telling reporters that the shifting of the blame toward Lion was "without any ethics" and that he planned to cancel the airline's further orders. Muilenburg coolly responded, via CNBC, that Boeing's contracts are "long-term arrangements" and "these are not things that can be exclusively canceled on either side."

In the absence of decisive leadership to address the malfunction, Boeing failed to act with sufficient speed and focus—even as the gravity of the problem became clear to at least some of its top executives. "Fairly early on, that assumption, that deadly assumption around what a pilot would do in that circumstance when that boundary condition was tested started to come to light," as Dave Calhoun, the lead director of Boeing's board, later put it. Keith Cooper, a vice president in the division where Mark Forkner had worked, asked his staff for a list of customers whose pilots might have trouble handling the MCAS software in a similar emergency. They named Russia's S7 and the Thai subsidiary of Lion Air among those in need of additional training, according to someone apprised of the discussions.

In early December, staffers in the FAA's Aircraft Certification Service concluded there might be fifteen more MAX crashes without a software fix, based on the future size of the fleet, the hours of anticipated flight, and a rough estimate that one in every hundred pilots might have trouble handling the rare sensor failure. The calculation was part of a spreadsheet intended to help the agency manage risk, the kind of bloodless analysis the industry had long been pushing for in its efforts to shake off governmental oversight.

Of course, in actual flights, only four pilots had faced the emergency at the controls, plus the deadheading pilot in the jumpseat. If you counted him, that was one crash for every five pilots. And even if the FAA's more generous analysis of the risk was accurate, it should have been eye-popping. Fifteen crashes would be comparable to the number for the Boeing 757, 767, 777, 787, and the newest 747s over the previous three decades combined.

Still the MAX kept flying. That "six weeks–ish" stretched into months.

11

"The Death Jet"

Sitting at the controls of a MAX at Chicago's O'Hare International Airport in January 2019, pilot Dennis Tajer and his first officer talked through their flight plan as they warmed up the plane at the gate, passengers filtering in behind them. Tajer, the American Airlines pilot union spokesman, had flown KC-135 tanker planes for the air force during the first Gulf War and had more than a decade of experience on the older versions of the 737. It was his first time in the MAX since that tense meeting with Boeing's Mike Sinnett in November. He and his copilot agreed that cutting power to the stabilizer with all those alerts going off sounded hairy. On the fly, they came up with their own checklist. They knew MCAS only worked when the flaps were up. They decided if everything went haywire, they'd just keep the flaps down and head back to the airport. Their flight was uneventful, but the improvising showed what little faith some of the most knowledgeable pilots had in what Boeing was telling them about a dangerous flaw in its most important product.

For Christmas that winter, Samya Stumo, a twenty-four-year-old from the Berkshires in Massachusetts, went to visit her grandparents in Iowa with her family. They took a minivan. It was a chance for more bonding time in an exceptionally close family. She and her brothers, Adnaan and Tor, all in their early twenties, had been

homeschooled by their parents, Michael Stumo and Nadia Milleron. The couple had lost a fourth child—a boy, Nels—to cancer
at two and moved to a farm soon afterward, resolving to soak in
every second of family life. The kids invented fantastical worlds in
the barn and eventually played gypsy jazz together, Samya on cello,
Adnaan on violin, Tor on the accordion.

Samya, the only daughter, had the confidence that comes from
supportive parents and fortunate circumstances. She taught herself to read at age four, proudly raised her own pig at seven, drove
a dump truck at ten, and enrolled in Mary Baldwin University's
program for "exceptionally gifted" students in Staunton, Virginia,
at fourteen. Samya studied Spanish and anthropology at the University of Massachusetts at Amherst and then got a master's degree
from the University of Copenhagen School of Public Health. For
her thesis, she led a multiyear study of viral hepatitis in twenty-five
countries. On the family's visit to Iowa over Christmas, she got
word she'd been hired for her dream job. It was at ThinkWell, a
Washington-based group that advised the Bill & Melinda Gates
Foundation and others on health policy. She'd be going to Kenya
for a project to broaden women's access to health care. Driving
home to Massachusetts in the minivan, her father, Michael, proudly
offered Samya advice about negotiating her salary.

Dennis Muilenburg was celebrating a milestone that month, too.
Century-old Boeing had just blown past $100 billion in annual rev-
enue. "Huge day," said CNBC reporter Phil LeBeau on January 30,
as Boeing shares rose 6 percent and Muilenburg once again basked
in Wall Street admiration. When the CNBC reporter brought up
forecasts suggesting that the stock, then $387, could hit $500, Muilenburg coyly deflected the question. "We're focused on sustained
long-term growth," he said. (Months earlier, his finance chief had
set the blistering internal target of $800 to $900.)

Boeing's engineers were still working on Sinnett's promised
update to the software. The FAA, with Ali Bahrami in charge of
safety, had given them a full ten months to finish the software and
test it again. Meanwhile, flights of the 737 MAX continued, and
Boeing's assembly lines strained to get more of them to airlines.

Even if the software update had been finished, the FAA wouldn't have had the staff in place to review it. Most of that month, federal workers were on furlough as part of the longest government shutdown in U.S. history. It stretched across thirty-five days, from just before Christmas to late January, as Trump, stung by criticism from Fox News commentators, tried to force through funding for his border wall with Mexico.

By the FAA's own analysis, the risk posed by the MAX was immense. A crash might happen every two to three years. There still wasn't any serious consideration given to grounding the planes, according to agency specialists informed of the discussions. The reason was clear enough: This wasn't something as important as a battery fire at Logan, on American soil. It was an accident in Indonesia. No Americans were killed. The pilots were foreign. It had vanished from the headlines. Boeing's executives, in PowerPoint presentations to the FAA, stuck to the argument that MAX pilots would recognize a misfire of the software in the ten seconds before the plane potentially became uncontrollable. They trusted in their new checklist.

As they made the rounds of the congressional committees that oversaw aviation, Boeing and FAA officials assured them that the Lion Air accident wasn't worth their scrutiny. Safety chief Bahrami met in February with Peter DeFazio, who chaired the U.S. House Transportation and Infrastructure Committee, and Rick Larsen, head of the aviation subcommittee. He called the crash a "one off" caused by poor pilot performance.

Former chief MAX manual writer Mark Forkner wasn't so sanguine. He already knew that his own actions—and particularly his statements, in those loose-tongued emails—may have left him exposed. Unusually for an aircraft accident investigation, two attorneys from the fraud section of the Justice Department, Cory Jacobs and Carol Sipperly, had started presenting subpoenas to people who'd been involved in the project. Not long after the Lion Air crash, an old Boeing colleague of Forkner's texted with the pilot, by then working at Southwest. They talked about the Seahawks, and then the friend remembered the controversy he'd been hearing about this MCAS software—what was going on with that? Forkner was cautious; he told his friend not to put anything in writing.

For now, the investigation was just one more bureaucratic annoyance. That February, Boeing handed over Forkner's internal messages to the Justice Department. Amid all the boasting of "Jedi mind tricks," the pilot's angst about having possibly misled the FAA—and the signs of a broken safety culture—were apparent to anybody who read them carefully. Muilenburg got a summary, as he described it later; he left Luttig and his Luttigators to handle it.

The CEO continued his relentless circuit of speeches and conferences, chewing up the miles on his bicycle when he wasn't working. With suppliers and some of his own employees counseling him to slow down, Muilenburg pushed to increase the MAX's production rate to fifty-seven planes a month from fifty-two. His board of directors never challenged him on any of the multiple red flags since the Lion Air crash. The Boeing board posts had become lucrative and coveted among political insiders and the corporate elite. Its directors included Dave Calhoun, McNerney's old friend from GE; Caroline Kennedy, the only surviving child of John F. Kennedy and a former U.S. ambassador to Japan; and Kenneth Duberstein, the onetime chief of staff for Reagan. Kennedy got more than $800,000 in compensation from 2017 to 2019 alone, and Duberstein—whose tenure stretched all the way back to McDonnell Douglas—made a total of $5.3 million. The board rewarded Muilenburg in turn. Two months after the Lion Air crash, it had awarded him the highest pay of his tenure: $31 million, including a $13 million bonus for performance.

In a phone call in March with her brother Adnaan, Samya Stumo told him about seeing a woman at an art gallery in Washington who was obviously having a bad day. She decided to play a game: Could she change this woman's mood? After first giving curt answers to Samya's small talk, the woman was soon showing family pictures and trying to add her on Instagram. Adnaan laughed; it figured. Everyone found his charming sister, six feet tall and blond, hard to resist.

A day after their phone call, Samya left for her dream job in Kenya from Washington's Dulles International Airport. "Just landed in Addis Ababa—another 2 hours to Nairobi," she texted her parents. She boarded the Ethiopian Airlines 737 MAX 8 bound for Nairobi at 8:30 a.m. that Sunday. It was a daily flight that often carried diplomats. Samya was in seat 16J.

One row up sat Kenyan electrical engineer George Kabau, twenty-nine, returning home after working for GE in Ethiopia. In front of him were a French couple, Suzanne and Jean-Michel Barranger, sixty-six, enjoying one of the annual trips they'd promised themselves since retirement. In 13L, Danielle Moore, twenty-four, was on her way to represent Canada as a youth ambassador at the UN Environmental Assembly in Nairobi. Farther back sat another of Canada's youth ambassadors, Angela Rehhorn, also twenty-four, and an American air quality expert, Matt Vecere, who would be appearing at the same UN conference. Spilling across two rows were three generations of a single family: Caroline Karanja, thirty-three, her three children, and her mother, Ann Karanja.

Ethiopian Airlines was considered perhaps the best-run carrier in Africa. At the controls, Yared Getachew, twenty-nine, lean and handsome, had flown more than eight thousand hours and had become the airline's youngest-ever captain two years earlier. Getachew's copilot, Ahmednur Mohammed, twenty-five, had only flown three hundred and sixty hours but was so dedicated to his craft that he often recruited a friend to sit beside him on a couch and rehearse cockpit checklists.

Seconds after the plane took off, the telltale signs of an MCAS malfunction revealed themselves. The control column began shaking in the captain's hands. Altitude and airspeed warnings appeared. Getachew reported a "flight control problem" to the tower. Then the nose pitched down. The angle-of-attack vane on the captain's side was reporting to the flight control computer that the jet was ascending at an almost-vertical seventy-five degrees, sixty degrees higher than the gentler, routine climbout that was actually taking place. The vane had developed some electrical issue, or perhaps a bird strike had sheared it away. As with the doomed Lion Air flight, MCAS—trying to avert what it perceived as an inevitable stall, on the basis of that one piece of bad data—took control of the plane. The only thing left was to start fighting the jet.

The pilots had the benefit of Lion Air's misfortune and had learned enough about the software to guess the problem. "Left alpha vane!" they called out simultaneously. Getachew flipped the cutout switches just as Boeing's advisory had recommended. But in the confusion he left the throttle open and the plane at takeoff speed; the indicators were showing disagreement, just as the Lion Air jet's had. When Getachew tried to use the manual trim wheel as the checklist had recommended, the force of the wind splaying against the stabilizer made it too hard to move. "Help me pull," he said to his copilot.

Lurching, the plane was still at eight thousand feet. The passengers should have been settling into their seats, flipping through a magazine or catnapping. Instead, they saw towns and fields blurring by uncomfortably fast. Sintayehu Shafi, a thirty-one-year-old Toyota mechanic on his way to Nairobi for a certification course, called his older sister, Konjit; the siblings were so close that he picked her up from work every day. Now his voice was unusually tight. The family's house happened to be under the flight path, and Sintayehu asked her to go outside and look for the plane. Baffled, she went to the front gate, but some kids were playing soccer there and she felt awkward about breaking through their game to scan the sky. She could hear the engines, though, so she told him, "You guessed right." Then she asked, how is your phone working while airborne? "I don't know," he answered, then suddenly called out, "Chaw!" Konjit heard a rising sound that immediately produced a pit in her stomach before the call abruptly ended.

In a simulator, the Ethiopian Air pilots probably wouldn't have needed more than a couple of tries to crack this particular non-normal situation. The instructor would have calmly stopped the demonstration and explained about the trim wheel, how they needed to make sure to slow down and neutralize the forces first. Back in the 1980s, the instructor might say, there was even a technique in the manual called the "roller coaster"—how you needed to take the counterintuitive step of first relaxing your grip on the control column, then release and crank the wheel a bit, and repeat, until you could move it freely. But that technique wasn't taught much anymore, because with each version of the 737, the need to use the trim wheel to arrest a runaway stabilizer—a ghost of the plane's analog past—had become less common.

The checklist didn't tell them any of that. It told pilots to move the stabilizer trim to cutout, just as the Ethiopian pilots had. Later, appearing as a less important afterthought, Boeing's bulletin mentioned that the electric trim switch "can be used" to neutralize the forces before cutting power. In fact, squeezing hard on the switch—the one under the thumb that Lion Air pilot Suneja had pressed twenty-one times—was the most important step, vital to keeping the MCAS software from pushing the plane into an uncontrollable dive.

But the pilots hadn't had the luxury of MAX simulator training. Unable to control the plane, they turned the cutout switches back on. Like a toy buzzer, MCAS kicked in again, tilting the nose down farther. People just waking up in the tiny town of Bishoftu, more than three hours on rutted roads from Addis Ababa, saw the jet pass hundreds of yards from their houses, making a terrifying sound of straining and shaking metal. Grazing cows ran in panic. White plumes trailed the plane until they heard a final echoing crash, leaving fire and black smoke. The almost brand-new plane and the 157 people it carried burrowed into a field of dull yellow teff, a grain cultivated for centuries around Bishoftu. The sky was so blue it was oppressive. This time the plane had killed its occupants in six minutes, half the time in which the MCAS software had brought down the Lion Air plane.

Samya's mother, Nadia Milleron, happened to be up again at two a.m. that Sunday in Massachusetts, just a few hours after exchanging texts with her daughter. She had just put on the BBC World Service in the kitchen when reports of a crash in Ethiopia came in. Ethiopian Airlines Flight 302. The same flight information was right there on her phone. Her body started shaking uncontrollably. All she could think was that it wasn't real if she didn't wake her family and tell them.

An operator at Boeing's twenty-four-hour crisis center was the first to tell its chief executive, Dennis Muilenburg. Two crashes in five months. It was the scenario every company fears: a public panic over product safety puncturing a carefully groomed reputation. When James Burke, the chairman of Johnson & Johnson, learned in 1982 that cyanide-laced bottles of Tylenol in Chicago had killed seven people, he asked two questions: "How do we protect people? And second, how do we save the product?" The answer to both questions turned out to be the same: By putting safety first, Tylenol saved the product. Burke told consumers to stop buying Tylenol, withdrew advertising, halted production, and pulled the pills off shelves. It was a huge financial blow—Tylenol accounted for 19 percent of the company's profits—but the swift action ensured no further loss of life. Burke's response is now considered a classic in corporate crisis management.

The test of faith and leadership Muilenburg had confidently talked about onstage had arrived. He led a late-night discussion soon after the crash with senior leaders including Anne Toulouse, the head of communications. Much like Burke, he zeroed in on two key questions, starting with safety. "Is the MAX safe? And was MCAS involved?" But unlike the Johnson & Johnson chairman, he'd already convinced himself of the answers—and protecting the product came before people. "We need to make a strong statement on the first, and be clear that there are no supporting facts on the second," Muilenburg wrote later that day to Toulouse, who was in the midst of drafting the company's response.

The statement Boeing released the Monday after the crash opened like a legal brief. "The 737 MAX is a safe airplane that was designed, built and supported by our skilled employees who approach their work with the utmost integrity," it said.

The rest of the release, echoing Muilenburg's comments to Maria Bartiromo on Fox Business, treated the regrettable incident as one that didn't accord with Boeing's procedures. "It is important to note," the statement said, "that the FAA is not mandating any further action at this time, and the required actions in AD2018-23.51 continue to be appropriate." Boeing went on to say—falsely—that the software only operates in "a non-normal part of the operating envelope." That was how it was supposed to work, but it had just fired at least three times on routine takeoffs, due to entirely foreseeable failures; and as Boeing lead director Dave Calhoun later said himself, the "deadly assumption" about how pilots might respond had already started to come to light within the company.

Regulators this time proved less willing to take Boeing at its word. The backlash began in China, not at the FAA; Chinese officials were the first to ground the MAX that Monday. Muilenburg talked to Trump and, as he described it later, encouraged the president to make his own decision based on data. It was the same argument that Ray LaHood, the Republican congressman and Obama-era transportation secretary, had heard after the second Dreamliner fire. Muilenburg went on about aviation system safety, the reasons it has worked, how aviation is the safest form of transportation. A Boeing statement said it had full confidence in the plane, but it understood if some regulators and customers had made decisions "they believe are most appropriate for their home markets." (In other words, blame China.)

Trump opted to let the planes stay in the air. His transportation secretary, Elaine Chao, said she had asked the FAA's deputy administrator to "continue to monitor this situation" and to update her "personally" on developments. Chao was married to Mitch McConnell, the powerful Republican majority leader of the Senate, and was one of the heirs to an international shipping business. That Tuesday, Chao boarded a Southwest 737 MAX 8 in Austin, Texas, returning with her staff to Washington after giving a speech at the South by Southwest festival about her efforts to streamline approvals of self-driving vehicles.

The same day, regulators in the European Union, India, Australia, Singapore, and Canada followed China's lead in grounding the MAX. Boeing and the slow-to-act FAA looked isolated in a new era of airline safety, one in which other countries no longer deferred to America for guidance. "What we're looking at here is almost a rebellion against the FAA," said Sandy Morris, an aerospace analyst at Jefferies International in London. "It's the first time I've ever seen this happen."

Ali Bahrami, the FAA's safety chief, kept taking calls from his foreign counterparts. They'd say, " 'Ali, 'I'm really sorry, minister asked us to ground the fleet,' " as he described it later. He insisted there was still no data. That Monday, the FAA had gotten the readout from the plane's satellite transponder, but the agency didn't have the expertise to analyze it. ("Other authorities may have," Bahrami later said. "We don't have any of that.") The FAA handed the readout to the NTSB, which delivered it to Boeing, whose engineers then examined it. They asked Bahrami for an urgent conference call on Wednesday morning.

Satellite transponders on aircraft record the position, altitude, direction, and speed every eight seconds. The Boeing officials showed Bahrami and his team a graphic that superimposed these traces from the flight in Ethiopia over the Lion Air plane's last moments. It was a match. In addition, a piece of the plane had been recovered that showed the flaps were in an "up" position— a precondition for MCAS to fire. There was nothing more to say; Bahrami walked out of his office and told his boss they needed to ground the fleet.

The FAA issued the order that Wednesday, three days after the crash. It was the second such admission of failure in just six years for a new Boeing model, following the Dreamliner—a grim milestone that even much-maligned McDonnell Douglas never reached. Its only grounding was the DC-10.

Boeing's stock fell 10 percent that first week, but investors largely took events in stride. The Wall Street analysts who advised them weren't terribly concerned, either. Estimates at the time suggested that a grounding might last three months, as with the Dreamliner fires, and cost Boeing $1 billion—a considerable loss but hardly a devastating one.

The Friday after the crash, Paul Njoroge, held up by his father-in-law, John, made his way to the yellow police tape blocking entrance to the field where his family had perished. He'd consumed nothing but water for days. The biting scent of freshly plowed dirt stung his nostrils. When they reached the tape, Paul crumpled and put his head into his hands. "I want to hear my kids talk to me," he said.

Njoroge, who was thirty-three, had met Caroline Karanja at the University of Nairobi in Kenya. Part of the country's emerging professional class, they'd immigrated to Toronto, where he worked as an investment analyst. His wife's trip home to Kenya by way of Addis Ababa that summer, accompanied by her mother, was a chance to show off their growing family. Six-year-old Ryan dreamed of being an astronaut. Kelli, four, was always beaming. Their nine-month-old, Rubi, sat in Caroline's lap. Paul had arranged the itinerary and bought the tickets; he'd planned to meet them later. He couldn't stop thinking about those final minutes when he wasn't there for them: Had Ryan and Kelli cried out for their father? "Everyone's telling me to be strong," he said quietly in the chaotic jumble of people piecing through wreckage. "I can't be. How can I be strong? How can I even live on? My family is my life."

Nadia and Michael, Samya's parents, had spent that week in hellish movement: The flight from New York to Addis Ababa via Qatar, whisked through airport security by a U.S. Embassy attaché, no passports, no shots. A run-down Hilton with cold water, then the Hyatt. Nadia's fury when one of the awkward young aides told her they couldn't get Samya's remains. But CNN was showing pictures of body bags! The embassy got the CNN reporter on the phone to explain that she didn't know what was in the bags, and then a Red Cross worker who said they'd found nothing bigger than a femur. Finally the long drive to the crash site in two embassy vehicles, Michael and Nadia and son Tor and Mike Snavely, Samya's boyfriend. Their other son, Adnaan, had been in New Zealand, and they'd sent him to California to be with Samya's grandmother, Laura, who was eighty-eight and an anthropology professor at Berkeley. She had adored Samya, and they thought the news might kill her.

At the crater—there was no other word for it—photographers and TV crews filmed them as they cried and tried to cover their faces. Skinny young guards with guns made a show of saying no when they went past the police tape into the crater—but it's my daughter, Nadia screamed—to leave white and yellow roses (not red; red is for the living). And no plane: it was gone. Giant backhoes were churning up mountains of dirt and only turning up tiny pieces of metal, clothing, suitcases, passports, and—as a Sky News reporter put it in language that is intolerably grim but sadly accurate—the remains of "decomposing bodies." The MAX had hit the ground with such speed that it had disintegrated, interring the fragments dozens of feet deep.

It was Lent, so Nadia and Michael, who are Orthodox Christian, took comfort in the services taking place every day in the majority Orthodox country. Strangers came up to them and grabbed their hands and bent their heads and cried. A muscular guy in a tight T-shirt who sold them black stone crosses wept when he heard why they were buying them.

That Sunday, mourners marched in the hundreds past the Library of Parliament in Addis Ababa to Selassie Cathedral, all in black or the sea-green uniforms of Ethiopian Airlines. Many carried photos of the dead, the scene gaining unearthly power from its complete silence. In the cathedral, after a priest read the victims' names aloud, the group carried empty coffins outside to a graveyard. The only sounds were sobbing, wailing, and chanting.

All over the world, thousands gathered in the months that followed to say goodbye to their husbands, wives, mothers, fathers, sons, daughters, sisters, brothers, lovers, friends, and coworkers.

At the United Nations building in New York, Secretary-General António Guterres laid a wreath, as he traditionally does, in honor of the employees who had died in the course of their UN duties over the previous year. Usually most of the fallen are the blue-helmeted peacekeepers killed in war zones. That year, twenty-one of the one hundred fifteen died in the MAX crash in Ethiopia.

In Toronto, a service for Danielle Moore, one of the twenty-four-year-old youth ambassadors to the UN Environment Assembly, drew two hundred people who sang songs, laid flowers, and left tea lights in a small pond. "From my daughter to you, I love you all," her mother, Clariss Moore, told the crowd gathered in steady rain under the flight path of a nearby airport.

Two brothers in California, Melvin and Bennett Riffel, had been on a last adventure together before Melvin's wife, Brittney, was due to have their baby. A thousand people mourned them at the St. Joseph Catholic Church in Redding, California, many joining a spirited wake afterward at the Redding Elks Lodge. A few men came in Hawaiian shirts like those Melvin had worn, and one couple wore shirts printed with the brothers' pictures. "Like I always told the boys—life isn't always fair and sometimes it will knock you on your butt," their father, Ike Riffel, told people at the Elks Lodge. "Let the healing begin. Let's get up. Let's start throwing punches." Brittney's baby, born two months later, was a girl.

Within days of the crash, at least one Boeing pilot got served with a federal subpoena while working at the training center in Miami. It sent a chill through the pilot fraternity, suggesting a deep level of familiarity with Boeing's operations and a shocking sign that the investigation had already escalated beyond anything in its history. British tabloids bestowed a name on the MAX—"the death jet," strange to see for a Boeing product.

Muilenburg and Boeing stuck to the script. He insisted, in prepared statements, that "safety is our highest priority," that every accident was a chain of events, and that people needed to let the investigation proceed before coming to any conclusion. On March 17, a *Seattle Times* story undercut the narrative by revealing what the FAA specialists had been saying privately for months—Boeing had screwed up. The story quoted anonymous engineers who said Boeing had provided the agency with a crucially flawed assessment of the MCAS software and drastically underestimated its power to push the plane into a nosedive.

In response, Muilenburg wrote a letter to airlines saying "our hearts are heavy" about the crash and that revisions to the software were coming. The CEO, chief lawyer Michael Luttig, and their public relations staffers still gave no indication they understood the maelstrom that was about to hit. In his brief comments to the press, Muilenburg claimed to be following a protocol of limiting communications about accidents until clues are painstakingly gathered.

The statements from Boeing read, as one PR expert put it, "like an engineer and a lawyer wrote it together"—a fair summation of the culture as it had evolved at Boeing. The clipped communications only deepened suspicions. Boeing was accustomed to coverage primarily in the trade press and sotto voce negotiations with compliant regulators. A shelf full of books had been written about its guts-and-glory past—at least one of them commissioned by Boeing itself. Now plaintiffs' lawyers, journalists, federal prosecutors, and congressional investigators were poring over every one of its assertions. A press officer warily counted the number of *New York Times* reporters descending on Seattle.

Too late to avert catastrophe, the software update that Sinnett had been promising since November was finally getting close to completion. Boeing had expected to hand over the final specifications to the FAA in April, six months (and not six weeks–ish, as Sinnett had said) after the first crash. A date had even been scheduled for Stacey Klein, the Aircraft Evaluation chief who'd worked with Forkner, to evaluate the revised software in a simulator in Miami. That date, March 13, turned out to be three days after the crash in Ethiopia. Boeing had been so confident MCAS was fixed that it was actually seeking training even *less* stringent than the couple of hours on an iPad already approved. This time it had asked for Level A training, the least intensive possible. Pilots simply would be provided with highlighted pages of the operating manual—no test or further practice required.

In late March, Boeing invited two hundred pilots, consultants, and regulators from around the world to Seattle to see the software changes for themselves. They couldn't all fit into the engineering simulator at the Systems Integration Laboratory, so Boeing broadcast a link from the lab to a room where they could suggest a scenario and watch how it played out. Just before the event, Boeing bused in reporters for a media session. Sinnett again took the lead in explaining the upgrade, saying it would limit the number of times the system could push down the nose, compare data from two angle-of-attack vanes instead of one, and turn it off in the event of a disagreement—the very things pilots at American, among others, had asked for after the Lion Air crash. "The emphasis is on dialogue, feedback, and complete understanding," he said.

The attempt at empathy fell flat. All at once, two decades of contained resentment—all the engineers it had tossed away, the regulators it had ignored, the customers it had demeaned—unloaded on Boeing like a crosswind gust on takeoff.

Rick Ludtke and other fired engineers came forward with accounts of how managers had pressured them to compromise the MAX's design at the expense of safety.

His young colleague Curtis Ewbank, who'd quit in 2015 after his proposed improvements to the plane were rejected, had returned to Boeing only the previous November to work on the latest version of the 777. Ewbank filed an internal ethics complaint saying managers were "more concerned with cost and schedule than safety and quality."

Mechanics at the Dreamliner plant in South Carolina described shoddy manufacturing, debris left on planes, and pressure not to report defects.

Pilots asked what else Boeing had hidden from them. American pilot spokesman Dennis Tajer came up with a list of memorable metaphors for MCAS—the rabid dog, the Tasmanian devil, the beast in the cage. "Every day brings news of another error or omission from Boeing," he said.

One stunning instance came in April, when Boeing acknowledged that some of its managers had known for a year before the first crash that the AOA DISAGREE warning, alerting crews to a bad angle-of-attack vane, wouldn't work for most airlines, who had acquired models that didn't include the corresponding indicator. Boeing's concession pointedly excluded "senior company leadership" (like Muilenburg and Luttig) from the group in the know.

That same day, at the annual shareholders meeting in Chicago, victims' family members held up photos of their loved ones and signs reading PROSECUTE BOEING & EXECS FOR MANSLAUGHTER and BOEING'S ARROGANCE KILLS. Muilenburg stood at a lectern before a room of reporters. One asked if he'd resign; another began pressing him to explain why he hadn't disclosed more about MCAS earlier. Dominic Gates, the *Seattle Times* beat reporter who would win a Pulitzer Prize for his reporting that year on Boeing, asked in his cutting Irish accent why Boeing couldn't just admit it had made a mistake. "Never mind the processes," he said. "What you came up with was flawed, was it not?" Muilenburg again couldn't muster an answer that sounded human or reflective. "We followed exactly the steps in our design and certification processes that consistently produce safe airplanes," he said. A Boeing representative cut the press conference short after fifteen minutes. Another reporter called out: "Three hundred and forty-six people died, can you answer a few questions here about that?" Muilenburg walked offstage, jaw clenched.

Belatedly, Boeing's public relations team tried to implement the strategy they should have implemented in the first place. Subsequent statements took on more obvious notes of contrition. Muilenburg was pictured leading from the front, sitting in the cockpit with pilots testing the latest software upgrades on the MAX. Wearing a pressed blue Oxford shirt on the factory floor, he said, "We own it" in a recorded video. He repeated the message a week later, in Dallas, at the George W. Bush Presidential Center forum on leadership. "That's what we do at Boeing: *We own it*. As our veterans know so well, how you respond to a tough situation will make all the difference to your organization and your country."

But the man and the mission were at odds. That spring, Muilenburg visited Boeing's commercial aircraft operations in Seattle, where the head of the company's commercial jet business, Kevin

McAllister, convened a group of flight controls engineers. McAllister gave an emotional speech, and a staffer wept in the background. When it was the CEO's turn to speak, he took five or six questions, revealing little. It could have been a moment to ditch the script, perhaps even reflect on those deeper worries about Boeing's engineering soul that had shadowed it ever since the McDonnell Douglas merger and still dominated conversations among the Boy Scouts in the aisles. Instead it was, as one engineer put it, "a nothingburger."

Despite the growing storm, Muilenburg, optimistic and schedule driven as always, refused to cut production. On East Marginal Way in Seattle, row after row of finished MAX jets in the bright livery of airlines around the world—billions of dollars in inventory—piled up behind chain-link fences. Within just a month of the plane's grounding, Boeing had to sell $3.5 billion in bonds and draw on a $1.5 billion line of credit from its banks to raise money, a sign of how close to the edge it operated, and how little it had set aside for such rainy days. So much cash had been shoveled back to shareholders—not to mention Boeing's board members and executives—that there was little left when MAX deliveries stopped and revenue dried up. Under Greg Smith, the chief financial officer, Boeing had even started pulling GE-like financial maneuvers to beat Wall Street's quarterly targets for cash, agreeing with some customers to pull forward anticipated payments for future deliveries in exchange for later concessions. By one analyst's measure, these "Houdini moments" had accelerated as much as $1.5 billion of payments in a single year.

Boeing's total equity—just like a house, a measure of its debt compared to its assets on hand—stood at $410 million by the end of 2018. It had been $13 billion in 1997, before Stonecipher and his successors started hollowing out the company in the drive to boost the all-important return on net assets.

Of course, the plane maker still had plenty of allies in Congress, and its almost fraternal relationship with the FAA held strong. At a hearing in May, Republican lawmakers led by Sam Graves, a representative from Missouri, suggested that it was foreign pilots rather than Boeing who were most to blame for the crashes. "You have to know how to fly the plane!" said Graves, a private pilot himself. He added that the Ethiopian pilots "were simply going too fast" and followed "no operating procedure that I know of or have ever heard of."

Once more, a lawmaker found himself preaching to the choir. The acting administrator representing the FAA at the hearing was Daniel Elwell, who had worked, just as Ali Bahrami had, as a vice president at the Aerospace Industries Association. Before that, Elwell had been an American Airlines pilot and managed the airline's government affairs. As the senior vice president of Airlines for America, a trade group, he'd served a stint as chairman of the Aviation Rulemaking Advisory Committee, the group whose closed-door meetings were the driving force in creating the alphabet soup of organizations—the ODA and the BASOO—that had put the industry firmly in control of aircraft certification.

"Absolutely," Elwell replied to Graves's criticisms of the pilots, saying he planned to "take a hard look at the training standards globally." The Republican congressman defended Boeing much as other lawmakers had after the Dreamliner fires, suggesting it would be a mistake to change anything about the way the FAA regulated Boeing. His rationale added a barely concealed nationalism. "It just bothers me that here we are, we just—we continue to tear down our system based on, you know, what has happened in another country," Graves said.

Muilenburg told analysts and airlines the plane would reenter service within months. Publicly, the FAA gave no such timeline. But Elwell met that spring with senior executives and pilots from the three U.S. operators of the MAX—Southwest, American, and United—and told them it was an all but foregone conclusion that the plane would be back in the air by the end of May, according to people familiar with the discussion. A PowerPoint presentation circulated by one FAA staffer in April, a month after the crash, focused on the plane's "Return to Service."

When the end of May came, the plane was still grounded. Bahrami, among other officials, continued sending positive signals. He told members of the International Civil Aviation Organization in Montreal in a private briefing to expect the FAA to approve the plane's reentry as early as June.

At the Paris Air Show that month, Muilenburg met with reporters in his gray power suit and purple tie. As the exposés kept coming, he'd started adopting a more chastened tone in public. "I'd say we come to this air show with a tone of humility and learning," he said. Later he joined Elwell inside the back of a parked military airplane, a location that allowed them to avoid being seen by the throngs of industry executives and journalists strolling around the exhibit halls on the Le Bourget airfield. Elwell told Muilenburg to moderate the talk of progress and give the FAA space to exercise scrutiny (or at least the appearance of it). "You're right," Muilenburg told him. "We're not going to push."

The following Saturday, ever fit, he climbed onto his bicycle for the Boeing Century Challenge, a 105-mile race through spectacular orchards and vineyards in the mountains surrounding Lake Chelan, carved from glaciers in central Washington. About fifty from Boeing joined him. He finished twenty-sixth out of twelve hundred riders.

12

Blood Money

Samya Stumo came from a family that had an unusually good grasp of how power is wielded in Washington. Her mother, Nadia Milleron, is the niece of Ralph Nader, the lawyer, former Green Party presidential candidate, and famed consumer crusader. His bestselling 1965 exposé of the automobile industry, *Unsafe at Any Speed,* led to seat-belt laws. The book had enraged General Motors and made the Chevrolet Corvair—the car whose steering wheel tended to impale its driver in crashes—infamous. Nader is perhaps more responsible than anyone else for the great number of consumer-focused regulatory agencies that emerged in the early 1970s—among them the National Highway Traffic Safety Administration, the Consumer Product Safety Commission, and the Environmental Protection Agency.

In the 1990s, Nader even took on the airline industry with a book called *Collision Course,* which argued that the FAA was too close to the industry it regulated. After Samya died, Nader blamed himself for not warning her about the MAX. He'd closely followed the Lion Air story and had his own doubts about the plane. Nader wrote a thundering open letter to Muilenburg after the crash: "You and your team should forfeit your compensation and should resign."

Nadia and her husband, Michael Stumo, had spent several of

the days since the loss of a second child unable even to get out of bed. But they resolved to make Samya's death have meaning. In late June, they held a remembrance—part eulogy and part campaign strategy session—at the American Museum of Tort Law, housed in a gray stone neoclassical building in Winsted, Connecticut. Nader had opened the museum in his hometown as a monument to plaintiffs' lawyers and his own brand of anticorporate populism. A cherry-red Corvair sat in the building's main hall. Only the previous December, Nader had convinced—really, commanded—his great-nephew Adnaan to play a solo fiddle concert there after learning the young man had been busking around the world.

Now they were all gathered in the same hall to mourn Adnaan's sister. Looking remarkably like he had in the presidential campaign twenty years earlier, Nader, then eighty-five, shuffled to the stage with his familiar stoop. He laid out the précis with a lawyerly command of the facts, his baroque formality touching and painful to hear because the client in this case was his own dead grand-niece. "The rule of law must be invoked to ensure justice for the deceased and the next of kin and explicitly signal strong deterrence to those who would be tempted to place material profits and short-term gains over the supremacy of life and safety," Nader said. "Can we do anything less for our beloved Samya and all the other passengers on those planes and their families?"

He beckoned his niece, Nadia, to the stage. She wore the same black stone cross she'd worn every day since returning from Ethiopia. Voice catching in her throat, she described her horror at walking amid the scraps of clothing at the crash site, and her bafflement when she learned that the plane had plunged into the ground because of a serious design error that had slipped past both Boeing and its regulator. "Two adult male pilots pulled back on the stick and could not move it because it was designed that the software would override the pilots," she said. "That that could go through the FAA and not be caught? That's crazy. That means that the FAA does not have the systems, the expertise, the oversight, to actually keep us safe."

Though his influence was fading, and the age of reforming zeal he'd inspired had long since passed in Washington, Nader still had clout. Richard Blumenthal, a Democratic senator from Connecticut, came to pay his respects. So did Joan Claybrook, a longtime associate of Nader's who had managed the National Highway Traffic Safety Administration for President Carter. She teared up as soon as she reached the lectern and started dabbing her eyes. "Dragon ladies cry," she said, a reference to the nickname bestowed on her by the automobile industry. Claybrook told the audience that Samya once came to a dinner party at her house in Washington; it snowed and one of her guests' cars got stuck. Samya went outside and started shoveling snow away from the tires with her hands, even though she was wearing a beautiful pair of red suede shoes. "I've never seen a more joyful person in my life," she said.

Then Claybrook brought the focus back to Boeing. Nader had called on the day of the crash to tell her Samya was dead. Claybrook remembered that her broker had invested $35,000 in Boeing stock for her retirement account three years previously. When she hung up, she called the broker to ask what the stock was now worth; it had appreciated by $100,000. "It just shows," Claybrook told the crowd, "that this company was not putting money into the airplane and into flying, it was putting the money into profit—of course, from which the members of that executive board and others profited as well." She said she could no longer see it as anything but "blood money." Claybrook sold the stock and donated the proceeds, in Samya's name, to the Nader museum.

Michael Stumo was no stranger to Washington himself, as head of the Coalition for a Prosperous America, a trade group backed by farmers, manufacturers, and labor unions. One of his first calls after he picked himself up off the floor had been to Stan Sorscher, the ex–Boeing engineer who had been instrumental in the labor walkout of 2000, and who also happened to be on the coalition's board. They'd known each other for years. Sorscher had seen the news of Samya's death when a text to all the board members went out. It was a gut punch. "Good people should have good lives," he remembers thinking. When Michael called, Sorscher immediately zeroed in on the deregulation that left the Boeing deputies primarily answering to bosses at Boeing, not at the FAA. The old system had resisted undue influence, he told Michael. The new one invited it.

Michael and Nadia had met Paul Njoroge, the father from Toronto who lost his entire family, through a WhatsApp chat thread the families started within days of the crash. They'd learned about it in Addis Ababa's Ethiopian Skylight Hotel, where the mourning relatives had gathered, sobbing on the lobby's purple couches. Veering between moments of bottomless despair and intense focus, Njoroge had been obsessively reading about Boeing—news stories, press releases, annual reports, quarterly financial statements. Consuming information was part of his job as an investment analyst.

Once he'd finished his investigation, the issues seemed so clear: The dangerous flaw revealed by the Lion Air crash. The pattern of rewarding shareholders and top executives while skimping on investments. The neutering of the FAA. It sent him into an even deeper depression, certain that he could have saved his family if only he had paid better attention. Representative Sam Graves's remarks at the May hearing, laying blame on the pilots, further disgusted him. "I felt that the reason why my family died was because when the first crash happened in October of 2018 it happened in Indonesia and not in the U.S. or Canada or the U.K., where lives matter more than in other places," he said. "The Indonesian people were seen as mere Indonesians. And that's why Boeing never felt compelled to ground the planes."

Paul began accompanying Michael, Nadia, and other relatives of victims on visits to congresspeople, walking the cold marble floors in the Cannon House Office Building or the Dirksen Senate Office Building amid the throngs of purposeful young staffers and lobbyists. Sometimes they only saw aides, but in many cases the members of Congress themselves sat and talked with them. They made it to fifty offices, Nadia eventually bowing out because the conversations brought such pain.

At the Transportation Department, another of their stops, Elaine

Chao and her staff were in tears, too; they had to send out for more Kleenex. The FAA appointed its first-ever family liaison to handle their requests for meetings and information, a manager named Michael O'Donnell. "They're not used to dealing with the very people they're supposed to protect," Stumo said.

Nadia's brother, Tarek Milleron, a PhD ecologist who lives in Berkeley, California, and works on forest conservation projects in South America, also turned his attention to the MAX campaign. He had some experience with the press from working for his uncle Ralph's presidential campaign. Tarek made the oversized poster showing photos of the victims that his sister held up for the cameras, and corresponded with experts in risk modeling to help understand where the FAA's analysis was lacking. Samya had stayed with his family for several months the previous year while her boyfriend was doing a medical residency at UC San Francisco. She had played a lot with Tarek's two young children. The hardest part was thinking about the world that was lost—the Thanksgivings, the stories she'd bring home about her accomplishments and travels, and, someday, kids of her own and more young cousins around the table. All gone.

To Tarek, the FAA managers were a crowd of dim bulbs, mindlessly repeating what Boeing had told them and promoting half-baked methods of statistical analysis, like the spreadsheet meant to calculate the risk of keeping the MAX flying. He couldn't believe the FAA had treated a very rough estimate—the guess that one out of one hundred pilots would struggle with the new checklist—as if it were a definitive, observed rate. When he raised his concerns in emails to FAA officials, the conversations went nowhere. "They say 'data-driven,' but they have no clue what it means," he said. "These are people who talk about science as though it's some type of magic power you sprinkle on things." As he tried to understand what went wrong at Boeing, he kept thinking about an engineering colleague of his father's. The man's pregnant wife had complained when her belly kept hitting the steering wheel. He cut the wheel in half—forgetting that she also had to make U-turns. It seemed to sum up the kind of overconfidence that could lead smart people to do dumb things.

Tarek sat in on one of the family meetings with the FAA, but couldn't shake the impression that they were only pretending to listen while planning to do exactly what they'd been working toward ever since the Lion Air crash: endorse Boeing's revised software and move on.

At one point, Nadia asked Michael O'Donnell, the FAA's family liaison, for a technical briefing about the plane. She asked if they could bring an aeronautical engineer to the meeting and he said no, families only. Nadia asked around to see who else among the grieving relatives had aerospace expertise. She connected with Javier de Luis, the MIT lecturer whose sister, UN translator Graziella de Luis y Ponce, had died in the Ethiopia crash. At the meeting, FAA officials explained how in the forthcoming, revised MCAS, the software would rely on two AoA sensors instead of one. In any cases of disagreement, it would shut down. De Luis listened in disbelief. Even the space shuttle, developed in the 1970s, had five redundant computers. Airbus planes typically used three sensors. The solution also seemed shockingly clunky: If the software was necessary to keep the plane's nose from pitching up in certain situations, what would happen in a flight that encountered one of those rare situations and *didn't* have MCAS available?

"If a student came in with this design, I wouldn't pass him," de Luis told them.

With officials still privately signaling the plane's imminent reapproval, testing of various scenarios continued at the Systems Integration Laboratory near Boeing Field that summer. The FAA was running through all of the contingencies that *hadn't* been considered in the first version of the MCAS software. They wanted to see, for instance, how the pilots would react to the rare possibility that the plane's microprocessor was scrambled by a cosmic ray at the same time as a misfiring MCAS.

One test included an FAA pilot and a second pilot from the agency's Aircraft Evaluation Group, who had airline experience. The airline veteran had only been invited because one of the FAA's usual test pilots became unavailable. "Remember, get right on that pickle switch," one of the Boeing officials reminded the two pilots, referring to the thumb switch Suneja had used in his attempt to control the Lion Air plane. Separately, they took turns gripping the wheel as their smooth flight was interrupted by the jarring stick shaker and blaring alerts announcing the malfunction. Boeing's own guidance said that the plane could enter an unstoppable nosedive if pilots didn't complete the proper checklist within ten seconds.

It took the test pilot just four seconds to spot the trim wheel moving, *get right on that pickle switch* (as the Boeing official had so helpfully reminded), and then hit the cutout. It was a maneuver he'd done probably hundreds of times over the years in the FAA's repetitive tests of various scenarios. Despite the coaching from Boeing, however, the airline veteran needed sixteen seconds. He was dead.

It was pure chance, and evidence of Tarek Milleron's point about the ridiculously small sample sizes and gut instincts ruling the FAA's supposedly rigorous decision making. But it made all the difference.

An FAA inspector who worked with Southwest crews in Dallas heard about the failure and conducted informal tests of his own in a simulator there. The three pilots he tested took forty-nine seconds, fifty-three seconds, and sixty-two seconds to complete a similar procedure. Those findings spooked even Elwell, the FAA's acting administrator.

That summer, Boeing was ordered to rewire the 737's two flight control computers more extensively to address the issue, so that they could continuously compare the values of any two sensors in the plane. This would make a runaway stabilizer caused by a failure of any of them—not just the AoA vanes, but also altitude or airspeed—far less likely. It was an additional requirement that would make the plane safer.

But it wouldn't help Muilenburg in his push to get it back in the air. Finally Boeing's seemingly unstoppable momentum had been slowed. Muilenburg's own crash was in motion.

—

Paul Njoroge appeared before the U.S. House Transportation and Infrastructure Committee on July 17, 2019, his eyes haunted, methodically turning the pages of a statement recounting the pain of a man who'd lost everything. Except his voice. Though it cracked when he talked about knowing that "my family's flesh is there in Ethiopia mixed with the soil, jet fumes, and pieces of the aircraft," it was clear and strong when he asked for a thorough investigation of the crashes. Congress, he said, should return the FAA to the system of oversight that had existed before the manufacturers co-opted it. He asked for criminal prosecution of Boeing and its executives, who, he pointed out, "have been the primary beneficiaries of this strategy to extract wealth from this storied company."

Peter DeFazio, the Democratic chair of the House committee, had long been a thorn in the side of the FAA, as well as Wall Street. Gnomish and intense, he had represented his Oregon district for more than thirty years. After the ValuJet crash in 1996, when it emerged that the FAA had failed to implement NTSB recommendations on storage of flammable materials, DeFazio pushed for a law changing the agency's mission from "promoting" aviation to merely "encouraging" it. In 2009, his proposal for a one-quarter of 1 percent tax on stock transactions drew the attention of Robert Mercer, the wealthy financier who later backed Trump. Mercer funded a research chemist who believes that climate change is a hoax to challenge DeFazio in subsequent elections. They'd been some of the closest of his career.

Already inclined to be skeptical of the FAA, DeFazio was even more irked after what he'd heard from safety chief Ali Bahrami, who had assured him in February there was nothing to worry about with the MAX. In addition to the hearings, the committee's staff was already hounding Boeing and the FAA for information, putting in requests that eventually forced them to yield hundreds of thousands of pages of documentation. The team was led by Doug Pasternak, a former NBC News investigative producer, and Alex Burkett, a lawyer who had worked in regulatory compliance at United Airlines.

Sitting beside Njoroge at the hearing, Michael Stumo neatly summarized what Sorscher had told him about how the FAA's oversight wasn't working at a Boeing no longer dominated by engineers as in the past. "It was difficult for the safety culture to stop something," he told the lawmakers. "Groupthink was encouraged."

Minutes before the testimony began, Boeing had announced that the lawyer Ken Feinberg would handle distributing $50 million it had allocated for "near-term financial assistance to families." Famous for managing the payments to September 11 victims, Feinberg had since become something of a go-to mediator in corporate scandals, from the BP oil spill to the Volkswagen emissions scandal. The families—and much of the media—portrayed it as a ham-handed effort to shape the public relations battle to Boeing's benefit. The money amounted to $144,500 per victim. It was part of a larger $100 million fund that Boeing had announced earlier that month, which was supposed to pay for community programs and economic development in addition to direct family payments. Boeing's initial statement on July 3 noted that it had created the fund "ahead of Independence Day in the U.S.," an oddly self-referring note for a global tragedy. Paul Njoroge told Congress he'd celebrated Canada Day—without his family.

On July 31, Ali Bahrami of the FAA appeared before the Senate. He spoke in the peculiar argot of lifelong bureaucrats, using two or three words—or five or six—when one would do. He had a fondness for, and seemed to enjoy explaining, the intricacies of *processes*. A sentence rarely passed his lips without the use of an obscure acronym. But there was an assuredness and a machismo to his delivery. Pressed on why the agency hadn't grounded the plane after the first crash, he answered the question just like the big dogs he regulated might: "Frankly, that's what I get paid for," he said. "That's what managers get paid for. To look at the facts and make decisions."

Finally, he was asked to say plainly why the FAA had only issued an advisory to pilots and given Boeing months to modify the MCAS software, when its own internal assessment found such a high risk of another incident. This time he gave a fuller answer, before trailing off into one more process. "We knew that [the] eventual solution would be to have the modification and based on our risk assessment, we felt that this, that we have sufficient time to be able to do the modification, ah, you know, and get the final fix," he said. "Which—what that means typically—we refer to it as 'closing action.' "

In Massachusetts, Nadia Milleron couldn't believe what she was hearing. She read the transcript again and again. He had just described with infuriating nonchalance how the FAA's "processes" had killed her daughter. It was noxious gaslighting of the kind then emanating from the White House every day. She wasn't crazy. He'd actually admitted to gambling with her daughter's life. She and her son Tor got in her car after midnight and, still in the clothes they had been wearing the day before, decided to hold a press conference at noon the next day outside the FAA's headquarters in Washington.

O'Donnell, the family liaison, suggested she meet with Bahrami instead. But then, in Milleron's recollection, he sounded almost wistful when he said "we"—meaning the FAA and Boeing—had hoped to get the plane flying by summer. Nadia and Tor talked to the reporters as planned, holding a sign that said KEEP BOEING 737 MAX 8 GROUNDED ALI BAHRAMI AND BOEING EXECS GO TO JAIL. O'Donnell brought them in to see Bahrami, and the conversation started out civilly. Bahrami said he had a daughter of his own and couldn't imagine losing her. Tor asked him if there was anything he'd learned from the accidents or wished he could have done differently. He said he couldn't think of anything. They left the office more enraged than ever.

Boeing's airline customers were getting angry too. They'd been strung along for months, Boeing assuring them the MAX's reapproval was imminent. The grounding played havoc with their schedules. (American Airlines passengers flying direct from Seattle to New York, for instance, found themselves making an unexpected stop in Charlotte.) Each missing MAX was costing Southwest $67,000 a day in lost revenue. McAllister, the commercial airplane chief, tried to placate them with offers of compensation. The conversations were especially tense with Ryanair's Michael O'Leary, the chief executive who had made the stunning below-cost offer to Albaugh a decade earlier, and who was brusque and demanding even on a good day. He went public with his dismay in September, telling the *New York Times* that he was "deeply disappointed" in Boeing's communication with its customers.

A group of aviation honchos, Muilenburg among them, gathered over Labor Day weekend at a ranch in Wyoming for the fall retreat of Conquistadores del Cielo, an exclusive and once all-male industry club dating to the 1930s. They engaged in the group's time-honored bonding rituals of throwing knives and drinking beer. (They even had their very own drinking song, adapted from a tune in the 1944 film *The Three Caballeros* about a trio of "gay Conquistadores"— "happy amigos" who are "always together.") Muilenburg's placid demeanor in the face of such controversy puzzled them. He frequently went for long bike rides.

After running out of space for the already-finished MAX jets around Seattle, Boeing began sending them to the high desert of eastern Washington, lining the planes up wingtip-to-wingtip in a regional airport that came to resemble a giant aircraft carrier in the aerial photos circulating on aviation websites. The lot eventually housed 250 factory-fresh MAX planes, inventory worth about as much as a mission to the moon. Maintenance workers powered them up every week and sampled the jet kerosene for bacteria. They soon found another issue—rags and other debris left in the fuel tanks, a sign of the hasty production ramp-up. By October, when Boeing reported a 51 percent drop in its third-quarter profit, the costs of the MAX delays and compensation for airlines had reached $9.2 billion, already nine times greater than analyst estimates from earlier in the year.

The elms on the National Mall were aglow when former NBC News producer Doug Pasternak and lawyer Alex Burkett, the investigative bulldogs on DeFazio's congressional staff, finally got something to chew on that fall.

It had taken months for Boeing to start producing documents to the Oregon Democrat's probe, on behalf of the House Transportation and Infrastructure Committee. But then the company's lawyers started regularly delivering stacks of them. One morning in October, Pasternak got a call from someone at the company who suggested they look at the one on the top. It was Forkner's instant messages with Gustavsson about the simulator, the ones the company had handed over to the Justice Department in February. They included the pilot's venting in which he appeared to be saying that he had trouble controlling the plane in a simulator after MCAS fired, and that he had unwittingly lied to regulators about how the system worked. Boeing sent the same batch of documents to the new administrator of the FAA, Stephen Dickson, another former airline pilot. "This is the smoking gun," DeFazio said.

Daylight at last opened between Boeing and the regulator, until then so cozily entwined.

"Dear Mr. Muilenburg," Dickson wrote. "Last night, I reviewed a concerning document that Boeing provided late yesterday to the Department of Transportation. I understand that Boeing discovered the document in its files months ago. I expect your explanation immediately regarding the content of this document and Boeing's delay in disclosing the document to its safety regulator." In a conversation, Dickson was even more blunt. He told Muilenburg that Boeing was effectively inviting stricter regulation. "You're forcing my hand," Dickson told him. The company's spokespeople claimed the delay had occurred because Boeing and the FAA were both subject to the same Justice Department inquiry into the plane's certification.

The lawyers and congressional investigators who'd been sparring with Boeing for months over access to documents were justifiably suspicious of the sudden transparency. It appeared less like an act of contrition and more as though the company was executing one more of Luttig's games of three-dimensional legal chess. By making a relatively low-ranking pilot the focus of attention, Boeing was drawing it away from the managers whose directives he was carrying out. "Strangely enough, out of five hundred thousand pages of documents, there doesn't seem to be a single email or document that goes up to Muilenburg or some of the other senior execs," DeFazio said.

If it helped shield the company, it didn't do much to quiet the public outcry and the escalating financial fallout, which would require Boeing's board to offer up for sacrifice more than just a middle manager. Commercial airplane chief McAllister, hired in 2016, was so new that he hadn't even moved his family to Seattle. At a board meeting that month, he was fired. (He'd made at least $28 million during his short tenure.) Muilenburg, too, suffered a public chastisement, losing the chairman title to lead director Dave Calhoun but remaining CEO. Boeing finally agreed that it would send executives to appear at publicly televised hearings of the Senate and House committees investigating the MAX in late October, the one-year anniversary of the Lion Air crash.

Thanks to the prodding from DeFazio and others in Congress, as well as the victims' families, Muilenburg—Boeing's Daniel—would soon be in the lion's den.

13

"Go Back to the Farm!"

Nadia and Michael were spending so much time in Washington that they got an apartment in the city's southwest, the sleepy quadrant that slopes down to the Tidal Basin and the Jefferson Memorial. Just before the October hearings, Nadia and Michael arranged for twenty-one family members of the victims to attend, some staying at a house near Howard University they rented on Airbnb. It was a consolation to be around people who shared the same grief and, now, the same purpose. But maintaining their stamina for the fight was difficult with so many reminders of their loss. Just as the grieving father who'd lost his daughter on a DC-10 had tried to say, in one of those infuriating sessions devoted to the industry's interests: The crash was only the first mugging. What happened next was the second.

Visiting the crash site in Ethiopia that October, Nadia and her son spotted bones washed up by recent rains. Distribution of the remains was coordinated by Blake Emergency Services, a London-based contractor hired by Ethiopian Airlines. ("In these cost-conscious times," Blake advises customers on its website, "our business model is straightforward: eliminate excessive costs, whilst maximizing the level of service and professionalism offered to our clients no matter where in the world they are.") Blake set up a website for people to claim the personal effects of their loved ones. Javier de Luis, the MIT lecturer whose sister, Graziella, died in the crash, scanned through it in horror, the items grouped into categories like "Toys," "Clothing," and "Photos." The only way to find anything was to look through it all. There was a passport-sized photograph of his sister; she'd been dutifully carrying an extra, as you're advised to do in emergencies.

The forensic exactitude made possible by science strained human decency. At one point Nadia and Michael received 122 formaldehyde-soaked bundles with labels like "arm" and "hair." Others got passports or papers still smelling of jet fumes.

That same month, the Indonesian Navy took the families of people who had died aboard Lion Air 610 to sea to leave memorial flowers and pray. When the boat got back to the pier, TV reporters and family members gathered around Edward Sirait, Lion Air's CEO. He introduced two men standing beside him as "our friends from Boeing" and said they had a message to convey. "We, Boeing, are here and have formed a financial-assistance fund," one of them said, adding that "Boeing extends its deepest condolences." He provided a phone number where people could contact him to claim the $144,500-per-victim in funds, "and also scholarships."

Sanjiv Singh and Michael Indrajana, the two plaintiffs' lawyers who had uncovered the scheme to coerce families into signing blanket releases, were dumbfounded. The men standing with Lion Air's CEO were lawyers for Jakarta-based firms, one of them styled as specializing in "legal intelligence." Neither of them mentioned Ken Feinberg, who was managing the supposedly independent assistance fund for Boeing. At least a dozen families had yet to file any legal claims. If those people went to Boeing after hearing the televised pitch, they'd be less likely to hire sharp-elbowed litigators like Indrajana and Singh, who were pushing for much higher settlements. "To me it looked like this very cleverly orchestrated dance where lawyers were out there going after these last remaining families to clean up liability for Boeing," Singh said. "They were not operating as a charity."

Singh e-mailed Feinberg and asked him to provide details about the two lawyers and his communications with Boeing, Lion Air, and their insurers—as well as his own compensation. Feinberg replied that the lawyers worked for him, not Boeing, and that "the other issues you raise in your email are unnecessary." (In an interview, Feinberg said Boeing had paid him a flat fee to administer the claims and they were separate from any legal settlements.)

For some families, Boeing's money was rupturing, not healing. Parents fought with in-laws over who was entitled to settlements, or long-lost relatives showed up to claim their share.

On October 29, it came time for the world to hear from the man in charge of Boeing, Dennis Muilenburg. At the Senate Commerce Committee hearing, seven months after the crash in Ethiopia, the Boeing chief executive (and, until days before, chairman) and his vice president of engineering, John Hamilton, sat at the table in the center, photographers kneeling around them. Other Boeing executives sat in the row behind them. Nadia, Michael, and the grieving relatives filled another one.

Connecticut's Richard Blumenthal, who had vowed at Samya Stumo's memorial service that her death would not be in vain, first had the families stand. The committee chairman, Mississippi's Roger Wicker, told them to hold up the oversized photos of their loved ones they held in their laps. Muilenburg craned around in his seat to look at them. Chief lawyer Brett Gerry and others in the Boeing contingent, perhaps sensing the made-for-camera moment, did the same and held their posture. Government Operations chief Tim Keating, chewing gum, turned his head halfway to look a couple of times but mostly stared straight ahead with his back to the families. That was how the photographs, blasted around the world, captured him.

"Mr. Muilenburg, as I watched those loved ones stand and frankly as I reviewed this file over the past week or so again, as I sit here today, my anger has only grown," Blumenthal began. "These loved ones lost lives because of an accident that was not only preventable, as the chairman said at the very start, but was part of a pattern of deliberate concealment. Boeing came to my office shortly after these crashes and said they were the result of pilot error. Those pilots never had a chance. These loved ones never had a chance. They were in flying coffins as a result of Boeing deciding that it was going to conceal MCAS from the pilots."

Muilenburg's eyes were wet, his features working painfully. Keating, sitting directly behind him, kept chewing gum, his expression suggesting he was watching an especially interesting movie. "When did you become aware of the fact that MCAS was not going to be included in the flying manual?" Blumenthal asked him. It was a kill shot for an opening question—this was, of course, the thing Muilenburg had lied about on Fox Business soon after the Lion Air crash, telling people MCAS *was* in the manual. The CEO looked down and said, "First if I could express my deep sympathies . . ." Blumenthal, a seasoned litigator, cut him off. "My time is limited, I apologize for interrupting you. I want to know when you specifically became aware of this effort?" Again, Muilenburg dissembled. "Senator, I can't reference that email, I'm not sure."

Blumenthal proceeded to answer his own question. He explained that in a sixteen-hundred-page manual, MCAS was mentioned only once—in the glossary, a pattern of deliberate concealment. "So when Boeing came to us and said it's the pilots, you were lying to us as well," the senator said. "Would you agree that this system of oversight is absolutely broken—that's the lesson here, isn't it? That Boeing lobbied the Congress for more delegation and now we have to reverse that delegation authority?"

Sitting behind Muilenburg, Boeing lawyer Gerry's eyes got wider as he watched the practiced trial attorney bore in on his client. "I'm asking you for a commitment here because you have the opportunity to make things right—will you commit to supporting reform efforts such as many of us on this committee have advocated?" Muilenburg started to say, "Senator, we'll commit to . . ." Behind him, his lawyer shook his head and all but mouthed "no." But Muilenburg finished ". . . to participating in those reform efforts and providing our inputs." Blumenthal sighed.

Senator Tammy Duckworth of Illinois brought the authority of a trained pilot—and, implicitly, her own sacrifice—to her own round of questioning. Duckworth lost her legs in combat in Iraq as a U.S. Army helicopter pilot. "Time and again Boeing has not told the whole truth to this committee and to the families," she said, her voice rising to a near shout. "A pilot's best friend is time and altitude. And on takeoff he's got no altitude, and he's got no time. You set those pilots up for failure."

Muilenburg's voice sounded unusually reedy. At times his eyes had a rabbity look of fear as the congresspeople, one by one, gave Boeing the tongue-lashing many of those in the audience had been itching to see. Surprisingly, an extended grilling by Ted Cruz, the Texas Republican who was otherwise an enthusiastic advocate of a limited government, did perhaps the most damage.

"Mr. Muilenburg, I have to say the testimony here today has been quite dismaying," he began, sounding like a lawyer giving the dramatic closing argument on a criminal procedural show. He picked up a copy of Forkner's instant messages, the paper cup of coffee at his arm making it clear that he was fully caffeinated. "So this exchange is stunning," Cruz said. "That exchange describes what happens in Lion Air and Ethiopian Air. Their loved ones are gathered here. Three hundred and forty-six people are *dead* because of what these chief pilots described as 'egregious' and 'crazy'—that's their language, that's Boeing's internal language." In the audience, one woman wiped away tears, her husband rubbing her back.

"Now what I find truly stunning," Cruz went on. "Boeing handed this exchange over to the Department of Justice in February. In March, I chaired a hearing of the aviation subcommittee on these two crashes. Boeing did not see fit to give us that exchange—nor did it give it to the FAA. Your testimony here today is that you first learned of this exchange a couple of weeks ago. I've practiced law a lot of years. Your lawyers read, after the crashes, your senior leaders saying they lied to the regulators. How in the *hell* did nobody bring this to your attention in February when you produced this to the Department of Justice? How did you just read this a couple of weeks ago?"

Muilenburg said he was made aware of it as part of the discovery process in the investigation early in the year and had counted on counsel to handle it. "'I was made aware,' passive voice, disclaiming responsibility," Cruz cut in, with a mocking tone. "You're the CEO, the buck stops with you," he thundered. "How did your team not put it in front of you, run in with their hair on fire saying, '*We've got a real problem here*'? How did that not happen and what does that say about the culture at Boeing if they didn't give it to you and you didn't read it and say, 'I want to see what happened!' How did you *not* in February send out a 911 fire alarm to say *we need to figure out exactly what happened,* not after all the hearings, not after the pressure, but because 346 people have died and we don't want another person to die?"

Muilenburg answered, disingenuously, "We're not quite sure what Mr. Forkner meant—his lawyer has suggested he was talking about a simulator that was in development."

The existence of a lawyer for the former chief MAX manual writer had only recently become public. And Forkner's representation was as blue-chip as anyone could find: David Gerger of Houston, whose clients have included the former chief financial officer of Enron and a BP engineer accused of manslaughter in the *Deepwater Horizon* blowout. Gerger had been quoted defending Forkner in newspaper coverage of the simulator emails. It was a wonder to the pilot's former colleagues, who talked among themselves about how the guy in the Seahawks jersey could afford such a high-powered attorney. Journalists waited for the day when Forkner would "flip"—turn on his superiors and show up on *60 Minutes*.

In fact, the lawyer was being paid by Boeing's directors' and officers' liability insurance policy, according to people familiar with the matter, part of an effort to keep the various inquiries into the company's actions under control. If the CEO had wanted to dig more deeply into what went wrong, as Cruz's question suggested, he very well could have.

As Gerger's online biography put it, "The biggest victory is quietly stopping a case." In that effort, thanks to former chief lawyer Michael Luttig, named "senior adviser" to the board on the crash investigations in May, Boeing was dealing with familiar faces across a government studded with "Luttigators" who'd once clerked for him. Those ranks included Christopher Wray, the director of the FBI. What's more, several people at the top of the Justice Department—including the head of the Criminal Division; the deputy attorney general; and the attorney general, William Barr—had previously worked for Kirkland & Ellis, the Chicago law firm that represented Boeing. Barr himself was an old friend of Luttig's, a colleague in the Justice Department in the 1990s. The Boeing lawyer had written a letter to the Senate gushing about Barr's qualifications to serve, saying "he will be the finest Attorney General in our Nation's history."

After the second crash, Barr told subordinates he was skeptical about the basis for a criminal investigation of Boeing, according to a person familiar with the matter. He relayed multiple questions to the line attorneys in the fraud section, who feared their probe would be shut down, this person said. By July, however, Barr had recused himself, citing his past ties to Kirkland & Ellis. (A Justice Department spokesman declined to comment.)

None of that was of any help in the moment to Muilenburg, squirming under the cross-examination by Cruz as to why he didn't investigate the pilot's concerns in the simulator. The CEO went on to explain that Forkner no longer worked at Boeing, as if that were another barrier to obtaining information. This argument was particularly feeble because the pilot on the other end of those messages, Patrik Gustavsson, still worked at Boeing—in Forkner's old job. Cruz immediately spotted the inconsistency. "Did you talk to him?" the senator asked, referring to Gustavsson. Muilenburg had to admit that he hadn't.

Once Cruz had finished, the buzz-cut Montana senator Jon Tester offered what sounded like the hard truth of a country-and-western song. "Probably a painful morning for you but the fact is, it's infinitely more painful for the folks that are sittin' a couple of rows behind you," he said, before giving the knife a final twist. "I would *walk* before I was to get on a 737 MAX," he said. "I would walk. There's no way."

After two and a half hours, Muilenburg got up to leave, eyes cast down. Nadia Milleron was a few feet away. "Turn and look at people when you say you're sorry," she blurted out. He stopped and turned, holding his body stiffly, knowing he was still on camera, and said clearly to her, maintaining his gaze: "I'm sorry."

Before the hearings, Boeing had agreed that Muilenburg would meet with the victims' relatives. It had become a public relations liability for the plane maker that he and other senior leaders had waited so long to speak directly with them; the families often mentioned it. So after his testimony they walked in separate groups—the ashen-faced corporate executives and the grief-stricken relatives—to their meeting at the Cannon House Office Building, just across the street from the Mall. Chairs had been lined up around a big wooden table, auditorium-style. When Michael walked in and saw that, he and others early to arrive shoved the table aside and started rearranging the chairs into a circle. Boeing's CEO wouldn't get to lecture them. Muilenburg entered with Tim Keating, his top executive in Washington, and Jennifer Lowe, the deputy who'd sat with the CEO only a year earlier, under more auspicious circumstances, at the Trump National Golf Club.

Many of the relatives clutched photos of their loved ones. They took turns telling the Boeing executives about their family members—killed, they said, because of the company's greed and callousness. Paul Njoroge brought pictures of four coffins instead of the faces of his wife, Caroline, and their children, Ryan, Kelli, and Rubi. Muilenburg knew the plane was flawed, Njoroge told him, and still he blamed foreign pilots; he hadn't seen the victims in Ethiopia and Indonesia as people just like his own children. "They're not human beings to you," Njoroge said, "so you can only see their coffins." He wanted to watch Muilenburg crack, to make the imperturbable engineer feel the weight of guilt. But as Njoroge talked about the daily pain his life had become, the anguish Boeing had caused, he broke down himself. What he got from Muilenburg was a look that in that moment, to him, felt pitying. It wasn't what he wanted at all.

—

DeFazio and his House committee had their turn to grill Boeing the next day. DeFazio released more emails showing that some of the company's engineers had worried about the reliance of MCAS on data from a single sensor, but their concerns had been ignored. Representatives pressed Muilenburg to resign. "You're the captain of this ship," Congressman Jesús García of Illinois said. "Cultural negligence, incompetence, or corruption starts at the top and it starts with you."

Muilenburg kept invoking the values he'd learned on an Iowa farm, to the point that it brought groans from Nadia and others in the rows of seats where the victims' family members sat, many of them leaning on each other or clasping hands. Her farm was a real place, where she'd raised her children. Muilenburg's was pure symbolism, a trick meant to invoke ethics and integrity and even the long-lost ghost of Boeing legend T. Wilson, another Iowa State graduate. None of that registered in his actions.

DeFazio picked up on it, too. "You're no longer an Iowa farm boy," he said. "You are the CEO of the largest aircraft manufacturer in the world, you're earning a heck of a lot of money."

Afterward, Nadia again approached Muilenburg. His security guard moved to body her away, but he leaned in to listen. She took the opportunity to ask about the MCAS software: Would it really be safe once Boeing finished making all of the changes? He assured her it would. Then she offered a review of his performance. "You talked about Iowa just one too many times and the whole group said, 'Go back to the farm, go back to Iowa,'" she said. "Do that!"

Muilenburg's performance—teary, sweaty, apologetic, but still robotically defensive of Boeing—was the lead story on websites and iPhone news alerts around the world. The narrative, which Boeing had so easily shaped to its benefit after the first crash, was now essentially the same, whether the stinging criticism came from a Republican like Ted Cruz or a Democrat like Debbie Mucarsel-Powell of Florida, who concluded, "This is a story about a company cutting corners, taking short cuts, sacrificing safety to achieve maximum profits." Muilenburg, once an eager young intern at the world's greatest aerospace company, had become the technocratic face of a deadly blunder. Among those joining in the calls for his resignation was the newspaper of his alma mater, Iowa State University. "As students, we must expect better from our esteemed alumni," wrote the *Iowa State Daily*.

A call went out to Alan Mulally, the long-retired leader whose reputation had only been burnished by his turnaround of Ford, to return and save Boeing. Then seventy-four, he was about Joe Biden's age, one retiree joked on an email thread that included Mulally. "If asked, I will serve," he replied.

But Muilenburg hadn't been forced out yet, and he still had a business to run, not to mention a growing pile of inventory to unload. He called Dickson of the FAA a couple weeks later and inquired whether he would consider letting the company deliver planes before they were cleared to fly. Considering Boeing's now-prickly relationship with the agency and Muilenburg's own diminished reputation, it was a sign of the pressure he was under that he would dare ask. Costs from the grounding had mounted to $18 billion; deliveries would be a way to recoup at least some revenue and shift inventory onto customers.

Dickson said he'd look into it, without committing to anything. Muilenburg read that as a green light, and Boeing put out a statement saying "it is possible" that deliveries would resume in December. The FAA chief felt manipulated. He sent a memo to safety chief Ali Bahrami telling his team to "take whatever time is needed" and, for good measure, recorded an unusual video message to all FAA employees that soon hit YouTube. "I know there's a lot of pressure to return this aircraft to service quickly," Dickson said from his desk in Washington, the monuments in soft focus behind him. "I've got your back."

Forrest Gump had finally spoken up to his drill sergeant. The next month, Dickson called the Boeing CEO into his office, and as he relayed it to congressional investigators in another email quickly made public, he reminded Muilenburg that the FAA was in charge of reviewing the MAX. "Boeing's focus," he said, "should be on the quality and timeliness of data submittals for FAA review."

Muilenburg at last, on December 16, said Boeing would halt production. He had been adamant that the MAX would fly by year's end. Missing the deadline finally ruined his credibility with the last and most critical corner of his constituency—investors. When a Boeing Starliner capsule, developed to ferry astronauts to the International Space Station, failed a rendezvous attempt in an unmanned test launch four days later, it was one last headline-grabbing embarrassment under Muilenburg's watch. The board met the next Sunday, December 22, and voted to fire him.

Luttig followed Muilenburg out the door; he retired the day after Christmas. Walking away with $59 million, he had earned more than enough to afford those college expenses for his children that he had fretted about in his letter of retirement from the federal bench.

With Muilenburg's ouster, Calhoun was installed as CEO. A board member since 2009, he had collected $3.4 million in compensation and served through every stage of the MAX's fraught birth and frenzied development. An old friend of Jim McNerney's, he used to play a regular foursome of golf with Jack Welch at GE.

The face at the top of Boeing may have changed, in other words, but the playbook had not.

14

"The Guy Most Like Jack"

Not many eighty-three-year-olds have occasion to don a headset with a small microphone, like a singer in a boy band, to give a crisp lecture on flight controls. That's what Peter Morton, Boeing's Pug Henry, the guardian of the engineers' virtue, was doing late in 2019, in a room of people—several older than him—at a retirement home in Seattle. Some were "Incredibles" who'd worked on the 747 with the great Sutter himself. (An actuary might cringe while calculating the defined benefits of all those pensions.) Morton played old movies—Tex Johnston's barrel roll of the Dash 80, the earnest Brien Wygle talking about the stopping power of the 737's thrust reverser, the Harlem Globetrotters zipping a ball around the capacious cabin of a 747. It was part of a road show Morton had worked up with a student at the high school across from Boeing Field, a new private pilot himself who hoped to become a third-generation Boeing employee.

But the bonds that had propelled Boeing to dominance in the jet age, when "functional fathers" like Sutter rode herd over its designs, had frayed. Morton had spent much of the past year writing closely argued memos to Muilenburg and other Boeing leaders about the "dysfunctional silo mentality," the "broken lines of communication," and the "misunderstanding and confusion" that had resulted.

He never heard back. To those who'd worked at Boeing before the McDonnell Douglas merger, it was unimaginable to thumb their noses at the FAA the way they were reading about in the papers. More unthinkable still was to design a hazardous flight control system with a single-point failure. It would have been a bad joke at a retirement party, said Frank McCormick, an engineer on the "Camelot" plane, the 777.

In 2019, some former Boeing engineers had been called to a rented office in a strip mall near a Hobby Lobby, not far from the factory in Everett, to answer questions from FBI agents and Justice Department lawyers assessing a potential criminal fraud on regulators. Other employees flew to Chicago to give sworn testimony. At least one manager talked with his family about the possibility of the FBI knocking on their door in an unannounced raid.

The next year, it turned out, would be worse.

On the first Sunday in March, Boeing summoned its vice presidents for an emergency conference call. The MAX was suddenly the least of their problems. A killer virus was sweeping through the Seattle area. After almost a year of relentless scrutiny, the firing of Muilenburg, and the hugely expensive halt in MAX production, some of those listening to the call did so in disbelief. It was like a biblical plague descending. Airlines (and consequently plane makers) were among the first businesses to feel the financial brunt of the virus. Already hamstrung, Boeing now had to choose from among only bad options. One alternative on the table was shutting down one of the last well-functioning parts of Boeing's battered commercial aircraft operation—the giant plant in Everett, Washington, that had helped produce a record number of Dreamliners the previous year.

Weeks earlier, Boeing's top market forecaster had told people at a Singapore conference that the novel coronavirus might have a temporary, manageable impact on travel, akin to the SARS epidemic of 2002. But after overwhelming hospitals in China, then Iran, and then Italy, the virus found its first U.S. epicenter in late February at a nursing home in a Seattle suburb (not unlike the place where Morton had only just made his presentation). Ambulances ferried away dozens of dying residents, their terrified family members forced to peer into the windows of the quarantined home. It was a perplexing threat, all the more so because even scientists didn't understand what to do. One resident of a nearby apartment complex donned gloves to walk his dog, attiring his companion in plastic booties. Boeing left the Everett plant open while cleaners wiped down handrails and set up hand sanitizer stations.

The pandemic would soon present an existential crisis for Boeing and its new chief, Dave Calhoun. Since taking over, Calhoun had struggled to contain the fallout over the internal conversations among pilot Mark Forkner and his colleagues. Congressional critics like DeFazio saw Calhoun, who had defended Muilenburg's actions almost to the last day of his tenure, as complicit. Among other questions, they wanted to know how much Calhoun himself knew about the decision to withhold the pilots' instant messages: When had he read them?

Asked that question on CNBC January 29, Calhoun answered vaguely. "We found out way too late," he said. On a call with analysts that day, he suggested Muilenburg had duped him and Boeing's board, in addition to the public. "I get a lot of media attention around the idea that I am somehow an insider," he said. "What if I changed that a little bit? What if I told you I simply had a front-row seat to everything you saw?"

A month later, three of the pilots who'd worked with Forkner—including Patrik Gustavsson, who'd commiserated with him over his trouble flying the MAX in the simulator—were called into a manager's office and read a prepared statement putting them on leave. As the federal investigation into the crashes continued, the move appeared to be part of a coordinated strategy to paint their actions as isolated, a bit of rot that Boeing was efficiently cutting out. (The messages were part of a "micro-culture" that didn't represent Boeing, as Calhoun put it in one of his few press conferences.) It left untouched managers like Michael Teal and Keith Leverkuhn, the men who had led the MAX program. The disasters had done nothing to slow their careers. Teal, who'd already collected a bonus for his work on the plane, moved on to become the chief engineer of Boeing's next new aircraft, a derivative of the 777. Leverkuhn became vice president of the propulsion division before retiring as planned.

Calhoun represented not just the latest in a long line of Jack Welch protégés to take the helm at Boeing; according to longtime Welch speechwriter Bill Lane, he was "the guy who was really the most like Jack." A cement salesman's son, Calhoun grew up in Allentown, Pennsylvania, and got an accounting degree from Virginia Tech before joining GE in 1979. He became known for his competitiveness—his "framework" for everything, as he once put it. In the late 1990s, Welch initially wanted Calhoun in the succession race. (When their foursome met for golf, they'd often play thirty-six or fifty-four holes in a single day.) One strike against him was that he had diabetes; while the disease is common now, it was seen as a liability for "a potential 20-year GE CEO" at the time, according to Welch's former speechwriter.

Later, as GE's vice chairman, Calhoun was in the running for the Boeing job that eventually went to his ex-colleague McNerney. In 2006, he made a leap then seen as unusual, taking the helm of an obscure Dutch publisher that had been taken over by a group of private equity firms. The lure was $100 million in compensation and a free hand to remake the company, which then housed a collection of media properties from *Hollywood Reporter* to *Billboard,* as well as the famed television-ratings company Nielsen.

He installed three of his former GE deputies in top management positions. In 2007 the company signed a $1.2 billion contract with Tata Consultancy Services, an outsourcing firm based in India. It was the largest such arrangement ever signed to that point, and it allowed Nielsen to replace more expensive employees who gathered market data in the United States. The deal caused controversy in Oldsmar, Florida, where the company had taken tax breaks to build a call center. It began laying off hundreds of people, while asking them to train their replacements at Tata. One city council member accused Nielsen, then the largest employer in the Tampa Bay suburb, of "making a joke of the tax-incentive program." Another said it was a poor corporate citizen. (Nielsen agreed to give up the tax breaks.) Over time Calhoun sold off most of the company's old-media print titles, while expanding its offerings in Internet advertising and measurement.

Nielsen went public in 2011, and three years later Calhoun became head of portfolio operations at Blackstone, one of the private equity firms that had backed the company. At a Blackstone investor conference in June 2014, he spoke immediately before Steve Schwarzman, the Blackstone chairman whose opulent birthday party at the Park Avenue Armory in Manhattan had become a symbol of excess during the financial crisis. (At the party, in 2007, orchids were scattered everywhere, and Patti LaBelle led the round of "Happy Birthday" for hundreds of guests including Donald and Melania Trump.) Calhoun described the experience at Nielsen as one of the most satisfying of his career.

"For five years of operating in a purely private environment before we went in the IPO, I got to do everything I ever wanted to do as fast and as hard as I ever wanted to do it," he said.

One of Calhoun's deputies, Steve Hasker, would later lavish praise on him for creating a "tremendous productivity engine." Calhoun, he told a McKinsey publication, had taken out 25 to 30 percent of Nielsen's cost base from 2006 to 2013. The company had "focused exhaustively on our internal costs, particularly those that are heavily people-dependent," Hasker said. "For a while, we did a lot of labor arbitrage and shipped a lot of activities offshore to lower-cost locations. That was highly productive and the cash it generated enabled us to truly become an 'investor' in new products."

In September 2016, just before Trump's election and in the critical last few months of the MAX's development, Calhoun joined Maria Bartiromo on Fox Business for a conversation in which the panelists hailed private equity investors for creating jobs. (There was no mention of labor arbitrage or offshoring, the other result of private equity investment.) With a tagline reading "Where's the Growth?" in the bottom third of the screen, Bartiromo asked if regulation and taxes were "the two big hammers" on the economy.

"It's real," Calhoun said. "We feel it every day. It's not getting any better. It's difficult to articulate each little item that sort of gets in your way, but it is slowing everybody down." Bartiromo clarified, "The bureaucracy, the regulation . . ." and Calhoun, nodding his head, said, "Oh, it's amazing bureaucracy." Another guest offered, "If you cut through the red tape we'd see even more amazing companies started." Calhoun answered, "Absolutely. I just look at governance in general as—it just slows down everything about a company's performance, both in the public and in some cases the private markets. It's just not helpful." (Amid the supposed hammering, the U.S. gross domestic product had grown almost 3 percent the previous year, the most since 2005.)

Two months after Calhoun's lament, engineers at Boeing handed over to the FAA their incomplete safety analysis of the MCAS software, a design that would have been questioned, the government later said, if the FAA's own flight controls experts had known the details of how it worked.

For all Calhoun's talk of bureaucracy and red tape, Boeing delivered its first MAX planes three months early.

Before the pandemic became all-consuming, the looming event preoccupying some at Boeing was the one-year anniversary of the Ethiopian Airlines crash that March 10. It had the potential to be a public relations disaster, rekindling global news coverage. Boeing and the families of the victims established an uneasy partnership to plan the memorial ceremony. The manufacturer agreed to put up the money, but to the families involved in planning the event, it began to feel like a commemoration of the BP oil spill stage-managed by BP.

One Friday in late January, Tim Keating, the head of Government Operations, and his deputy, Jennifer Lowe, met with relatives

and representatives of the victims at Ethiopian Airlines' headquarters next to the Addis Ababa airport. The offices had the drab
appearance of a government embassy, except for the walls of the
conference room where they met, which were painted a bright sea-
green. Keating, who'd attended a Jesuit college, the University of
Scranton in Pennsylvania, struck a tone of pastoral generosity and
said Boeing wanted to do everything it could to make the event
meaningful for the grieving families.

But he quickly laid down some ground rules. Boeing would pay
for no more than two representatives per family. It would cover
their hotel and food for three nights. The anniversary landed on a
Tuesday, and he instructed everyone to fly in on Sunday and out
Wednesday, no exceptions. It was an incongruous note after the
generous opening, and people started raising objections. Families
would have to choose if parents or siblings, for instance, could
attend. What about divorced couples—could all the stepparents
come? And what if someone from, say, Canada, wanted to arrive on
Saturday instead? Boeing had already pledged to spend $100 mil-
lion to support families and communities after the crashes, and now
it was setting limits like a corporate benefits manager.

The main reason for his interest in planning every detail, as one
person there saw it, was to minimize the potential for embarrassment to Boeing. "He had that Catholic sensibility of grief and sor-
row," the person said, "but his mission was a corporate mission. His
mission was to manage the anniversary event with the least amount
of cost and the least amount of media coverage." On every question, Keating made clear that Boeing would control access, not the
families. When one family asked to bring along a therapist, Keating
said Boeing had already hired a firm that would have therapists on-
site. He rejected an independent videographer to record the event
for those who couldn't attend; Boeing had taken care of that, too.
Journalists were out of the question.

The meeting got especially testy when the conversation turned
to planning the memorial service itself. Multiple family members
said they didn't want anyone from Boeing inside the tent for the

eulogies; already, it felt as if the killer was planning the funeral. That came as a surprise to Keating, who said, "If we're paying for it, we'll be there."

Negotiations over the monetary relief Boeing had pledged proved just as fraught. On January 30, Samya's father, Michael Stumo, met with Ken Feinberg, the lawyer distributing the Boeing funds, for a get-acquainted lunch at the Willard Hotel in Washington. It could hardly have started more awkwardly. As they headed for the elevator, Stumo mentioned that his daughter had actually met Feinberg once, at a UMass alumni event in 2017. The famous mediator preened. "Oh yeah, I remember that speech—how's your daughter?" he asked automatically. "She's fifty feet under the ground in Addis Ababa," Stumo answered tersely.

Feinberg continued as if he hadn't made a self-centered social blunder that also suggested he hadn't done his homework on Stumo's family. Once they sat down, he lavished praise on Stumo for the work he and his wife, Nadia Milleron, had done in organizing the families. In his baritone Boston brogue that lent everything he said an avuncular air, Feinberg said he wanted to hear their thoughts on how to distribute the funds. At the time the couple had already been talking to Boeing's Keating about company support for a nonprofit group they had helped start, the ET302 Families Foundation; Keating had asked for a budget proposal. Feinberg and Stumo agreed to continue the conversation.

It was on Valentine's Day when Michael and Nadia sat down again with Feinberg and his colleague, Camille Biros, at their offices next to the Willard, filled with framed degrees and photos of Feinberg shaking hands with presidents.

A documentary called *Playing God* had once been made about Feinberg, who'd handled settlements for BP, Volkswagen, and the Catholic Church after his star turn as the September 11 claims administrator. It depicted him as a modern-day King Solomon for the way he assigned a value to individual lives after tragedies. When the couple brought up their earlier conversations about the foundation with Keating, Feinberg told them his efforts were completely independent of Boeing. What's more, his job was to distribute immediate relief to families, not the community funds. Still, he said the couple's work was so important that he offered to advocate with Boeing for them to get the funds.

A Boeing press release went out February 17 saying Feinberg's brief had been expanded and he'd now be in charge of distributing the entire $100 million fund, not just the half that had been promised as direct relief. But it was Keating, not Feinberg, who declined the foundation's $400,000 budget request, telling the nonprofit's director that he was hearing from "a lot of groups" and wasn't sure the foundation represented a majority of them. "It felt like the D.C. shuffle," said one person involved in the negotiations with both men. They'd meet and get information, "but in retrospect, it became clear they didn't have any intention of accepting our proposals," this person said. ("All I will tell you from 30,000 feet really is we haven't heard any real criticism that our program has not been independent of Boeing," Feinberg said.)

Days before the March 10 anniversary event, Boeing CEO Calhoun provided attendees one more reason for heartburn when he gave an interview to the *New York Times* that pinned much of the blame for the company's troubles on the ousted Muilenburg, whom he'd so assiduously defended. "It's more than I imagined it would be honestly," he said. "And it speaks to the weaknesses of our leadership." He met the *Times* reporters at the Boeing Leadership Center, the training center in a historic mansion near St. Louis that Harry Stonecipher had insisted on completing after the McDonnell Douglas merger. Photos of Muilenburg still adorned the walls. In a conversation about incentives, the new CEO stuck another knife in his ousted predecessor. "If anybody ran over the rainbow for the pot of gold on stock, it would have been him," Calhoun said, disingenuously for someone who'd made a fortune in private equity to pass to his grandchildren.

Even more painful was the suggestion that Boeing still hadn't internalized the lessons about its flawed design. At another point in the conversation, he implied that the pilots from Indonesia and

Ethiopia, "where pilots don't have anywhere near the experience that they have here in the U.S.," were part of the problem too. Asked whether he believed American pilots would have been able to handle a malfunction of the software, Calhoun asked to speak off the record. "Forget it," he said, when the reporters refused. "You can guess the answer." As for the larger message about Boeing's own culture: "I see a couple of people who wrote horrible emails."

On March 10, the grieving relatives filled the 373-room Ethiopian Skylight Hotel, the same place where many had gathered in the days after the crash. Since then, they'd connected through activism, countless emails, and their WhatsApp chat thread. They came from twenty-six countries. As the families had wished, no one from Boeing was at the memorial, held under a tent at the crash site, where the dirt was laid with the petals of more than a hundred thousand roses. They gave tributes to the victims, in a program deliberately free of any mention of the company that had brought them together, and then had six minutes and forty-three seconds of silence—the exact length of the flight from takeoff to crash. They planted seeds in small ochre pots arrayed on wooden boxes, each for a different crash victim. The only jarring note was a newly erected chain-link fence around the site. "They're terrified that you guys are going to find bones," the event planner Boeing had hired told Samya's mother, Nadia.

The families returned home to a changed world: On March 11 the National Basketball Association canceled the rest of its season, and actor Tom Hanks said he and his wife had contracted the virus, the developments that, strangely, finally underlined its severity to a media-saturated populace. Theaters, music venues, bars, and restaurants emptied. Intensive care units started filling, and governments issued the first "stay-at-home" orders in living memory. Scientists gave crash courses in "respiratory droplets" and "flattening the curve." After Samya's death and the intense confrontations that followed, Michael and Nadia weren't scared; the worst thing had already happened to them. They were relieved to have more time at home with their sons, Adnaan and Tor.

Boeing's stock meanwhile went into free fall. It had already dropped 20 percent since the second crash a year earlier. The shares fell another 50 percent that March, touching a low of $89, amid eerie scenes of deserted airports and empty city plazas. Early that month, Boeing's Puget Sound–area managers got expanded authority to let office workers stay home, while the production team kept coming into the Everett plant. The machinists warily eyed each other, some in masks, others not. Increasing numbers began using vacation time to stay home. Others who crowded into meeting rooms for teleconferences, joined by people already working from home, began wondering why they were still there at all.

At least twice, ambulances appeared in the huge open bays of the Everett factory taking away workers who'd fallen sick; their sections were cleaned and work continued. Auto plants in Detroit closed on March 18. Everett remained open. Boeing finally said it would shut the plant five days later, a day after a fifty-seven-year-old worker there died from the coronavirus and his family sent out a plea for its closure over Facebook.

In April, at the height of lockdowns around the world, passenger traffic fell a stunning 95 percent from the same month a year earlier. Airlines parked two-thirds of their global fleet, the brightly painted planes stretching for miles in neat formation in one desert storage yard in California. The industry *was* in fact cyclical, not the picture of everlasting growth Muilenburg had painted—one last judgment he got wrong.

It was a terrible outcome for Boeing and Calhoun, of course. Boeing had to draw down a $13.8 billion bank loan just to keep operations running. Calhoun even considered taking a federal bailout, conversations serious enough that Nikki Haley, Boeing's former champion in South Carolina and a potential Republican presidential candidate in 2024, quit the board with a statement about her free-market principles. Instead of orders, Boeing tracked cancellations—more than one thousand in 2020. Even if it could get the four hundred MAX planes in storage flying—and after a year on the ground there was still no assurance of that from the FAA—cash-strapped airlines couldn't afford to pay for them.

In other ways, the pandemic opened new possibilities, as Calhoun eventually acknowledged himself. The MAX scandal was swept from the front pages. In the dark calculus of twenty-first-century corporate management, a global tragedy was also an opportunity, a chance to reset expectations for Boeing on Calhoun's own terms. Boeing was no longer a corporate pariah whose mismanagement had contributed to a catastrophic loss of life; it was an endangered American manufacturer working to secure the livelihoods of tens of thousands of employees in the midst of a national emergency. "We can't lose Boeing," President Trump said.

The company ultimately managed to avoid a bailout by raising $25 billion in debt in April from private lenders, who clearly viewed the last U.S. builder of commercial jets and number two defense contractor the same way as the president did: too big to fail. At the same time, Boeing benefited from the tens of billions of dollars in aid that Congress authorized to fund the payrolls of some of its largest customers, the U.S. airlines. The air force, Boeing's ever-loyal supporter, quietly found another way to assist: in April, it agreed to release $882 million in funds that had been withheld for technical deficiencies on thirty-three KC-46 tanker planes, problems severe enough that software, cameras, and computers needed to be completely redesigned.

Calhoun was back on familiar ground, after twenty-eight years of parachuting into various divisions at GE and more than a decade running private-equity-backed companies. This time, he would get a chance to tear down Boeing and build it back up in his own image. "We'll never have another opportunity to evaluate like we do now, both near-term and medium-term," he said in July, while announcing plans to cut 19,000 of Boeing's 160,000 jobs and consolidate production of larger jetliners either in Everett or in South Carolina.

—

After all the indignation, the two ranking senators on the Senate Commerce Committee, Roger Wicker of Mississippi and Maria Cantwell of Washington, that summer proposed bipartisan FAA reform legislation that made tough-sounding changes but, in the view of some of Boeing's engineers and the MAX victims' families, wouldn't shake the agency's subservience to the plane maker. Instead of going back to the old system, in which the deputies formally reported to the FAA, the lawmakers kept the confusing alphabet soup that left Boeing in charge of its own safety organization. Most significantly, they preserved the BASOO, the group created by Ali Bahrami that had arrayed just forty FAA staffers against fifteen hundred at Boeing.

The lawmakers did return to the agency the power to appoint the deputies. But at a hearing of Wicker and Cantwell's Commerce Committee that June, Stephen Dickson, the FAA administrator, said he envisioned continuing to leave those roles largely up to Boeing. Until Michael Stumo and other relatives of crash victims complained, Dickson was going to be the only person to testify at the hearing. It was a sign of how much momentum had been lost to the pandemic that the FAA was coming out of the spotlight more or less unscathed. Michael sat alone at a table in the nearly deserted hearing room, his wife, Nadia, standing behind him in a face mask, holding up her oversized poster with photos of the crash victims. Despite another moralizing speech from Texas senator Ted Cruz— "You do not work for Boeing," he reminded Dickson—the hearing drew little attention.

Mostly working from home, Boeing's engineers and FAA managers exchanged documents and held teleconferences about the last steps needed to return the MAX to the skies, as all the final changes were made to the software. While the pandemic added some complications—planes had to be wiped down and sealed between flights—the team working on the project was generally pleased that the worldwide scrutiny had died down.

A third crash of the MAX (even if not Boeing's fault) would have the potential to be devastating for the plane's reputation—similar to the McDonnell Douglas DC-10, whose crash in Paris, in an eerie coincidence, had cost exactly the same number of lives, 346, and whose commercial prospects were finished by a later accident.

Calhoun raised hell in Boeing's pilot ranks, telling Mike Fleming, an executive he put in charge of an effort to raise maintenance and pilot training standards among Boeing's customers, that he'd be fired if Boeing sold a single airplane to an unsafe airline. The phrasing, again, suggested an inability to accept the need to stamp out unsafe practices at Boeing itself.

The unit of technical pilots where Mark Forkner had worked was moved into the same organization with the test pilots, an attempt to keep them in the loop and prevent communications breakdowns like those on the MAX. Boeing's engineers, too, began reporting directly to a vice president of engineering, who answered to Calhoun instead of to business unit leaders—preventing another situation like the one on the MAX in which its chief engineer, Michael Teal, had no staff of his own and reported to a business-unit vice president.

The CEO and his board considered writing minimum safety standards into Boeing's contracts, according to someone apprised of the deliberations. There would also be a formal mechanism for pilots to report any safety concerns they encountered while instructing airlines in the field. A safety committee on the board, led by a retired navy admiral, was working out the new policies. That effort was moving slowly in part because of liability concerns about how much data to collect, how to share it—and whom to tell. One constituency that might *not* learn the full details: Calhoun and the board themselves. The thinking was to give them anonymized data.

As part of a new cadre of "Global Engagement Pilots," Boeing hired 160 to fly with airlines reintroducing the MAX, embedding them for thirty-five-day assignments at an equivalent annual salary of $200,000. They came from Cambridge Communications, the pilot recruitment company based in the Isle of Man—more of the "dirtbag contractors" whose hiring had so infuriated Boeing's longtime pilots and, in a way, helped create the bad feelings and lousy communications loop that contributed to the whole mess.

The effort was led by Carl Davis, Forkner's former boss, who doubled down on a strategy to remove the union-represented pilots who had flown in the field with customers. The last seven were laid off in September. "The loss of this critical coordinating function between the Boeing employees who design and manufacture aircraft and the customer air crews who fly them is incalculable," said Ray Goforth, executive director of the engineers' union. "For customers and regulators, the face of Boeing will now be contractors masquerading as genuine Boeing pilots."

In October, Calhoun chose South Carolina for its wide-body jetliner operations, completing the decade-long exodus to the nonunion South. Boeing lost $11.9 billion in 2020. (The loss that Harry Stonecipher had shamed Boeing employees for back in 1997 had been a comparatively modest $178 million.) Burning through cash at $4 billion a quarter, Calhoun shuttered the Leadership Center and, with it, the "Harry's Place" dining room. A manufacturing R&D center on East Marginal Way—the name of the street finally befitting Boeing's growth prospects there after a hundred years—was shuttered. The last of the 747s built by the "Incredibles" at Joe Sutter's Everett factory will roll off the lines in 2022, with no new wonder to fill the world's most vast empty space. Finally, the Longacres building was put up for sale—not just the simulator bays that Peter Morton had inaugurated with a specially commissioned orchestral work, but the offices for Boeing's commercial aircraft operations, where the WORKING TOGETHER sign used to be.

It wasn't private equity, but "the guy most like Jack" got to do everything just as fast and as hard as he ever wanted.

EPILOGUE

The very air they breathed was unsafe. In the concourse at Miami International Airport four days after Christmas in December 2020, the president of American Airlines, Robert Isom, stood wearing a mask, keeping his distance from the reporters around him, also wearing masks. They were there to cover the return to U.S. skies of the MAX, the "death jet" of the tabloids, the doomed plane that had, indeed, cost lives and reputations just as Boeing's overworked engineers in the pews had warned. The pandemic, of course, had revised everyone's thoughts about risk.

In the concourse, Isom explained how confident American was in the improvements made to the plane, and at the gate, when it was announced as a MAX flight, nobody ran. (In fact, some thrill seekers had specifically booked it.) Isom sat in one of the first rows himself when the plane took off, at 10:30 a.m., and landed at New York's LaGuardia Airport two and a half hours later. Just another routine flight.

A low-cost airline in Brazil, GOL, had been the first to bring back the MAX a few weeks earlier, and by midyear, the plane was in service with carriers worldwide, from United Airlines to Ryanair to Air Canada. The Boeing team working to recertify the plane grumbled that while Canadian regulators held their feet to the fire on the final design changes, Air Canada pilots had continued flying the plane without passengers to keep their licenses current. Some death trap.

Many people in the industry—and especially at Boeing—still believe the twenty-month grounding was an overreaction, Boeing the fall guy for lousy overseas pilots and sanctimonious whistle-blowers. One of the most pointed comments to the final Airworthiness Directive published by the FAA came from an American Airlines pilot: "Interesting that none of the three major airlines had any problems with MCAS. Let's get her back in the AIR!"

For airlines confronting their own existential crisis after the pandemic, the MAX, for all its infamy, is a moneymaker. Those giant engines—no longer soda cans, now more resembling Big Gulps—save 15 percent on fuel costs for every flight. And instead of tiny winglets raked at the tips of the wings, as on the earlier 737 Next Generation, there were "split scimitars" in each direction, sluicing every last percentage point of efficiency from the airflow.

American had another reason to be the first in the United States to fly the MAX in the last days of 2020, one that it hadn't stated publicly: the terms of its bank financing were tied to the plane's use on paid routes that year. Renegotiating them would have been more costly than being first to put the MAX back in the skies and taking whatever public-relations flak came with it. In the end there was little of that, with cost-sensitive fliers seeing few hassle-free ways to avoid the MAX. That first week, even during the pandemic, the flights were more than 90 percent full. People reflexively trusted in the industry's safety record.

As pilots at Boeing liked to tell each other (similar to how people at McDonnell Douglas used to talk about the DC-10), every day a MAX doesn't crash is a day the plane gets back a bit of its reputation.

Floyd Wisner is a lawyer from Chicago who's handled crash cases for twenty-five years and represented some of the families of the victims in Indonesia and Ethiopia. He had the impression, before he first started taking depositions of Boeing engineers, that they'd be rocket scientists. "And they're not, they're ordinary guys," he said. "They take a design like the 737, and they make some changes. I'm concerned that they don't put *enough* thought into it. Sometimes I think they don't have the big picture: Who's watching over everybody?"

Congress, after more prodding from the victims' families, decided that it shouldn't be any yea-saying Forrest Gump, the character the frustrated FAA specialist Richard Reed felt like as he watched lawmakers strip him of power. A law passed at the end of 2020, in a rare moment of bipartisanship, did away with the extreme delegation of authority enacted only two years previously. It mandated the assignment of safety advisers from the FAA to work directly with the deputies at Boeing, similar to the system before it was co-opted. Approval of any design would henceforth require a separate examination of the human factors. The law provided for civil penalties for corporate managers found to be pressuring the FAA's deputies. It also barred managers at the regulatory agency from receiving any compensation based on meeting manufacturer-driven schedules.

Those new powers still depend on how they're implemented by the agency itself, and in March 2021, Michael Stumo, Samya's father, received a letter that a whistleblower in the FAA had sent to the new transportation secretary, Pete Buttigieg. The author of the letter, a current FAA staffer, wrote that managers had told engineers to expect little change as a result of the law. "Posing for the cameras" is how the top certification official, Earl Lawrence, had summed up the congressional inquiry in one staff meeting. Like Bahrami, Lawrence came from an industry trade group (the Experimental Aircraft Association). "Clearly, 'helping' industry by delegating approvals and removing FAA certification engineers from the process actually is 'loving' the industry to death," the whistleblower wrote.

Some of the families in Indonesia who signed those blanket releases after the first crash got a measure of vindication, settling their cases for well in excess of $1 million. The amounts were the most anyone could remember for an accident in Indonesia. Sanjiv Singh and Michael Indrajana, the lawyers who had been so incensed by what they saw as the selective and racist use of the releases, aren't letting the matter drop. They believe the families got less than they could have, victims of a system that treats the lives of people in Indonesia and other developing countries as inherently less valuable. In January, they emailed Cory Jacobs, the attorney in the Justice Department's fraud section who opened the criminal probe of Boeing, and asked for a second phase to investigate who coordinated the effort to get families to sign the forms. "We know for a fact that large carriers and manufacturers have benefited from this practice (though they deny orchestrating it) repeatedly in the past and it must be brought to a stop," they wrote.

There's also the matter of the redheaded stepchild that already went out the door. Even after all the cancellations, MAX orders number more than three thousand, and the plane will likely become common in airline fleets over the next several years. Ryanair and Alaska Airlines lent their support with additional orders, undoubtedly at deep discounts.

In the view of some of the engineers who know the plane best, who can picture its systems just as clearly as the wires and pipes in an old basement, not enough has been done to fix what might go wrong. "With its unique systems design, the 737 operates in some scenarios at reduced safety margins compared to modern aircraft," as one Boeing employee, less eager to get the plane back up in the air, wrote in his own comments to the FAA.

That person was Curtis Ewbank, the young engineer who had tried to get his bosses to listen to his concerns about the MAX's design, quit in frustration, and eventually rejoined Boeing. His comments painstakingly laid out the scenarios where the plane is lacking. The rudder cables remain vulnerable to engine shrapnel, the issue that thirteen FAA specialists wanted fixed before they were overridden by managers. In a jam of the elevator system, the crew is expected to "literally learn on the fly," while reading notes from the checklist—something pilots don't train for in a simulator, he said.

Some of the cockpit alerts, he added, leave the crew to interpret and deal with erroneous information instead of removing it automatically as in a more modern design; the MAX remains the only large commercial airliner without an electronic checklist to guide pilots.

Thirty years after the 1986 *Challenger* disaster, an engineer at Morton Thiokol, the firm that had designed the shuttle's infamous O-rings, called one of his former managers. Bob Ebeling was eighty-nine now, and in hospice. Before the infamous launch, both had tried to alert NASA to the risks the *Challenger* faced, to no avail. Nearing death, Ebeling told the former manager, Allan McDonald, that he'd never stopped replaying the events of the tragedy in his head. He wished he'd made his case better. He asked why God had chosen a loser like him for such an important job.

"I said, 'Bob, a loser is a person who does nothing,'" McDonald recalled. "You did something and you really cared."

McDonald went on to write a book, *Truth, Lies, and O-Rings,* about the lessons to be drawn from the disaster. He lectured at universities and tried to get engineering schools to make courses in ethics a requirement of graduation.

By many accounts, a cultural reckoning like the one that followed the *Challenger* disaster never took place at Boeing and its regulator.

Answering questions from House Transportation and Infrastructure Committee investigators, Ali Bahrami, the FAA safety chief and former industry lobbyist, said he wasn't familiar with the details of the FAA assessment that had warned of the risk of additional crashes after the Lion Air accident. He said he hadn't seen the subsequent bulletin pointing pilots to the emergency checklist. He couldn't recall any conversations with Boeing in the five months between the two accidents, although his emails showed a call had been scheduled with at least one high-ranking executive. He couldn't even recall the right movie when they asked him about

Mark Forkner, the Boeing pilot who'd been so fond of quoting the phrase "Jedi mind tricks" from *Star Wars*. "I guess I'm not a *Star Trek* guy or whatever it comes from," he said.

Keith Leverkuhn, the MAX's program manager, told the House investigators he would consider the program a success.

Conceived in haste to avoid losing market share, the MAX ended up putting Boeing into the deepest hole in its history. The American export champion delivered 157 planes in 2020 compared to 566 for Airbus. Even by one of its own design ambitions—avoiding simulator training—the MAX was a failure. Pilots transitioning from the previous 737 will now need to train in a simulator, a welcome requirement for safety but one that will hamper its commercial prospects. Boeing faces competition from not just Airbus but also an emboldened aircraft maker from China, Comac, whose government by midyear had yet to unground the MAX.

Meant to cost $2.5 billion—a simple derivative of a model updated a dozen times since the 1960s—the MAX easily exceeded the $20 billion Boeing might have spent on an all-new program. The direct cost was $21 billion, including compensation to customers, aircraft storage, pilot training, and settlements to the families. Through the end of 2020, more than six hundred MAX orders had been canceled, a loss of another $33 billion at typical selling prices. If buyers don't return, the Boeing MAX debacle could approach the more than $65 billion that BP lost in the *Deepwater Horizon* blowout, the most expensive corporate disaster in history.

Yet the people who made the most damaging decisions, and laid on the impossible demands, kept rising to the top. Like Jack Welch's General Electric before it, Boeing became a collection of assets to be shuffled as managers saw fit to make the most beneficial combination for stockholders, not for customers or employees. Welch died, at eighty-four, from kidney failure early in 2020; but he was still selling his management secrets in a $48,695 online MBA course.

"Winning is good," declares the familiar hoarse voice. "Winning is *wonderful*. Winning is fun."

The Boeing leaders he inspired went on to create great wealth—for their own families, if not their company. Jim McNerney, born to command, became chief executive of the U.S. Equestrian Team Foundation and retired to two adjoining multimillion-dollar homes in Wellington, Florida.

Phil Condit, who launched the merger with McDonnell Douglas and hosted sessions about the corporate soul at a forested mansion, built a second mansion with his fourth wife.

The former McDonnell Douglas chief Harry Stonecipher is still raising hackles—most recently in a suburb of Asheville, North Carolina, where he and his second wife sued the town over an ordinance preventing them from keeping twelve cats in their sixty-seven-hundred-square-foot home. (Baby, Dante, Duchess, and the other felines had their own kitchen.)

Dennis Muilenburg did go back to the farm, as the grieving Nadia Milleron urged him. He's an investor and adviser at Monarch Tractor, which sells a $50,000 electric model and is trying to become the Tesla of agriculture.

After an investigation lasting almost two years, the Justice Department levied what it called a $2.5 billion fine on Boeing and agreed to a deferred prosecution of one count of criminal fraud conspiracy, stemming from its two pilots' inaccurate representations to the FAA about how the MCAS software worked. The bulk of the fine, though, came from compensation payments of $1.77 billion to customers and $500 million in settlements to victims' families—most of which it was likely to pay anyway. The amount of the criminal penalty was only $243.6 million, which, as the complaint noted, was about what it would have cost Boeing to let MAX pilots train in a simulator in the first place.

Like Calhoun, the government saw a couple of pilots who wrote horrible emails. The only people cited in the complaint were the two 737 technical pilots, Mark Forkner and Patrik Gustavsson, though not by name. To their coworkers, it was bizarre that the managers—

men who heaped on the pressure, reaped the rewards, and then disappeared when the whole deadly blunder was exposed—never paid any price.

After seeing the Justice Department's settlement of "the 737 Max Fraud Conspiracy," as the press release put it, a pilot who worked with Forkner and Gustavsson suggested a different headline. It would say that Boeing got away with murder.

ACKNOWLEDGMENTS

I am grateful to the many people who generously offered their time and wisdom to help with this project, none more so than the families of those who died on Lion Air Flight 610 and Ethiopian Airlines Flight 302. Their courage in sharing their personal suffering, and persistence in learning the truth of what happened, were an inspiration. In particular, I would like to thank Nadia Milleron, Michael Stumo, Tarek Milleron, Paul Njoroge, Rini Soegiyono, Konjit Shafi, and Javier de Luis.

This research would have been impossible without the assistance of many dedicated employees of Boeing and the FAA, who believed that an independent journalistic investigation would ultimately help both institutions learn from the tragedies, not harm them. They showed great trust and candor in speaking with me, often multiple times. A special thanks to Richard Aboulafia, who was one of the first analysts I got to know when I started writing about aerospace twenty-five years ago and has been a perceptive guide to its forces and actors. I also spoke to aerospace analysts, executives, pilots, engineers, machinists, lawyers, and many others whom I can't thank by name, who contributed immeasurably to my understanding of a complex and indispensable industry.

Bloomberg Business News, as it was called back then, advertised for positions in London, Paris, Copenhagen, and other European bureaus in a three-ring binder I came across at my college's career placement center—the start of a journey that's taken me around the world and taught me how to write about companies with rigor and fairness. While many news organizations are shrinking, John Micklethwait, Reto Gregori, and Otis Bilodeau have shown sustained commitment to serious journalism of all kinds. Robert Blau leads the investigations team with unerring instincts and high standards, and I'm thankful to all of them for the freedom to pursue this project.

Flynn McRoberts, our 737 MAX czar, guided coverage of the crashes, made thoughtful suggestions on the manuscript, and has been a valuable mentor. Dan Ferrara at *Bloomberg Businessweek* deftly edited the feature articles that informed my thinking for this book. Joel Weber, Kristin Powers, Jim Aley, and the talented team at the magazine were supportive from the beginning. I am consistently awed by Julie Johnsson and Alan Levin's reporting on Boeing and the FAA, and their work appears frequently in the endnotes. Over the years, Andrea Rothman, Anthony Effinger, John Coppock, Reed Landberg, Rachel Layne, Jim Gunsalus, Susanna Ray, Pham-Duy Nguyen, and Dina Bass have provided inspiration and support. The incredible journalists turned authors Liam Vaughan, Susan Berfield, and Bryan Gruley generously helped me navigate the journey.

Specialized as it is, the aerospace beat has produced an unusually large share of talented reporters—among them Jeff Cole, Stanley Holmes, Ralph Vartabedian, Byron Acohido, Andy Pasztor, Dominic Gates, and Jon Ostrower—whose work has resonated with a general audience and been recognized for its quality. I've learned a lot from all of them, and if Jeff's life hadn't been sadly cut short, he might have written a book like this one.

At the Museum of History & Industry in Seattle, Adam Lyon and Anna Elam ably assisted with my many requests. The tranquility of the Whiteley Center, at the University of Washington's Friday Harbor Laboratories on San Juan Island, was essential during the pandemic. Thank you to Kathy Cowell, who facilitated my stays there.

There were many people who saw the need for a book-length exploration of this subject and helped make it happen. It's been a delight to discover a kindred spirit in Yaniv Soha, my meticulous editor at Doubleday, who helped shape the manuscript with precision, grace, and good humor. Cara Reilly made discerning comments that opened my eyes to more of the book's potential. Nora Reichard helped guide it across the finish line. Thanks to Scott Waxman and Andrew Stuart for placing the book with a great publisher. John Fontana and Matt Dorfman produced the indelible and haunting cover.

My family has experienced the writing of this book viscerally, and their support through the highs and lows has meant the world. My mother, Constance Robison, is always there with unconditional love. It's an intense joy that my sons Emmett and Spencer, who were building with blocks when I started it, are now embarking on their own projects—plays, stories, poems, histories of castles. They lost some of dad's attention right in the midst of the pandemic, and I hope the result makes them proud. Finally, thank you to Leslie, whose boundless reserves of strength, humor, wisdom, love, kindness, and patience made it all possible.

A NOTE ON SOURCES

This book is based on hundreds of hours of interviews with current and former employees of Boeing and the FAA, industry executives and analysts, and family members of the victims, as well as thousands of pages of published materials—including court records, meeting transcripts, emails and instant messages, news accounts, documents released by congressional investigators, and official accident reports. I also drew on oral histories and public appearances by the major players, as well as my own experiences covering Boeing as a beat reporter during the pivotal years of the McDonnell Douglas merger and engineers' strike.

Anything appearing between quotation marks comes from my own reporting, a published account, or a recorded appearance. While I have quoted people by name whenever possible, in some cases people asked to remain anonymous because of their fear that making comments seen as critical of Boeing or the FAA would harm their career prospects or expose them to retribution. The company and the agency both declined my requests for interviews. Presented with detailed questions, Boeing provided no on-the-record response, other than to defend its accounting practices. The FAA declined to answer questions, as did other key figures.

I benefited from the contemporaneous coverage of publications including the *Seattle Times,* the *Wall Street Journal,* and the *New York Times,* in addition to that of my colleagues at Bloomberg, and have taken care to cite those instances in the notes. I would have been lost without a seminal history of the aircraft industry: John Newhouse's *The Sporty Game.* Memoirs by Tex Johnston and Joe Sutter were especially helpful for the early history of the jet age. Finally, I drew on an excellent technical monograph by the Southwest Airlines pilot Dan Dornseif, *Boeing 737: The World's Jetliner.*

NOTES

INTRODUCTION

2 sent his family a choppy WhatsApp: Brooke Rolf, "Doomed Passengers' Final Moments," *DailyMail.com,* October 31, 2018.

2 texted a selfie: Fergus Jensen, "Indonesian Aircraft Was New, Fell Out of a Clear Sky Minutes After Takeoff," Reuters, October 29, 2018.

2 Wahyu Aldilla sat: Angela Dewan et al., "Lion Air Plane Crashes in Indonesia," CNN, October 31, 2018.

2 A grieving family: "Lion Air Crash: Indian Pilot and Husband of Mystery Pair Among Victims," BBC News, October 30, 2018.

2 Twenty employees of: "Lion Air Crash."

2 At thirty-one, he had already: My descriptions of the pilots and the last moments of Lion Air 610 are drawn from the final Aircraft Accident Investigation Report published by the Komite Nasional Keselamatan Transportasi (KNKT), Transportation Building, Jakarta, Indonesia, October 2019.

4 Horrified fishermen: Jensen, "Indonesian Aircraft Was New."

4 "I'm sure Dad": Riska Rahman, "Lion Air Crash: 'I'm Sure Dad Could Swim His Way Out and Survive the Crash,'" *Jakarta Post,* November 1, 2018.

5 "What's MCAS?": Andrew Tangel, Andy Pasztor, and Mark Maremont, "The Four-Second Catastrophe: How Boeing Doomed the 737 MAX," *Wall Street Journal,* August 16, 2019.

5 Pilots for American: Author interview with Dennis Tajer, spokesman, Allied Pilots Association, May 2020.

5 A Boeing manager asked: Author interview with anonymous source, January 2020.

5 The 157 people aboard: Elias Meseret, "Jetliner Crashes in Ethiopia, Killing 157 from 35 Countries," Associated Press, March 10, 2019.

6 In shocking emails: The "Jedi mind tricks" and other quotes from Boeing employees are drawn from emails provided to the House Committee on Transportation and Infrastructure that were released in January 2020. They are available in a searchable format as "Boeing Emails Handed Over to Congress in January 2020" at the nonprofit Internet Archive, https://archive.org.

8 Muilenburg made more: The Boeing CEO's compensation was detailed in a lawsuit filed by Seafarers Pension Plan against Boeing, Muilenburg, and other top executives in the U.S. District Court for the Northern District of Illinois, 19-cv-08095, December 11, 2019.

8 The group declared: Business Roundtable, "Statement on Corporate Governance," September 1997, https://www.rivistaianus.it/.

9 "If this continues": Morgan Radford and Aaron Franco, "Inspectors Warn Unsafe Pork Could Make Its Way to Consumers Under Trump Rule Change," NBC News, December 16, 2019.

10 "How unlucky": Author interview with Javier de Luis, November 2019.

10 The 737 remains: Final Committee Report on the Design, Development & Certification of the Boeing 737 Max, House Committee on Transportation and Infrastructure, September 2020, https://transportation.house.gov, p. 17.

10 approximates a 1990s Nintendo: Darryl Campbell, "The Ancient Computers in the Boeing 737 Max Are Holding Up a Fix," *Verge,* April 9, 2020.

10 once in every three million: David Shepardson, "Fatalities on Commercial Aircraft Rise in 2018," Reuters, January 1, 2019.

10 But there were forty-one: This analysis of total accidents in 2018 is drawn from the Boeing Statistical Summary 2018, published September 2019.

11 By the count: Edward F. Pierson, "Statement of Edward F. Pierson Before the House Transportation and Infrastructure Committee," December 11, 2019, https://www.whistleblowers.org/whistleblowers/edward-pierson/.

1. THE INCREDIBLES

13 One massive building: Colin Diltz, "Boeing Made an Entire Fake Neighborhood to Hide Its Bombers from Potential WWII Airstrikes," *Seattle Times,* June 9, 2016.

13 Days after Germany's: The description of how Boeing made use of Nazi aeronautical research comes from Robert J. Serling, *Legend and Legacy: The Story of Boeing and Its People,* 84, and Eugene Rodgers, *Flying High: The Story of Boeing and the Rise of the Jetliner Industry,* 99.

14 At $3 million apiece: Serling, 95.

14 He never traveled: Serling, 251.

14 "Be considerate of": Rodgers, *Flying High,* 78.

15 The conditions inside: Joe Sutter, *747: Creating the World's First Jumbo Jet and Other Adventures from a Life in Aviation*, 26.

15 "There isn't much": Harold Mansfield, *Vision: A Saga of the Sky*, 10.

15 Flying it over Seattle: Mansfield, 13.

15 Boeing took it out himself: Walt Crowley, "Boeing-Built Airplane, the B&W, Makes Its Maiden Flight from Seattle's Lake Union on June 15, 1916," *History Link.org*, November 23, 1998.

16 By 1928, almost one-third: Rodgers, *Flying High*, 43.

16 Boeing himself was grilled: The transcript of the hearing appears in *Investigation of Air Mail and Ocean Mail Contracts, Hearings Before a Special Committee on Investigation, United States Senate*, U.S. Government Printing Office, 1934.

17 As was common: The text of the racially restrictive covenants attached to property deeds in Boeing developments from 1935 to 1944 read, "No property in said addition shall at any time be sold, conveyed, rented, or leased in whole or in part to any person or persons not of the White or Caucasian race. No person other than one of the White or Caucasian race shall be permitted to occupy any property in said addition of portion thereof or building thereon except a domestic servant actually employed by a person of the White or Caucasian race where the latter is an occupant of such property." Catherine Silva, The Seattle Civil Rights & Labor History Project, University of Washington, https://depts.washington.edu.

17 Allen and his deputies: Serling, *Legend and Legacy*, 123.

18 So in April 1952: Eugene E. Bauer, *Boeing: The First Century*, 138.

18 Ten days after the board's: A. M. "Tex" Johnston, *Tex Johnston: Jet-Age Test Pilot*, 172.

18 This exciting new way: British Movietone, "Queen Mother and Princess Home from Rhodesia—1953," https://www.youtube.com/watch?v=rWMql0FA4XY.

18 One of the elegant-looking: Robert G. Pushkar, "Comet's Tale: A Half Century Ago, the First Jet Airliner Delighted Passengers with Swift, Smooth Flights Until a Fatal Structural Flaw Doomed Its Glory," *Smithsonian*, June 2002.

18 Then, in 1954: Pushkar.

19 He got his nickname: Johnston, *Tex Johnston*, 1.

20 The film showed giant: Serling, *Legend and Legacy*, 127, and *Tex Johnston*, 191.

20 But one evening: Johnston, *Tex Johnston*, 251.

20 Days earlier a 707: Daryl McClary, "Boeing 707 Jetliner Crashes Near Oso in Snohomish County, Killing Four Crew Members and Injuring Four Passengers," *HistoryLink.org*, July 23, 2017.

20 "It is obvious": Johnston, *Tex Johnston*, 252.

21 "When something goes wrong": Serling, *Legend and Legacy*, 91.

21 Passenger travel was increasing: John Newhouse, *The Sporty Game*, 110.

22 The Boeing workforce: Jim Kershner, "Boeing and Washington's Aerospace Industry, 1934–2015," *HistoryLink.org*, September 8, 2015.

22 "We hire engineers": Newhouse, *Sporty Game*, 137.

22 An early propulsion engineer: Granville Frazier tells the story on his personal website, www.grannyfrazier.com.

22 Boeing's designers worked: Author interview with Fred Mitchell, March 2020.

22 "functional fathers": Author interview with Peter Morton, January 2020.

22 "Sutter's runaways": Jeff Cole, "Boeing's 79-Year-Old Engineer Is Jet Maker's Secret Weapon," *Wall Street Journal*, January 10, 2001.

22 "the college of jet knowledge": "Boeing & Douglas: A History of Customer Service," Boeing Corporation, Seattle, WA, 1998. Available at https://www.boeing.com.

22 Boeing put mechanics: Bauer, *Boeing*, 242.

23 "it was not the Wild West": Author interview with Peter Morton, December 2019.

23 "sell, sell, sell": Jonathan S. Leonard and Adam Pilarski, "Overwhelmed by Success: What Killed Douglas Aircraft" (working paper, Haas School of Business, 2018).

23 One internal study: Serling, *Legend and Legacy*, 253.

24 Boeing had shipped to Cologne: Serling, 253.

24 "It's like a shitty pickup": Author interview with Gordon Bethune, December 2019.

24 Boeing pitted two engineering teams: The descriptions of the design are drawn from *747* by Joe Sutter (pp. 76–79) and *Boeing: The First Century* by Eugene Bauer (p. 183).

24 "the flying football": Sutter, *747*, 76.

25 Two handles on the floor: Most of the details about the 737's earliest iterations were drawn from Dan Dornseif's *Boeing 737: The World's Jetliner*. I also relied on a series of 1988 interviews with test pilots at the Museum of Flight in Seattle, compiled by Boeing and the museum into a DVD called *Boeing First Flights: The Jet Age.*

25 "'I know it's a big chunk'": Interview with Brien Wygle, *Boeing First Flights: The Jet Age,* Museum of Flight, May 3, 1988.

26 "overly sales-oriented operating management": Quoted in Leonard and Pilarski, "Overwhelmed by Success."

26 A self-proclaimed "practicing Scotsman": Ralph Vartabedian, "John McDonnell's Bumpy Ride: Pentagon Contracts Are Evaporating, Thousands Have Been Laid Off, the Competition Is Stepping Up the Pressure—Is the Family Heir the Right Man to Pilot McDonnell Douglas Through the Storm?" *Los Angeles Times,* December 1, 1991.

27 "You know, Bill": Serling, *Legend and Legacy,* 285.

27 "Sutter, do you realize": The accounts of 747 budget meetings in these pages are from Sutter, *747,* 143–48.

28 They built and tested: Dwight Bates, "'Incredible' Saga," March 2016, https://www.boeing.com.

28 "I told 'em point blank": Sutter, *747,* 115.

28 two months from running short: Rodgers, *Flying High,* 293.

29 "Guys were walking through": Author interview with Fred Mitchell, March 2020.

29 Boeing offered to sell: *Boeing First Flights,* May 3, 1988.

29 In 1972, just fourteen: Bauer, *Boeing,* 186.

2. MEA CULPA

30 Debris was scattered: Moira Johnston, *The Last Nine Minutes: The Story of Flight 981,* 100.

30 At a stockholders' meeting: Harold Evans, *Good Times, Bad Times,* 31; Johnston, *Last Nine Minutes,* 199.

31 "It was high summer": Glenn C. Graber and Christopher D. Pionke, "DC-10 Problems: Whose Responsibility?" University of Tennessee.

31 "The press, too": Johnston, *Last Nine Minutes,* 220.

31 A federal judge: Douglas B. Feaver, "Possible Design Problem Grounds All U.S. DC-10s," *Washington Post,* June 7, 1979.

31 The plane was the first: PowerPoint presentation by Peter Morton, "757/767 Flight Deck Evolution," November 2017.

32 Over lunch at the Jolly Boy: Author interview with Peter Morton, January 2020.

32 "Votre EICAS": PowerPoint presentation by Morton.

33 "I know who the hell": Author interview with anonymous former Boeing executive, March 2020.

33 During a party: Eric L. Flom, "Wilson, T.A. (1921–1999)," *HistoryLink.org,* April 30, 2006.

33 The Boeing chief was well paid: "For 12 Executives, '78 Was a $1 Million Year," *New York Times,* May 5, 1979.

33 But Wilson had little use: The personality traits of the former Boeing CEO are drawn from author interviews with former Boeing executives and Andrew Pollack, "Putting Boeing in a Class by Itself," *New York Times,* September 8, 1985.

34 The Seattle plane maker surprised: Richard Witkin, "Boeing Says Repairs on Japanese 747 Were Faulty," *New York Times,* September 8, 1985.

34 "the most honest, reputable": Author interview with Gordon Bethune, December 2019.

35 "We are fighting": Quoted in Mark A. Lorell, "Multinational Development of Large Aircraft: The European Experience," Rand Corporation, July 1980.

35 "the biggest foreign penetration": Richard Witkin, "Eastern Accepts $778 Million Deal to Get 23 Airbuses," *New York Times,* April 7, 1978.

35 When a McDonnell Douglas: John Newhouse, *The Sporty Game,* 206.

35 "went to the White House": Author interview with C. Fred Bergsten, December 2017.

35 Prices at the time: Thomas Petzinger Jr., *Hard Landing: The Epic Contest for Power and Profits That Plunged the Airlines into Chaos,* 65.

36 unique flat-tire look: Dan Dornseif, *Boeing 737: The World's Jetliner,* 111.

36 Internal forecasts: Dornseif, 121.

36 United had been reducing: Robert J. Serling, *Legend and Legacy: The Story of Boeing and Its People,* 402.

37 The A320, by contrast: Kevin Michaels, *Aerodynamic: Inside the High-Stakes Global Jetliner Ecosystem,* 217; Chris Clearfield and Andras Tilcsik, *Meltdown: What Plane Crashes, Oil Spills, and Dumb Business Decisions Can Teach Us About How to Succeed at Work and Home,* 89.

37 By 2019, Airbus estimated: "Loss of Control In-flight (LOC-1) Accident Rates," *A Statistical Analysis of Commercial Aviation Accidents 1958–2019,* Airbus, 2019, https://accidentstats.airbus.com.

37 "The 757 would sell": Peter Rinearson, "Making It Fly: The Boeing 757," *Seattle Times,* June 19–26, 1983.

38 "Sutter had a hate": Author interview with anonymous former Boeing executive, February 2020.

38 On the first occasion: Joe Sutter, *747: Creating the World's First Jumbo Jet and Other Adventures from a Life in Aviation,* 247.

38 "In the aviation industry": Quoted in Pollack, "Putting Boeing in a Class."

39 In spring 1988: *Boeing First Flights: The Jet Age,* Museum of Flight, May 3, 1988.

39 The runt of Boeing's fleet: Serling, *Legend and Legacy,* 401.

39 It lacked a device: Byron Acohido, "Safety at Issue: The 737," *Seattle Times,* October 27, 1996.

39 "We believe the airplane": Quoted in Jon Hilkevitch, "U.S. Panel Questions Safety of 737s," *Chicago Tribune,* March 24, 1999.

3. "JACK WELCH, LOOK OUT"

40 He was an only child: My portrait of Phil Condit is drawn from the following sources: Karen West, "Condit at the Controls," *Seattle Post-Intelligencer,* November 11, 1993; Polly Lane, "Phil Condit: Taking Boeing's Controls," *Seattle Times,* April 28, 1996; Stanley Holmes, "Boeing: What Really Happened," *BusinessWeek,* December 14, 2003; and interviews with former Boeing executives.

41 "good on people skills": Quoted in Eugene Rodgers, *Flying High: The Story of Boeing and the Rise of the Jetliner Industry,* 420.

41 Boeing didn't have its first: Polly Lane, "Boeing's Top Female Executive Resigns," *Seattle Times,* June 19, 1992.

41 In the 1970s: Steve Wilhelm, "100 Years of Male Domination Not Yet Over at Boeing, New Book Says," *Puget Sound Business Journal,* October 16, 2015.

42 The highlight was always Tuesday: Author interviews with anonymous former Boeing executives, February 2020; Lane, "Phil Condit."

42 A mid-1990s internal analysis: John Newhouse, *Boeing Versus Airbus: The Inside Story of the Greatest International Competition in Business,* 126.

43 "I *hate* this new": Author interview with Stan Sorscher, November 2019.

44 Teams of lawyers: Karl Sabbagh, *Twenty-First-Century Jet: The Making and Marketing of the Boeing 777,* 53.

44 "In order to launch": Rodgers, *Flying High,* 423.

45 no room on the corporate jet: Author interview with anonymous former Boeing executive, June 2020.

45 Mulally always projected: Sabbagh, *Twenty-First-Century Jet,* 161.

45 When his temper flared: Author interview with anonymous former Boeing engineer, November 2019.

45 "Accountability is huge": Author interview with anonymous former Boeing executive, May 2020.

46 "No expense was spared": Author interview with Akshay Sharma, July 2019.

46 every person there: Author interview with Paul Russell, December 2019.

46 "My first project": Author interview with Kenneth Schroer, March 2019.

48 Bethune guaranteed that: The descriptions of the 737 Next Generation models come from Dan Dornseif's *Boeing 737: The World's Jetliner* (pp. 141–43) and from my interview with Fred Mitchell in March 2020.

49 A quirky strain: Colin Leinster, "The Odd Couple at McDonnell Douglas," *Fortune,* June 22, 1987.

49 "The Five Keys": Vartabedian, "John McDonnell's Bumpy Ride," *Los Angeles Times,* December 1, 1991.

50 "I sent mine back": Vartabedian.

50 "Our investment is only": Steven Greenhouse, "Dicey Days at McDonnell Douglas," *New York Times,* February 22, 1987.

51 The bitter joke: Richard W. Stevenson, "Breathing Easier at McDonnell Douglas," *New York Times,* September 29, 1991.

51 Some did exactly: Author interview with anonymous former Boeing executive, March 2020.

51 The classes put them through: Vartabedian, "John McDonnell's Bumpy Ride."

51 "We were fragged": Vartabedian.

51 Most of the nine: David J. Lynch, "Flying Out of Turmoil—McDonnell Douglas Is Beginning to Recuperate from Dramatic Change, But Challenges Still Ahead," *Orange County Register,* August 4, 1991.

51 "Where is everybody?": Author interview with Rick Caldwell, October 2019.

51 began their first tentative: Newhouse, *Boeing Versus Airbus,* 134.

52 Stonecipher, then fifty-eight: Author interview with anonymous source, June 2020.

52 The force of nature: My description of Harry Stonecipher is drawn from Jonathan R. Laing, "Taking Flight: A No-Nonsense CEO and the Promise

of the 7E7 Have Boeing Climbing Again," *Wall Street Journal,* July 5, 2004; Patricia Callahan, "So Why Does Harry Stonecipher Think He Can Turn Around Boeing?" *Chicago Tribune,* February 29, 2004; and interviews with former Boeing executives and other anonymous sources.

53 "Tell me what": Callahan, "So Why Does Harry."

54 "Although production of": Quoted in Edward Wyatt, "A Winning Formula: Forget Timing, Forget Technology," *New York Times,* May 28, 1995.

54 Stonecipher in 1996: Newhouse, *Boeing Versus Airbus,* 136.

54 They wrote down four: Callahan, "So Why Does Harry."

55 "like a couple of cats": Eugene E. Bauer, *Boeing: The First Century,* 325.

55 "And rightly so!": Jerry Useem, "Boeing vs. Boeing," *Fortune,* October 2, 2000.

55 GE met or beat: David Henry, "SEC Fines GE $50 Million for Accounting Misdeeds," Bloomberg, August 4, 2009.

55 Welch was an innovator: Bryan Gruley, Rick Clough, and Polly Mosendz, "GE's Larry Culp Faces Ultimate CEO Test in Trying to Save a Once-Great Company," *Bloomberg Businessweek,* June 12, 2019.

55 The unit might sell: Thomas Gryta and Ted Mann, "GE Powered the American Century—Then It Burned Out," *Wall Street Journal,* December 14, 2018.

55 GE workers finishing: Bill Lane, *Losing It! Behaviors and Mindsets That Ruin Careers: Lessons on Protecting Yourself from Avoidable Mistakes,* 40.

55 "bent the accounting rules": In paying the $50 million fine, GE neither admitted nor denied the SEC's allegations. The four violations cited by the SEC: "Beginning in January 2003, an improper application of the accounting standards to GE's commercial paper funding program to avoid unfavorable disclosures and an estimated approximately $200 million pre-tax charge to earnings; a 2003 failure to correct a misapplication of financial accounting standards to certain GE interest-rate swaps; in 2002 and 2003, reported end-of-year sales of locomotives that had not yet occurred in order to accelerate more than $370 million in revenue; and in 2002, an improper change to GE's accounting for sales of commercial aircraft engines' spare parts that increased GE's 2002 net earnings by $585 million." U.S. Securities and Exchange Commission, "SEC Charges General Electric with Accounting Fraud," August 4, 2009.

56 "giddy school kids": Bauer, *Boeing,* 325.

56 "Gosh, I guess": Bauer, *Boeing,* 325.

56 Woodard told people: His quotes are from an August 11, 2016, interview for the Boeing 100 Voices Oral History Project Collection, Museum of History & Industry, Seattle.

57 "If the merger": Newhouse, *Boeing Versus Airbus,* 135.

57 "McDonnell Douglas has bought": Author interview with Larry Clarkson, February 2020.

57 T. told at least: Author interviews with anonymous former Boeing executives, 2020.

4. HUNTER KILLER ASSASSINS

58   "About half": Knute Berger, "The Burden of the 787," *Crosscut*, January 18, 2011.

58   "What you had": Leon Grunberg and Sarah Moore, *Emerging from Turbulence: Boeing and Stories of the American Workplace Today*, 33.

58   In a parking lot: Author interview with former Boeing engineer Cynthia Cole, March 2021.

59   In the information: I obtained a copy of a January 9, 1998, email summarizing a staff meeting led by Gary Hart, manager of Information & Communication Systems, Business Resources. Hart "shared that Heritage McDonnell has been using a '5/15' (five minutes to read, fifteen minutes or less to write) status reporting method. He asked his staff to use this method . . ."

59   One quirk Stonecipher: Author interview with Peter Morton, January 2020.

59   He laminated: Jeff Cole, "Two Share Cockpit as Boeing Works to Tighten Controls," *Wall Street Journal*, December 1, 1999. In a later telling, the laminated card is four-by-six and he carries it in his briefcase (Callahan, "So Why Does Harry Stonecipher Think He Can Turn Around Boeing?," *Chicago Tribune*, February 29, 2004).

59   Stonecipher actually made: Callahan.

59   "Michael Eisner, for all": Richard Aboulafia, letter, April 2005, http://www.richardaboulafia.com.

59   After a months-long: John Newhouse, *Boeing Versus Airbus: The Inside Story of the Greatest International Competition in Business*, 137.

60   Managers there always: Author interview with Fred Mitchell, March 2020.

61   In Stonecipher's first appearance: Author interviews with anonymous former Boeing executives.

61   That day in Boca: Robert Slater, *Jack Welch and the GE Way: Management Insights and Leadership Secrets of the Legendary CEO*, 289.

62   "First he's going to": Author interview with Gordon Bethune, December 2019.

62   Whenever Stonecipher said: Author interview with anonymous source, June 2020.

62   "Phil was a mouse": Author interview with anonymous former Boeing executive, February 2020.

63   Obediently, Condit called: Sources for the description of this episode: Author interviews with anonymous former Boeing executives; Jerry Useem, "Boeing vs. Boeing," *Fortune*, October 2, 2000; Jeff Cole, "Boeing's Cultural Revolution—Shaken Giant Surrenders Big Dreams for the Bottom Line," *Seattle Times*, December 13, 1998.

63   "Tell them not": Useem, "Boeing vs. Boeing."

63   "CFO???": Roy Harris, "New Boeing CFO: Fearless in Seattle," *CFO*, April 1, 1999.

63 "Do you have any": Author interview with anonymous source, June 2020.

64 "Have you ever seen": Peter Robison, "New Cost-Cutter Shakes Up Boeing with Tough Financial Standards," Bloomberg, January 24, 2000.

64 At the Boeing management retreat: Peter Robison, "Boeing's Condit Warned Managers Jetmaker Could Face a Takeover," Bloomberg, February 5, 1999; Jeff Cole, "New Boeing CFO's Assignment: Signal a Turnaround Quickly," *Wall Street Journal*, January 26, 1999.

64 "I was comfortable": Author interview with Richard Glasebrook, April 2021.

64 "It has not gone": This is from a transcript of the Senior Finance Managers' meeting on May 4, 1999, later distributed to employees.

65 "You dumb": Author interview with anonymous former Boeing executive, March 2020.

66 The important thing: Quoted in Robison, "New Cost-Cutter."

66 Condit at first: Author interview with former Boeing executive Larry Clarkson, February 2020.

67 As a consolation: Author interview with former Lazy B union president Wayne Ridenour, December 2020.

67 At first, engineers: Author interviews with former Boeing employees.

67 Miscommunications led: Peter Robison, "Boeing-Buffett Training Venture Draws Some Complaints," Bloomberg, January 24, 1999.

68 The company was also: Author interview with Cynthia Cole, former Speea president, May 2019.

68 It didn't help: The account of the dispute over the "correction action memo" given to Stan Sorscher comes from author interviews with Sorscher, November 2019, and from records of the complaint before the National Labor Relations Board, Region 19, Boeing and Seattle Professional Engineering Employees Association, Case 19-CA-26679, formerly 27-CA-16562-1.

69 late in 1999: The conversation with Dagnon was described by Morton in an author interview, January 2020. Morton also discussed it during an interview with Delmar Fadden, another former flight deck engineer, for the Boeing 100 Voices Project, Museum of History & Industry, Seattle, May 16, 2016.

69 On the morning: Bill Dugovich, "Stan Sorscher, Longtime Union Activist, Retires," SPEEA IFPTE Local 2001, Monthly Publication, December 2019.

69 The difference in money: Peter Robison, "Boeing Engineer Leaves Picket Lines—for Microsoft," Bloomberg, March 3, 2000.

70 "We're concerned": Robison.

70 Others told university professors: Peter Robison, "Boeing's Mulally Urges Strikes to Stop 'Malicious' Attacks," Bloomberg, March 15, 2000.

70 Three federal mediators: Author interview with Cynthia Cole, May 2019.

70 In late February: The account of Speea's salon at the Silverado is drawn from author interviews with Stan Sorscher (November 2019), Byron Callan (August 2020), Joe Campbell (October 2020), Charles Bofferding (March 2021), and Richard Glasebrook (April 2021).

71 "We're going after": This phrasing is in Sorscher's recollection. In Bofferding's

memory, he brought up the potential loss of the production certificate as a natural consequence if the striking workers didn't return soon: "If this keeps up, Boeing could lose its production certificate."

73 The episode had cost: Author interviews with Stan Sorscher, Cynthia Cole, and Charles Bofferding, 2019 and 2021.

5. *"EVERYBODY* THINKS THEY'RE DIFFERENT"

75 "All of us have": Sam Howe Verhovek, "Tentative Pact Made to End Boeing Strike," *New York Times,* March 18, 2000.

75 In private, he had: Author interview with anonymous former Boeing executive, May 2020.

75 Using the metaphor: Clayton M. Christensen, Michael Raynor, and Matthew Verlinden, "Skate to Where the Money Will Be," HBR OnPoint, *Harvard Business Review,* November 1, 2001.

76 white roses: Jerry Useem, "Boeing vs. Boeing," *Fortune,* October 2, 2000.

76 Condit began using: Author interview with anonymous former Boeing executive, June 2020.

77 "It's more of": Bryan Corliss, "Boeing's Star Turn," *HeraldNet,* November 14, 2000.

78 It had a master: Sandy Angers, "Number of Orders for Boeing Business Jet Hits Triple Digits," Boeing Frontiers, December 2005/January 2006, https://www.boeing.com.

78 "The BBJ lets": "Boeing Business Jets Debuts at Farnborough 2000," July 24, 2000, https://boeing.mediaroom.com.

78 A partner company: Jeff Cole, "Group Devises Showers for Airliners, But Will Fliers Accept Recycled Water?" *Wall Street Journal,* August 4, 2000; Tom Buerkle, "Boeing Backs Start-Up's Project: In-Flight Shower: Ultimate Perk?" *International Herald Tribune,* July 31, 2000.

78 It was a startup: The corporate filings of Knowledge Training LLC are available at the Washington State Office of the Secretary of State, Corporations & Charities Division, https://ccfs.sos.wa.gov.

78 "I only regret": Author interview with anonymous former Boeing executive, June 2020.

78 "It was a golden": Author interview with anonymous former Boeing executive, June 2020.

78 "Any rewards I got": Author interviews with Granville Frazier, May 2020 and April 2021.

79 Late in the summer: Peter Robison, "Boeing Picks Chicago for New Base, Leaving Seattle," Bloomberg, May 10, 2001.

79 "Headquarters is supposed": Steve Wilhelm, "Phil Condit, Who Took Boeing to Chicago, Reflects on How a Different Home Changed the Company," *Puget Sound Business Journal,* June 17, 2011.

79 The secret had been: Kyung M. Song, "New Boeing Job Tests Watt's Power; Ex-City Official Takes on Tough Task of Rehabilitating Company's Image," *Seattle Times,* February 10, 2002.

79 The executive that Condit: Interview with James T. (Jim) Johnson, Boeing 100 Voices Project, Museum of History & Industry, Seattle, May 24, 2016.

80 "Where's Phil?": Jeff Cole, "Boeing's Cultural Revolution—Shaken Giant Surrenders Big Dreams for the Bottom Line," *Seattle Times,* December 13, 1998.

80 He spent the equivalent: Peter Robison, "Boeing to Move Corporate Headquarters from Seattle," Bloomberg, March 21, 2001.

80 "As long as": Robison.

80 "We're going to Chicago": "Boeing Officials Land in Chicago," *Chicago Tribune,* May 10, 2001.

80 The Boeing World Headquarters: Stanley Ziemba, "Morton Thiokol Moving Headquarters to W. Loop," *Chicago Tribune,* September 14, 1988.

81 Boeing's new, supposedly "leaner": Boeing, *Boeing World Headquarters: Our Home in Chicago,* 2003.

81 "big, hairy, audacious": James C. Collins and Jerry I. Porras, *Built to Last,* 91.

81 "If in fact": Useem, "Boeing vs. Boeing."

82 suspicious lack of: Peter Robison, "Boeing Pushes New Plane and Analysts Ask: What About Windows?" Bloomberg, May 31, 2001.

83 "We're number two": Author interview with anonymous former Boeing executive, June 2020.

83 "There is the question": Quoted in J. Lynn Lunsford, "Losing Ground to Airbus, Boeing Faces a Key Choice, *Wall Street Journal,* April 21, 2003.

83 The analysis found: John Newhouse, *Boeing Versus Airbus,* 200.

83 His legacy also: Caroline Cole, "Winging It at Boeing's Leadership Center," *Workforce.com,* September 29, 2000.

84 "every bell and whistle": Quoted in Peter Robison, "Boeing's Harry Stonecipher Leaves, Testing New Company Culture," Bloomberg, May 31, 2002.

84 "Very functional": Peter Robison, "Boeing CFO Gets Thrills from Takeoff in Stock, Not Just Planes," Bloomberg, August 28, 2000.

84 "a math guy": Robison.

84 They told fellow: Lunsford, "Losing Ground to Airbus."

85 Among those circulating: Stanley Holmes, "Getting In on Boeing's Name Game," *BusinessWeek,* June 1, 2003.

85 Dissidents inside Boeing: L. J. Hart-Smith, "Out-Sourced Profits—the Cornerstone of Successful Subcontracting," Boeing Third Annual Technical Excellence Symposium, February 14–15, 2001.

86 One executive raised: Author interview with anonymous former Boeing executive, June 2020.

86 At the air force: George Cahlink, "Fallen Star: The Cautionary Tale of a Celebrated Federal Executive's Corporate Flameout," *Government Executive,* February 1, 2004.

86 "I was hired to win": Anne Marie Squeo and Andy Pasztor, "U.S. Probes Whether Boeing Misused a Rival's Documents," *Wall Street Journal,* May 5, 2003.

87 He sent an email: United States of America v. Michael M. Sears, United States District Court for the Eastern District of Alexandria, Criminal No. 04-310-A.

87 Druyun ultimately confessed: United States of America v. Darleen A. Druyun, United States District Court for the Eastern District of Alexandria, Criminal No. 04-150-A.

87 "She immediately went": Stanley Holmes, "Boeing: What Really Happened," *BusinessWeek,* December 14, 2003.

88 An internal analysis: Dominic Gates, "Boeing Celebrates 787 Delivery as Program's Costs Top $32 Billion," *Seattle Times,* September 24, 2011.

88 "When people say": Patricia Callahan, "So Why Does Harry Stonecipher Think He Can Turn Around Boeing?" *Chicago Tribune,* February 29, 2004.

88 As Boeing ramped: Report to Congress of the U.S.-China Economic and Security Review Commission, November 2005, http://www.uscc.gov.

88 "In the old days": Maureen Tkacik, "Crash Course: How Boeing's Managerial Revolution Created the 737 MAX Disaster," *New Republic,* September 18, 2019.

89 When they reached: Karl Sabbagh, *Twenty-First-Century Jet: The Making and Marketing of the Boeing 777,* 162.

89 At his wit's end: Klaus Brauer tells the story, up to the inflatable gorilla, for the Boeing 100 Voices Project, Museum of History & Industry, Seattle, May 31, 2016.

90 The chemistry was: Author interview with anonymous former Boeing executive, June 2020.

91 "His team is": Author interview with anonymous former Boeing executive, June 2020.

91 He'd been on Boeing's board: Author interview with anonymous source, June 2020.

91 This time the board: Julie Creswell, "Pay Packages Allow Executives to Jump Ship with Less Risk," *New York Times,* December 29, 2006.

91 "It wasn't even": Author interview with anonymous former board member, June 2020.

91 The influential recruiter: Peter Robison and James Gunsalus, "Boeing Stock, Orders Soar as McNerney Fights Legacy of Missteps," Bloomberg, May 26, 2006.

91 "The mere mention": Brian Hindo, "3M: Struggle Between Efficiency and Creativity," *BusinessWeek,* September 17, 2007.

92 "the board couldn't take": Author interview with anonymous former Boeing executive, March 2020.

92 "If you hire": Author interview with anonymous former Boeing executive, June 2020.

92 "Let's say we": Quoted in Robison and Gunsalus, "Boeing Stock, Orders Soar."

92 The chart showed: Author interview with anonymous former Boeing executive, October 2020.

93 Within a day: Author interview with anonymous former Boeing executive, June 2020.

93 "The idealism just": Author interview with anonymous former Boeing executive, June 2020.

93 The supplier was planning: Michael Leon v. Securaplane Technologies Inc., U.S. Department of Labor, Case No. 2008-AIR-00012.

94 When firefighters arrived: Carli Brosseau, "2006 Fire Under NTSB scrutiny," *Arizona Daily Star,* January 27, 2013.

6. THE CORPORATE PLAYBOOK

95 "He liked to": Judith Crown, "Jet Setter," *Chicago,* May 27, 2007.

95 "A sizable unmet need": Recommendations of the Task Force on Medicaid and Related Programs, Department of Health, Education, and Welfare, 1970, https://www.ssa.gov.

96 "Because of his drive": Charles S. Lauer, "Remembering a Renaissance Man; Walter McNerney Left a Legacy in Administration, Education and Policy," *Modern Healthcare,* August 15, 2005.

96 "Whatever you do": Crown, "Jet Setter."

96 Downy and Bounce: Julie Dunn, "Private Sector; This Time, Keys to the Executive Washroom," *New York Times,* March 16, 2003.

96 "Take a look": Thomas F. O'Boyle, *At Any Cost: Jack Welch, General Electric, and the Pursuit of Profit,* 68.

97 Welch had admired: O'Boyle, 68.

97 "We have the commitment": Jack Welch, *Jack: Straight from the Gut,* 451.

98 The Hollywood star toured: O'Boyle, *At Any Cost,* 26.

98 The week before: The AFL-CIO meeting at the White House is recounted in Joseph A. McMartin, *Collision Course: Ronald Reagan, the Air Traffic Controllers, and the Strike That Changed America,* 320–25.

99 "Ideally, you'd have": Interview with Lou Dobbs, *CNN Moneyweek,* December 13, 1998.

99 In a dizzying: Harry Bernstein, "2 Faces of GE's 'Welchism': One Dr. Jekyll, One Mr. Hyde," *Los Angeles Times,* January 12, 1988.

99 The deregulatory fervor: John H. Cushman Jr., "Safety in the Sky: Where the Gaps Are—A Special Report; F.A.A. Staggers Under Task of Monitoring Airline Safety," *New York Times,* February 13, 1990.

99 The tax rate: David Wessel, "What We Learned from Reagan's Tax Cuts," Brookings, December 8, 2017.

99 "stock buybacks have channeled": William Lazonick, "The Curse of Stock Buybacks," *American Prospect,* June 25, 2018.

100 McNerney impressed him: Peter Robison and James Gunsalus, "Boeing Stock,

Orders Soar as McNerney Fights Legacy of Missteps," Bloomberg, May 26, 2006.

100 "We're taking a different": O'Boyle, *At Any Cost,* 9.

100 "GE screwed him up": Author interview with anonymous recruitment consultant, September 2020.

100 "Jack got outlandish": Crown, "Jet Setter."

101 From 1994 to 2004: The figures are drawn from the company's December 10, 2004, release on Business Wire: "Since 1994, GE has returned more than $75 billion to shareowners through dividends and the repurchase of more than 1.1 billion shares." GE reported $134.19 billion in free cash flow in annual filings from 1994 to 2004.

101 Welch left with: "Top 10 Largest CEO Severance Packages of the Past Decade," *Forbes,* January 19, 2012.

101 "This guy looks half-dead!": Welch, *Jack,* 163.

101 Just after Thanksgiving: Welch, 426.

101 He got $34 million: Julie Creswell, "Pay Packages Allow Executives to Jump Ship with Less Risk," *New York Times,* December 29, 2006.

102 He did it by: The figures are from Brian Hindo, "3M: Struggle Between Efficiency and Creativity," *BusinessWeek,* September 17, 2007.

102 "We should be": U.S. Equal Employment Opportunity Commission, "3M to Pay $3 Million to Settle EEOC Age Discrimination Suit," August 22, 2011.

102 "What's remarkable is": Hindo, "3M: Struggle Between Efficiency."

102 McNerney won praise: "Boeing CEO Apologizes for Lapses, Scandals," NBC News, August 1, 2006.

103 "These are not ZIP": Dominic Gates and Alicia Mundy, "Boeing Lawyer Warns of Company's Legal Peril," *Seattle Times,* January 31, 2006.

103 The answer came: These events are described in United States of America, ex. rel. Edward Quintana vs. The Boeing Company, United States District Court for the Western District of Texas, No. SA-06-CA-1029-FB.

103 Justice Department later joined: "Boeing to Pay $2 million over Whistleblower Claims," *Seattle Times,* August 11, 2009.

103 In the year McNerney: The figures are from the Center for Responsive Politics, https://www.opensecrets.org.

103 "We used to have": Author interview with anonymous former Boeing executive, June 2020.

103 "We are right": Steve Harding, "Army Demonstrates Future Combat Systems," *Army News Service,* September 28, 2005.

103 Four years later: Mark Thompson, "The Army's Lousy Tracked Record," Project on Government Oversight, March 16, 2020, https://www.pogo.org.

103 "I think this program": Thompson.

104 "There wasn't a lot": Don Tapscott and Anthony C. Williams, *Wikinomics: How Mass Collaboration Changes Everything,* 226.

104 One major supplier: Michael Hiltzik, "787 Dreamliner Teaches Boeing Costly Lesson on Outsourcing," *Los Angeles Times,* February 15, 2011.

104 At a meeting with top: Author interview with Cynthia Cole, former Speea president, May 2019.

104 Managers hadn't thought: Author interview with Cynthia Cole, March 2021.

105 McNerney finally had to: Jon Ostrower, "At Boeing, Innovation Means Small Steps, Not Giant Leaps," *Wall Street Journal,* April 2, 2015.

105 "I used to get calls": Author interview with Joe Campbell, October 2020.

105 The SEC later opened: Robert Schmidt, Julie Johnsson, and Matt Robinson, "Boeing to Face SEC Probe of Dreamliner and 747 Accounting," Bloomberg, February 11, 2016.

105 "We lost control": John Lippert and Susanna Ray, "Boeing Rally Raises Doubt Dreamliner Justifies Profit Estimate," Bloomberg, April 25, 2010.

105 "It was a real": Peter Sanders, "Boeing Brings in Old Hands, Gets an Earful," *Wall Street Journal,* July 19, 2010.

106 "He was pretty sure": Author interview with anonymous former Boeing executive, June 2020.

106 They'd have to spend $1.5 billion: Susanna Ray, "Boeing Papers Say 787 Plant Site Gave Upper Hand with Labor," Bloomberg, September 23, 2011.

106 Boeing got more than: "Boeing's Charleston Tax Break Tops $800M; 60 Years and Counting for Airplane Tax Break," *Seattle Times,* January 23, 2010.

106 Workers there would make: Danny Westneat, "Boeing, Machinists and Denial," *Seattle Times,* October 28, 2009.

107 Luttig was Republican royalty: Tom Schoenberg, Julie Johnsson, and Peter Robison, "Boeing Has Friends in High Places, Thanks to Its 737 Crash Czar," Bloomberg, July 20, 2019.

107 An online law journal: David Lat, "Supreme Court Shortlister Turned General Counsel Calls Out the Court (Plus Presidents and Congress Too)," *Above the Law,* May 8, 2017.

107 At a hearing: U.S. Senate Committee on Health, Education, Labor and Pensions, "Fairness for Employees? Harkin Questions Huge Pay Gap between Employees and Executives," May 12, 2011.

107 The previous May: David Lat, "Lawyerly Lairs: Luttig in Lap of Luxury (Plus Info About His Current Compensation)," *Above the Law,* July 27, 2010.

108 The profit on each: Benjamin Zhang, "Here's How Much Boeing Is Estimated to Make on Each 737," *Business Insider,* March 13, 2019.

109 One day in 2010: Author interview with anonymous former Boeing executive, March 2020.

109 Ryanair would later buy: David M. Ewalt, "Boeing Lands $15.6 Billion 737 Order from Ryanair," *Forbes,* March 19, 2013.

109 A backup fire extinguisher: Hiroko Tabuchi and David Gelles, "Doomed Boeing Jets Lacked 2 Safety Features That Company Sold Only as Extras," *New York Times,* March 21, 2019.

109 In another fateful: Thomas P. DiNapoli, comptroller of the state of New York, v. Boeing, in the Court of Chancery of the State of Delaware, Verified Stockholder Derivative Complaint, No. 2020-0465-AGB, June 30, 2020.

109 It reached the point: Author interview with John Leahy, May 2020.

110 Another design under consideration: Author interview with former Airbus executive, May 2020.

111 "I probably would have": Author interview with John Leahy, May 2020.

111 The airline was such an important: The account of the American Airlines order is based on author interviews with multiple industry executives with direct knowledge of the events.

112 Ryanair's O'Leary called: Avi Salzman, "Does Airbus Have the Edge over Boeing?" *Barron's*, May 16, 2011.

112 A small but telling: Author interview with anonymous industry executive, October 2020.

113 Albaugh predicted "quite a number": Jeremy Lemer and Mark Odell, "Customers Forced Boeing's Hand on New Engine Option," *Financial Times*, July 24, 2011.

114 "Instead, we have status quo": Lemer and Odell.

114 "Stingy with a purpose": Cited in Thomas P. DiNapoli, comptroller.

114 In a 2014 piece: Clayton M. Christensen and Derek van Bever, "The Capitalist's Dilemma," *Harvard Business Review*, June 2014.

115 "Safety was just a given": Douglas MacMillan, " 'Safety Was Just a Given': Inside Boeing's Boardroom amid the 737 Max Crisis," *Washington Post*, May 5, 2019.

7. THE FORREST GUMPS

117 Joe Sutter and other engineers: Joe Sutter, *747: Creating the World's First Jumbo Jet and Other Adventures from a Life in Aviation*, 68.

118 Reed started telling colleagues: Author interviews with Richard Reed, October and November 2019.

118 Hikers still come across: Alexis England, "60 Years Ago, 2 Planes Collided over the Grand Canyon and It Changed the World," *Arizona Republic*, June 30, 2016.

118 Employees began moving: Federal Aviation Administration, "A Brief History of the FAA," https://www.faa.gov.

118 In part citing cost: Stephen Mihm, "The FAA Has Always Played Cozy with the Aviation Industry," Bloomberg, March 21, 2019.

119 Among those the FAA: Federal Aviation Administration, Fact Sheet—FAA's Response to NTSB's "Most Wanted" Safety Recommendations, March 16, 2020, https://www.faa.gov.

119 "There was a direct": Author interview with Mike Collins, December 2019.

119 Five months after: Edwin Chen, "Gingrich Stresses Need to Remake Government: Address: Speaker Asks Public for Help in Solving Budget Problems. He Calls for 'New Birth of Freedom,'" *Los Angeles Times*, April 8, 1995.

120 That year, Thomas McSweeny: Terry McDermott, "Is the FAA Up to the

Job—A Question of Safety—Do Airplane Makers Dominate Regulators?" *Seattle Times,* June 4, 1995.

120 The "superior contribution increase": U.S. Department of Transportation, "FAA Reforms Have Not Achieved Expected Cost, Efficiency, and Modernization Outcomes," Office of Inspector General, Audit Report, January 15, 2016.

120 "earliest possible issuance": Federal Aviation Administration Aviation Rulemaking Advisory Committee, "Aircraft Certification Procedures Issue Area Delegation Systems Working Group, Task 1—Delegation Functions," *Federal Register,* June 19, 1998, https://www.faa.gov.

121 The influence war: Federal Aviation Administration, 2001 Aviation Rulemaking Advisory Committee meeting, Hyatt Regency Crystal City at Reagan National Airport, Washington, D.C., February 7, 2001, transcript available at https://www.faa.gov.

123 A native of Gadsden: Hearing Before the Committee on Commerce, Science, and Transportation, U.S. Senate, September 3, 2002, https://www.congress.gov/.

123 "I want to bring": Marion Blakey, "The Spirit of December 14th," Aero Club, Washington, D.C., February 20, 2003, https://www.faa.gov.

124 The formal rule: Establishment of Organization Designation Authorization Program, Federal Aviation Administration, *Federal Register,* October 13, 2005, https://www.federalregister.gov.

124 "The primary reason": Jim Morris and Frank Koughan, "Waiting to Happen: With Overseas Mechanics and Overstretched Inspectors, FAA Oversight of the Airlines Is an Accident . . . ," *Mother Jones,* July/August 2006.

124 "There is nothing": Hearing Before the Committee on Transportation and Infrastructure, House of Representatives, April 3, 2008, https://www.govinfo.gov.

125 It was the largest fine: Andy Pasztor, "Southwest's Cozy Ties Triggered FAA Assault," *Wall Street Journal,* April 3, 2008.

125 McSweeny left that same: Author interview with anonymous FAA official, November 2019.

125 Boeing offered more: Paul Lowe, "Former FAA Staffer Joins Boeing," *AIN Online,* October 9, 2007.

126 "From top down": Author interview with anonymous FAA official, November 2019.

126 "I've heard cash incentives": Author interview with Marc Ronell, November 2019.

126 In fiscal 2007: Federal Aviation Administration, 2007 AVS Business Plan, https://www.faa.gov.

127 Giving the lie: *Aircraft Certification "Transformation" Pre-Decisional Involvement Report: Union Recommendations and Dissenting Opinion,* National Air Traffic Controller Association, PASS, AFSCME, February 6, 2017.

127 "It was push, push": Author interview with Steve Foss, May 2019.

127   One senior manager: Author interview with anonymous former FAA manager, March 2019.

127   The fragmentation of responsibilities: Author interview with Ken Schroer, March 2021.

128   Early on, one: Author interviews with anonymous current and former FAA officials, 2019 and 2020.

128   "had not always supported": U.S. Department of Transportation, Office of Inspector General, memorandum, June 22, 2012, https://www.oig.dot.gov.

128   "There was nothing": House Committee on Transportation and Infrastructure, Interview of Ali Bahrami, December 5, 2019, https://transportation.house.gov, p. 114.

128   They suspected him: Author interviews with anonymous current and former FAA officials, 2019 and 2020.

129   "It speaks to": Author interview with anonymous FAA official, November 2019.

129   A week later: Monica Langley, "Chief of Embattled Boeing Steers Clear of the Spotlight," *Wall Street Journal,* February 22, 2013.

129   The agency's administrator: This account is drawn from interviews with Michael Huerta in September 2020 and with Ray LaHood in May 2020 and March 2021.

130   "Michael, it's my call": Author interview with Ray LaHood.

130   "I know you're not happy": Author interview with Ray LaHood.

130   The employees entrusted: National Transportation Safety Board, Office of Aviation Safety, Interim Factual Report, March 7, 2013, NTSB Case Number DCA13IA037.

130   "This wasn't rocket science": Author interview with anonymous FAA engineer, November 2019.

130   Documents submitted: Jad Mouawad, "Report on Boeing 787 Dreamliner Battery Flaws Finds Lapses at Multiple Points," *New York Times,* December 1, 2014.

131   "Would you feel comfortable": "Lessons Learned from the Boeing 787 Incidents," Hearing Before the Subcommittee on Aviation of the Committee on Transportation and Infrastructure, House of Representatives, June 12, 2013, https://www.govinfo.gov.

131   "They should be handling": "Review of FAA's Certification Process: Ensuring an Efficient, Effective, and Safe Process," Hearing Before the Subcommittee on Aviation of the Committee on Transportation and Infrastructure, House of Representatives, October 30, 2013, https://www.govinfo.gov.

131   "Our members have": "Review of FAA's Certification Process."

8. THE COUNTDOWN CLOCK

132   "fly the biggest piece": Author interview with Rick Ludtke, April 2019.

133   "Why does Boeing": Author interview with Stan Sorscher, November 2019.

133 Boeing had introduced: "White-Collar Union at Boeing Files Age-Bias Complaint," *Seattle Times,* July 24, 2014.

133 It echoed the strategy: U.S. Equal Employment Opportunity Commission, "3M to Pay $3 Million to Settle EEOC Age Discrimination Suit," press release, August 22, 2011.

134 "We no longer think": Interview with Jim McNerney, CEO, the Boeing Company, Harvard Business School, Alumni Interview Series, *The Harbus,* April 16, 2013.

134 "a bundle of compromises": Byron Acohido, "Safety at Issue: The 737," *Seattle Times,* October 30, 1996.

135 Boeing had computer software: Author interview with former Boeing engineer, September 2019.

135 After one early: Mike Barber, "MAXimum Performer: New 737 MAX Will Build upon a Legacy of Accomplishment and Success," *Boeing Frontiers,* December 2011/January 2012.

135 Whoever yelled loudest: Author interview with anonymous industry source, July 2019.

135 "We're going to make this": Barber, "MAXimum Performer."

135 a "countdown clock": Final Committee Report on the Design, Development and Certification of the Boeing 737 Max, House Committee on Transportation and Infrastructure, September 2020, https://transportation.house.gov, p. 17.

135 The program's chief engineer: House Committee on Transportation and Infrastructure, Interview of Michael Teal, May 11, 2020, https://transportation.house.gov, p. 13.

136 The 737 by then: Estimates by analysts including Goldman Sachs, Bank of America Merrill Lynch, and Melius Research were that the 737 accounted for between 33 percent and 40 percent of Boeing's profit. Melius analyst Carter Copeland estimated the 737 generated $1.8 billion a quarter in profit, 37 percent of Boeing's $19.6 billion 2018 gross profit. Cited in Peter Robison and Julie Johnsson, "Two 737 Max Crashes in Five Months Put Boeing's Reputation on the Line," *Bloomberg Businessweek,* March 13, 2019.

136 "It's a pig": Interview with anonymous former Boeing pilot, May 2020.

136 Boeing had promised: The $1 million–per–airplane promise was communicated to employees as a summary of the contract. In practice, the agreement stipulated that Boeing would pay Southwest $1 million per MAX airplane delivered if pilots were unable to operate the 737 NG and 737 MAX interchangeably for any reason. If the FAA required more than ten hours of pilot training and/or flight simulator training, Boeing also agreed to reimburse Southwest for any direct training expense greater than ten hours. Final Committee Report, p. 24.

137 Paying for pilots: "Alteon President Urges Aviation Training Industry to Lower Costs and Improve the Quality of Pilot Training," PR Newswire, Seattle, June 13, 2007.

137 "It's such a kludge": Author interview with Rick Ludtke, May 2019.

137 "I was saying, 'Guys' ": Author interview with Richard Reed, November 2019.

138 The MAX was actually: Final Committee Report, p. 5.

138 For marketing: "Boeing Introduces 737 MAX with Launch of New Aircraft Family," August 30, 2011, https://boeing.mediaroom.com.

138 Over the next two years: Final Committee Report, p. 47.

138 The proposal they sent: Dominic Gates, "Boeing Pushed FAA to Relax 737 MAX Certification Requirements for Crew Alerts," *Seattle Times,* October 2, 2019.

138 Early testing revealed: Dominic Gates, "The Inside Story of MCAS: How Boeing's 737 MAX System Gained Power and Lost Safeguards," *Seattle Times,* June 22, 2019; Jack Nicas et al., "Boeing Built Deadly Assumptions into 737 Max, Blind to a Late Design Change," *New York Times,* June 1, 2019.

139 Managers talked frequently: Author interviews with multiple anonymous former Boeing engineers and pilots.

140 Test pilots, for instance: Author interview with anonymous former Boeing pilot, May 2020.

140 At a budget meeting: Final Committee Report, p. 17.

140 one of a half dozen "risks": House Committee on Transportation and Infrastructure, Interview of Keith Leverkuhn, May 19, 2020, https://transportation .house.gov, p. 33.

140 They decided in June 2013: Final Committee Report, p. 92.

141 The FAA's deputies at Boeing: Final Committee Report, p. 100.

141 In 2014, Ewbank was among: Dominic Gates, Steve Miletich, and Lewis Kamb, "Boeing Rejected 737 MAX Safety Upgrades Before Fatal Crashes, Whistleblower Says," *Seattle Times,* October 2, 2019.

141 FAA records showed: Curt Devine and Drew Griffin, "Boeing Relied on Single Sensor for 737 Max That Had Been Flagged 216 Times to FAA," CNN, April 30, 2019.

141 "People have to die": Dominic Gates, "Boeing Whistleblower Alleges Systemic Problems with 737 MAX," *Seattle Times,* June 18, 2020.

142 he never even heard: House Committee, Interview of Keith Leverkuhn, p. 38.

142 "Dogs have fleas": Author interview with Naj Meshkati, professor of civil and environmental engineering, University of Southern California, October 2019.

142 "They were targeting": Author interview with Rick Ludtke, May 2019.

142 Overall, Boeing's workforce fell: Peter Robison, "Former Boeing Engineers Say Relentless Cost-Cutting Sacrificed Safety," *Bloomberg Businessweek,* May 8, 2019.

142 The climate didn't reward: Author interview with Mark Rabin, April 2019.

143 "Bill, you know we can't": William Hobek v. The Boeing Company, United States District Court of South Carolina, Charleston Division, Case No. 2:16-cv-3840-RMG.

143 caught some employees on tape: Will Jordan, "The Boeing 787: Broken Dreams," Al Jazeera, July 20, 2014.

144 The "more-for-less": Dominic Gates, "McNerney: No More 'Moonshots' as Boeing Develops New Jets," *Seattle Times,* May 22, 2014.

144 In a 2015 filing: Dominic Gates, "Boeing CEO's Compensation $29M, Including $14M Bonuses," *Seattle Times,* March 13, 2015.

144 McNerney himself made: The executive compensation was detailed in a lawsuit filed by Seafarers Pension Plan against Boeing and other top executives in the U.S. District Court for the Northern District of Illinois, 19-cv-08095, December 11, 2019.

144 Mondays at 6:30 a.m.: Author interviews with Greg Atchison, small group leader, Biblical Business Training, November 2017, and Brandon Mann, founder, Biblical Business Training, December 2017.

145 milked the cows: "Dennis A. Muilenburg, President, Chairman, and CEO, the Boeing Company, Discusses Boeing's Success, Leadership, and Bicycling" (Q&A transcript), Economic Club of Washington, D.C., May 9, 2018, https://www.economicclub.org.

145 Sioux Center's Dordt University: Jenna Johnson, "Donald Trump: 'They Say I Could 'Shoot Somebody' and Still Have Support," *Washington Post,* January 23, 2016.

145 He was one of the best: Author interview with Ted De Hoogh, June 2020.

146 In college at Iowa State: Author interview with Steve Haveman, June 2020.

146 He played pickup basketball: Dominic Gates, "Boeing's Budget Ax Falls on Popular Gym for Employees," *Seattle Times,* April 26, 2017.

146 When his career ascent: Dennis Muilenburg, remarks at "What's Next?" tech summit, Chicago, October 4–5, 2016, https://www.theatlantic.com.

147 "When I daydream": "Battle of the X-Planes," *Nova,* PBS, February 4, 2003, https://www.pbs.org.

147 By the mid-2000s, Muilenburg's picture: Author interview with anonymous former Boeing executive, July 2020.

147 With his blond: Robert Wright and Peggy Hollinger, "New Boeing CEO Dennis Muilenburg Eyes Jet Production Challenge," *Financial Times,* June 24, 2015.

147 In his own supplier squeeze: Julie Johnsson and Peter Robison, "Boeing Is Killing It by Squeezing Its Suppliers," *Bloomberg Businessweek,* February 14, 2018.

148 "How long do you want": Robison, "Former Boeing Engineers."

148 "Idea's [*sic*] are measured": Robison.

148 "That culture is new": Author interview with Adam Dickson, November 2019.

148 Boeing was in the midst: The rudder cable and fuel pump issues are laid out in a statement by Michael Collins to the House Committee on Transportation and Infrastructure on December 11, 2019.

149 Boeing surveyed the FAA: Final Committee Report, p. 165.

9. HUMAN FACTORS

151 Forkner's group reported: Julie Johnsson and Peter Robison, "Boeing Is Killing It by Squeezing Its Suppliers," *Bloomberg Businessweek,* February 14, 2018.

151 "I just like airplanes": Dominic Gates, "Beyond Pilot Trash Talk, 737 MAX Documents Reveal How Intensely Boeing Focused on Cost," *Seattle Times,* January 10, 2020.

151 One person who served: Author interview with anonymous former Boeing employee, November 2020.

151 Forkner was such a fan: Author interview with anonymous former Boeing pilot, May 2020.

152 "It's like swapping fries": Justin Wastnage, "Interview with Sherry Carbary, President of Alteon Training," *FlightGlobal,* March 13, 2007.

152 Carbary wasn't a pilot: The descriptions come from author interviews with multiple former Boeing pilots.

153 After a visit: Author interview with anonymous former Boeing pilot, May 2020.

153 One high-ranking Boeing executive: Author interview with anonymous former Boeing executive, July 2020.

153 "We felt like shortcuts": Author interview with Charlie Clayton, December 2019.

153 "You're giving us too many": Author interview with Mike Coker, December 2019.

153 "We're not going to have": Author interview with anonymous former Boeing pilot, November 2019.

153 Others talked about: Author interview with anonymous former Boeing pilot, November 2020.

154 The building was shopworn: Author interview with anonymous former Boeing pilot, October 2019.

154 One longtime airline pilot: Author interview with anonymous former Boeing pilot, November 2019.

155 Behind an innocuous-looking: Boeing, "737 Max E-cab Construction Underway," June 25, 2014, https://www.boeing.com/features/2014/06/bca-737max -ecab-06-25-14.page.

156 "right at first flight": Boeing, "The 'e-cab': A Test Flight Deck," November 30, 2015, http://www.boeing.com/commercial/737max/news/the-e-cab -a-test-flight-deck.page.

156 "With all the inexperience": "Boeing Emails Handed Over."

156 "dogs watching TV": "Boeing 737 MAX."

156 When someone wrote: "Boeing 737 MAX," Hearing, p. 228.

156 Forkner got nervous enough: House Committee on Transportation and Infrastructure, Interview of Michael Teal, May 11, 2020, https://transportation .house.gov, p. 17.

156 "new interpretations of existing": House Committee, Interview of Michael Teal, p. 17.

157 they'd forgotten to set: Author interviews with anonymous former Boeing pilots.

157 In one 2006 test: Jeff Wise, "Introducing the Airplane of the Future," *Popular Mechanics,* June 5, 2006.

157 Once, one of the Boeing trainers: Author interview with anonymous former Boeing pilot, May 2020.

158 A month after: House Committee, Interview of Michael Teal, p. 26.

158 In the back: Boeing offered a tour of a similar airplane—the 737 MAX 7—outfitted with test equipment at the 2018 Farnborough Air Show and broadcast it live on Facebook. See the Boeing Company, "Tour of the 737 MAX 7 Test Airplane," www.facebook.com.

159 The pilots told Teal: House Committee, Interview of Michael Teal, p. 83.

159 "All changes are minimal": Final Committee Report on the Design, Development and Certification of the Boeing 737 Max, House Committee on Transportation and Infrastructure, September 2020, https://transportation.house.gov, p. 111.

159 The same day Leverkuhn and Teal: Final Committee Report, pp. 100 and 119.

159 To his boss Leverkuhn: House Committee, p. 70.

160 So the chief pilot: The actions taken to investigate failure scenarios of MCAS are described in Joint Authorities Technical Review of the Boeing 737 MAX Flight Control System, Observations, Findings, and Recommendations, October 11, 2019, p. 33; House Committee, Interview of Keith Leverkuhn, p. 66.

160 "What happens when": Final Committee Report, p. 110.

160 "I don't think": Final Committee Report, p. 100.

161 "There had been an issue": House Committee on Transportation and Infrastructure, Interview of Keith Leverkuhn, May 19, 2020, p. 32.

161 "We're not leading the market": Interview with Steve Taylor, Boeing 100 Voices Project, Museum of History & Industry, Seattle, June 3, 2016.

161 "Okay, Sean": Interview with Suzanna Darcy-Henneman, Boeing 100 Voices Project, Museum of History & Industry, Seattle, May 27, 2016.

162 That August of 2016: Tee times at Boeing Classic Korean Air Pro-Am, 7:45 AM Shotgun Start, August 23, 2016, http://www.boeingclassic.com.

162 On August 15, 2016: Boeing Response to Question 7 and Related Questions, House Committee on Transportation and Infrastructure, https://transportation.house.gov.

163 One salesperson wrote: Boeing provided additional emails to the House Committee on Transportation and Infrastructure that were released in January 2020. They are available in a searchable format as "Boeing Emails Handed Over to Congress in January 2020" at the nonprofit Internet Archive, https://archive.org.

163 Finally, in November 2016: Boeing Response to Question 7 and Related

Questions; Joint Authorities Technical Review of the Boeing 737 MAX Flight
Control System, Observations, Findings, and Recommendations, October 11,
2019, p. 34.

163 "I was getting too expensive": Author interview with Rick Ludtke, April 2019.

163 "Oh I'm sure": "Boeing Emails Handed Over."

163 Boeing's engineers decided to defer: Final Committee Report, p. 124.

164 "Things are calming down": "Boeing 737 MAX," Hearing, p. 64.

164 Sitting in a hotel room: Boeing provided the instant messages to the House
Committee on Transportation and Infrastructure and they were released in
October 2019. They are available in a searchable format as "Boeing Instant
Message Exchanges" at the nonprofit Internet Archive, https://archive.org.

164 In a conversation with Klein: United States of America v. The Boeing Company, United States District Court for the Northern District of Texas, Fort
Worth Division, Deferred Prosecution Agreement, 4:21-CR-005-O, Attach-
ment A-11.

164 "Idiots!" he wrote: Final Committee Report, p. 140.

165 "sick amount of $$$$": Final Committee Report, p. 141.

10. CRASH

166 The captain, Bhavye Suneja: The details about the captain and his copilot,
Harvino, appear in the final Aircraft Accident Investigation Report published
by the Komite Nasional Keselamatan Transportasi (KNKT), Transportation
Building, Jakarta, Indonesia, October 2019.

166 He loved to cook: Joanna Slater, "'Playing with Lives': Widow of Pilot on
Doomed Lion Air Flight Says Direct Appeals Made to Ground Boeing
Model," *Washington Post*, March 30, 2019.

166 Machines were another: Liu Chuen Chen, "Bhavye Suneja Had Asked Us
to Get Ready for a Party in Delhi: Friends of Indian Pilot Killed in Lion Air
Flight Crash," *Indian Express*, October 30, 2018.

167 He had started out: Nicholas Ionides, "Kirana's Lion Appetite for Success,"
FlightGlobal, September 25, 2006.

167 "only stupid people": Ionides.

168 "Airbus helps us to be better": Quoted in Ulisari Eslita, "Rusdi Kirana Has
Lion-Size Ambitions for Indonesia's Largest Airline," *Forbes Asia*, February 2015.

168 "It just faded away": Author interview with John Goglia, July 2020.

168 "Zero," as a Boeing employee: The emails and instant messages regarding the
simulator all appear in "Boeing Emails Handed Over to Congress in January 2020" at the nonprofit Internet Archive, https://archive.org.

169 In his late forties: Author interviews with anonymous former Boeing pilots,
May–June 2020.

170 Half-finished planes stacked: Dominic Gates, "Boeing's 737 Ramp-Up Shows Signs of Strain as Unfinished Planes Pile Up in Renton," *Seattle Times,* August 2, 2018.

170 At town hall meetings: Edward F. Pierson, "Statement of Edward F. Pierson Before the House Transportation and Infrastructure Committee," December 11, 2019, https://www.whistleblowers.org/whistleblowers/edward-pierson/.

170 "We can't do that": Pierson, "Statement of Edward F. Pierson."

171 Not long after: Author interview with anonymous former Boeing executive, June 2020.

171 "Our aspiration is no longer": Quoted in Paul Roberts, "Boeing's CEO faces Questions About His Own Future amid 737 MAX Crisis," *Seattle Times,* May 7, 2019.

171 Just before Enron crashed: Adam Levy, "Enron CEO Skilling Takes Company in New Directions," Bloomberg, May 1, 2001.

172 "Can anybody go faster": "Dennis A. Muilenburg, President, Chairman, and CEO, the Boeing Company, Discusses Boeing's Success, Leadership, and Bicycling" (Q&A transcript), May 9, 2018, https://www.economicclub.org /sites/default/files/transcripts/Dennis_Muilenburg_Edited_Transcript.pdf.

172 "We used to measure success": Ali Bahrami, "Turning the Corner," speech, Federal Aviation Administration, Air Cargo Safety Forum, Herndon, Virginia, August 17, 2017, available at https://www.faa.gov.

173 "It appeared they were looking": Natalie Kitroeff and David Gelles, "Before Deadly Crashes, Boeing Pushed for Law That Undercut Oversight," *New York Times,* October 27, 2019.

173 "It's basically putting": Author interview with Marc Ronell, November 2019.

174 "Is Boeing here?": Julie Johnsson and Peter Robison, "Boeing Is Killing It by Squeezing Its Suppliers," *Bloomberg Businessweek,* February 14, 2018.

174 Trump let Muilenburg listen: Anthony Capaccio, "Trump's F-35 Came with a Surprise: Rival CEO Was Listening," Bloomberg, February 15, 2017.

174 By one high-ranking executive's: Author interview with anonymous industry source, May 2020.

175 After weeks of high-level: Adrian Morrow and Nicolas Van Praet, "Boeing Abandoned C Series Talks Weeks Before U.S. Duties Imposed," *Globe and Mail,* October 23, 2017.

175 "We're going to build": Donald J. Trump, "Remarks Prior to a Dinner with Business Leaders and an Exchange with Reporters in Bedminster, New Jersey," transcript, August 7, 2018, https://www.govinfo.gov.

176 "Surprises happen a lot": The interview appeared on the *Point Taken* podcast series as "Episode 4—Faith at Work: An Interview with Dennis Muilenburg, CEO of The Boeing Company," October 3, 2018, https://pointtaken.libsyn .com/category/Leadership.

176 The piece Muilenburg published: "Pursuing God's Mission," September 24, 2018, https://b-b-t.org/.

176 In front of cameras at Luke: A transcript and video of the event is at C-SPAN: "President Trump Remarks at Defense Roundtable," October 19, 2018, https://www.c-span.org.

177 "The cash is the cash": Julie Johnsson, "Boeing Rallies on Surge in Cash Flow, Boost in 2018 Forecast," Bloomberg, October 24, 2018.

177 The first drop: "Anomalies Felt by Lion Air Passengers on the Denpasar-Jakarta Route Before the Plane Crash," *Tribun-Bali.com,* November 1, 2018.

178 "Is that the instruction book": "Anomalies Felt by Lion Air."

178 At least one person: Jane Onyanga-Omara and Thomas Maresca, "Previous Lion Air Flight Passengers 'Began to Panic and Vomit,'" *USA Today,* October 30, 2018.

179 A third, off-duty pilot: Alan Levin and Harry Suhartono, "Pilot Who Hitched a Ride Saved Lion Air 737 Day Before Deadly Crash," Bloomberg, March 19, 2019.

179 The captain's note: The maintenance steps undertaken on the plane are described in the final Aircraft Accident Investigation Report published by the Komite Nasional Keselamatan Transportasi (KNKT), Transportation Building, Jakarta, Indonesia, October 2019, p. 36.

179 At eight a.m. in Jakarta: Lewis Kamb, "A Lion Air Crash Victim, His Family's Loss and a Year of Quiet Mourning," *Seattle Times,* October 29, 2019.

180 The pilot Suneja's father: Riska Rahman, "Lion Air Crash," *Jakarta Post,* November 1, 2018.

180 During the search: Nur Asyiqin Mohamad Salleh, "Lion Air Crash: Indonesian Diver Dies During Search and Rescue Operation," *Straits Times,* November 3, 2018.

180 "We quickly identified": "The Boeing 737 MAX: Examining the Design, Development and Marketing of the Aircraft," Hearing Before the Committee on Transportation and Infrastructure, House of Representatives, October 30, 2019, https://www.govinfo.gov, p. 54.

180 He stood and bowed: Associated Press, "Grief and Fury Overflow as Families Confront Lion Air Owner Rusdi Kirana. He Stays Silent, Then Flees," November 6, 2018.

181 "When they changed": Author interview with anonymous FAA official, November 2019.

181 The empathy that Boeing's aviators: Author interviews with anonymous former Boeing pilots and other sources, 2020.

182 The FAA went along: FAA Aviation Safety, Emergency Airworthiness Directive, November 7, 2018, AD #: 2018-23-51, available at https://theaircurrent.com.

183 Earlier models had two: Mike Baker and Dominic Gates, "Boeing Altered Key Switches in 737 MAX Cockpit, Limiting Ability to Shut Off MCAS," *Seattle Times,* May 10, 2019.

183 Boeing had reports: Final Aircraft Accident Investigation Report published by the Komite Nasional Keselamatan Transportasi (KNKT), 169.

183 "I think it is unconscionable": Quoted in James Fallows, "Here's What Was on the Record About Problems with the 737 Max," *Atlantic,* March 13, 2019.

184 "withheld information about": Andy Pasztor and Andrew Tangel, "Boeing Withheld Information on 737 Model, According to Safety Experts and Others," *Wall Street Journal,* November 13, 2018.

184 "I am sure you have already": Thomas P. DiNapoli, comptroller of the state of New York, v. Boeing, in the Court of Chancery of the State of Delaware, Verified Stockholder Derivative Complaint, No. 2020-0465-AGB, June 30, 2020. The email records were produced for this case.

184 "New questions this morning": Fox Business, "Boeing CEO: The 737 MAX Is a Very Safe Airplane," November 13, 2018.

185 "Press is terrible": Cited in Thomas P. DiNapoli, comptroller.

185 Muilenburg told him: Cited in Thomas P. DiNapoli, comptroller.

185 "million-dollar corner": The description of the event was drawn from Ted Gallagher, "Boeing CEO Jets Home to Christen Sioux County Regional Airport," *Sioux County Journal,* November 15, 2018, and author interviews in June 2020.

186 The first victim: Kurniawan/Xinhua/Alamy Live News, "Relatives Carry the Coffin of Jannatun Cintya Dewi," November 1, 2018.

187 "I was not in": Author interview with Rini Soegiyono, May 2021.

188 "Oh my God, this": Author interview with Michael Indrajana, March 2021.

189 "We wanted the psychological pressure": Hannah Beech and Mukita Suhartono, "Lion Air Crash Families Say They Were Pressured to Sign No-Suit Deal," *New York Times,* March 21, 2019.

190 After those crashes: In Re: Air Crash Near Medan, Indonesia, on September 5, 2005, United States District Court for the Northern District of Illinois, 07-cv-04845; In Re: Air Crash Disaster Over Makassar Strait, Sulawesi, United States District Court for the Northern District of Illinois, 09-cv-3805.

190 "The underbelly of aviation": Author interview with Sanjiv Singh, August 2020.

191 "Interviews with dozens": Hannah Beech and Mukita Suhartono, "'Spend the Minimum': After Crash, Lion Air's Safety Record Is Back in Spotlight," *New York Times,* November 22, 2018.

191 "Because the MAX": Julie Johnsson, "Boeing Tumbles as Bad News Multiplies for Cash Cow 737 Max," Bloomberg, November 13, 2018.

191 Muilenburg held a briefing: Cited in Thomas P. DiNapoli, comptroller.

191 "You may have seen": Cited in Thomas P. DiNapoli.

191 In Shanghai that fall: Author interview with anonymous former Boeing pilot, November 2020.

192 "One of the things": My account of Boeing's meeting with the American Airlines pilots is from the audiotape and transcript provided by the pilots' union.

194 Boeing put out its own statement: "Boeing Statement on Lion Air Flight 610 Preliminary Report," November 28, 2018, https://boeing.mediaroom.com.

194 "The trust in the machine": Euan McKirdy, "Lion Air Crash: Pilots Fought Automatic Safety System Before Plane Plunged," CNN, November 29, 2018.

194 He dropped multiple f-bombs: Peter Robison and Margaret Newkirk, "Boeing Charted Own Safety Course for Years with FAA as Co-Pilot," Bloomberg, March 23, 2019.

195 He went public: Harry Suhartono and Julie Johnsson, "Lion Air Stands Firm on Canceling $22 Billion Boeing Jet Orders," Bloomberg, December 11, 2018.

195 Muilenburg coolly responded: Suhartono and Johnsson.

195 "Fairly early on": "CNBC Excerpts: Boeing Chairman Dave Calhoun Speaks with CNBC's Phil LeBeau Today on 'Squawk Box,'" CNBC, November 5, 2019.

195 asked his staff for a list: Author interview with anonymous source, January 2020.

195 In early December: The FAA certification memo was produced during a U.S. House Transportation and Infrastructure Committee hearing, December 11, 2019.

195 the kind of bloodless analysis: Ali Bahrami described the tool as a way to assess priorities among 150 to 200 airworthiness directives in a given time. "What we decided to do is develop a tool that helps us with that decision-making—because we were becoming a data-driven, risk-based decision-making organization." House Committee on Transportation and Infrastructure, Interview of Ali Bahrami, December 5, 2019, https://transportation.house.gov, p. 141.

195 Fifteen crashes would be: Andy Pasztor and Andrew Tangel, "Internal FAA Review Saw High Risk of 737 MAX Crashes," Wall Street Journal, December 11, 2019.

11. "THE DEATH JET"

196 Sitting at the controls: Author interview with Dennis Tajer, May 2020.

196 For Christmas: Author interview with Michael Stumo, October 2020.

197 She taught herself to read: Author interview with Michael Stumo, October 2019.

197 "Huge day": "CNBC Exclusive: Boeing CEO Dennis Muilenburg Speaks with CNBC's Phil LeBeau Today," CNBC, January 30, 2019.

197 The FAA, with Ali Bahrami: Andrew Tangel and Andy Pasztor, "Regulators Found High Risk of Emergency After First Boeing MAX Crash," Wall Street Journal, July 31, 2019.

198 Most of that month: House Committee on Transportation and Infrastructure, Interview of Ali Bahrami, December 5, 2019, https://transportation.house .gov, p. 153. Bahrami made a reference to the shutdown in his interview with House investigators: "Remember, we were shut down to begin. But right after about December timeframe, once the AD was issued, we were working the corrective action, and people were working it with Boeing."

198 Boeing's executives, in PowerPoint: The Boeing "MCAS Development and Certification Overview" presentation appears in "The Boeing 737 MAX: Examining the Design, Development and Marketing of the Aircraft," Hearing Before the Committee on Transportation and Infrastructure, House of Representatives, October 30, 2019, https://www.govinfo.gov, p. 180.

198 He called the crash: Final Committee Report on the Design, Development & Certification of the Boeing 737 Max, House Committee on Transportation and Infrastructure, September 2020, https://transportation.house.gov, p. 213.

198 Unusually for an aircraft: Steve Miletich, "Kirkland Consultant Questioned for Six Hours in Criminal Probe of Boeing 737 MAX Crashes," *Seattle Times,* May 20, 2019.

198 Not long after: Author interview with anonymous former Boeing pilot, May 2020.

199 Kennedy got more than: Cited in Thomas P. DiNapoli, comptroller.

199 Two months after: His compensation is detailed in Seafarers Pension Plan vs. Boeing, U.S. District Court for the Northern District of Illinois, 19-cv-08095, December 11, 2019.

198 In her last conversation: Hannah Shirley, "Samya Stumo Remembered as a Crusader for Healthcare," *Berkshire Record,* March 21, 2019.

200 "Just landed in Addis": Statement of Michael Stumo Before the United States Senate Committee on Commerce, Science and Transportation, Examining the Federal Aviation Administration's Oversight of Aircraft Certification, June 17, 2020, https://www.cliffordlaw.com.

200 One row up sat: David Gelles, "The Emotional Wreckage of a Deadly Boeing Crash," *New York Times,* March 9, 2020. My description uses the seating layout that appears in this article.

200 At the controls: Maggie Fick, "Youngest Captain, Loving Son: Ethiopian Pilots Honored in Death," Reuters, March 20, 2019.

200 Seconds after the plane: The actions of the pilots are described in the interim report of the Federal Democratic Republic of Ethiopia, Ministry of Transport, Aircraft Accident Investigation Bureau, Report No. AI-01/19, March 10, 2019.

201 Baffled, she went: Author interview, October 2019.

202 the "roller coaster": Dominic Gates, "Why Boeing's Emergency Directions May Have Failed to Save 737 MAX," *Seattle Times,* April 3, 2019.

202 People just waking up: "'Loud Rattling Sound': Witnesses Say Ethiopian Plane Trailed Smoke," SBS News, March 12, 2019.

202 just a few hours: Simon Browning, "Boeing 737 Max: 'I Lost My Family in the Ethiopian Plane Crash,'" BBC News, July 4, 2019, and author interviews.

203 An operator at Boeing's: Andrew Tangel, Alison Sider, and Andy Pasztor, "'We've Been Humbled': Boeing's CEO Struggles to Contain 737 MAX Crisis," *Wall Street Journal,* December 22, 2019.

203 When James Burke: Dieudonnee Ten Berge, *The First 24 Hours: A Comprehensive Guide to Successful Crisis Management;* Andrew Caesar-Gordon, "The Perfect Crisis Response?" *PR Week,* October 28, 2015.

203   He led a late-night: Cited in Thomas P. DiNapoli, comptroller. The email records produced in this lawsuit included one from Muilenburg to communications chief Toulouse on the day of the crash: "Anne, I think this note is solid, but it lacks a statement about our confidence in the fundamental safety of the MAX. . . . I would like to add a specific statement regarding the MAX focused on this fundamental safety and confidence point. I also think we need to be stronger regarding the Lion Air point. . . . e.g., any speculation attempting to link the two accidents is not supported by facts. This goes back to our discussion last night on answering two basic questions: is the MAX safe? And was MCAS involved? We need to make a strong statement on the first, and be clear that there are no supporting facts on the second."

203   The statement Boeing released: Boeing, "Boeing Statement on 737 MAX Software Enhancement," March 11, 2019, https://boeing.mediaroom.com.

204   Muilenburg talked to Trump: Interview with Andrew Ross Sorkin, DealBook conference, *New York Times,* November 6, 2019. "The first time I called him," Muilenburg said, "it was to compare notes just after the second accident, to find out what was going on, convey our concerns, and to encourage that any decisions be made based on data. The system safety, aviation system safety, the reason it's worked, the reason it is the safest form of transportation in the world, is because we make decisions based on data. That was the subject of my first call."

204   A Boeing statement: Boeing, "Boeing Statement on 737 Max Operation," March 12, 2019, https://boeing.mediaroom.com.

204   His transportation secretary: Kathryn A. Wolfe, "Chao Flew on a Boeing 737 MAX from Austin Festival," *Politico,* March 12, 2019.

204   That Tuesday: Renzo Downey, "Secretary Chao Announces New Transportation Technology Council at SXSW," *Austin American-Statesman,* March 12, 2019; Wolfe, "Chao Flew on a Boeing."

205   "What we're looking at": Peter Robison and Julie Johnsson, "Two 737 Max Crashes in Five Months Put Boeing's Reputation on the Line," *Bloomberg Businessweek,* March 13, 2019.

205   " 'Ali, I'm really sorry' ": House Committee, Interview of Ali Bahrami, p. 63.

205   "Other authorities may have": House Committee, p. 63.

205   Satellite transponders: Jonathan Amos, "Satellite Plane-Tracking Goes Global," BBC News, April 2, 2019.

205   Estimates at the time: Robison and Johnsson, "Two 737 Max Crashes."

206   "I want to hear my kids": Susan Ormiston, " 'My World Went Silent,' Says Grieving Father Who Lost 5 Family Members As They Flew from Toronto to Nairobi," CBC, March 17, 2019.

206   Nadia and Michael: These descriptions are from an author interview with Nadia Milleron, March 2021.

207   Giant backhoes were: "You Can Smell the Scorched Earth," Sky News, March 11, 2019.

207   That Sunday, mourners: Peter Robison and Alan Levin, "Boeing Had Too

Much Sway Vetting Own Planes, FAA Was Warned," Bloomberg, March 17, 2019.

207 At the United Nations: "UN Honours Fallen Colleagues and Friends Who 'Risk All to Promote Peace,'" *UN News,* May 6, 2019.

208 In Toronto: Bryan Passifiume, "Friends, Family Pay Tribute to Toronto Woman Lost in Ethiopia Air Disaster," *Toronto Sun,* March 15, 2019.

208 Two brothers in California: Mike Chapman, "Friends, Family Give Colorful Send-Off to Riffel Brothers Who Died on Ethiopian Flight," *Record Searchlight,* March 16, 2019.

208 Within days of the crash: Author interview with anonymous source, September 2020.

208 The story quoted: Dominic Gates, "Flawed Analysis, Failed Oversight: How Boeing, FAA Certified the Suspect 737 MAX Flight Control System," *Seattle Times,* March 17, 2019.

209 "like an engineer": Robison and Johnsson, "Two 737 Max Crashes."

209 A shelf full of books: *Legend and Legacy,* by Robert J. Serling, brother of the *Twilight Zone* creator Rod Serling, was published by St. Martin's Press but commissioned by Boeing, according to a later book, *Flying High,* by Eugene Rodgers, and Byron Acohido's 1993 *Seattle Times* article "Piloting Plant Through Change: Boeing Executive to Lead the Everett Division Through Layoffs, 777 Launch, Other Challenges."

209 A date had even: Final Committee Report on the Design, Development & Certification of the Boeing 737 Max, House Committee on Transportation and Infrastructure, September 2020, https://transportation.house.gov, p. 30.

209 In late March: Julie Johnsson and Mary Schlangenstein, "Boeing Was Close to Software Fix Before Second 737 Max Crash," Bloomberg, March 27, 2019.

210 Ewbank filed: Dominic Gates, Steve Miletich, and Lewis Kamb, "Boeing Rejected 737 MAX Safety Upgrades Before Fatal Crashes, Whistleblower Says," *Seattle Times,* October 2, 2019.

210 Mechanics at the Dreamliner: Natalie Kitroeff and David Gelles, "Claims of Shoddy Production Draw Scrutiny to a Second Boeing Jet," *New York Times,* April 20, 2019.

210 One stunning instance: Boeing, "Boeing Statement on AOA Disagree Alert," April 29, 2019, https://boeing.mediaroom.com.

211 PROSECUTE BOEING & EXECS: Rupert Neate, "Boeing Boss Rejects Accusations About 737 Max Jets That Crashed," *Guardian,* April 29, 2019.

211 "Never mind the processes": "Boeing CEO Dennis Muilenburg Answers Questions at the Company's Shareholder Meeting," CNBC, April 29, 2019, https://www.cnbc.com.

211 Wearing a pressed: "Boeing CEO Dennis Muilenburg Addresses the Ethiopian Airlines Flight 302 Preliminary Report," *PR Newswire,* April 4, 2019.

211 He repeated the message: Boeing, "Boeing Co. Introductory Remarks: Afternoon Sessions at George W. Bush Presidential Center's Annual Forum on Leadership—Final," *FD (Fair Disclosure) Wire,* April 11, 2019.

212 McAllister gave an emotional: Peter Robison, "Former Boeing Engineers Say Relentless Cost-Cutting Sacrificed Safety," *Bloomberg Businessweek,* May 8, 2019.

212 "Houdini moments": Dominic Gates, "For Boeing, Juggling Cash Flow Means Another 'Houdini Moment,'" *Seattle Times,* February 8, 2019.

213 "You have to know": "Status of the 737 Max," Hearing Before the Subcommittee on Aviation of the Committee on Transportation and Infrastructure, House of Representatives, May 15, 2019, https://www.govinfo.gov/, p. 5.

213 "Absolutely": "Status of the 737 Max," p. 36.

213 But Elwell met: Author interviews with anonymous sources, October 2020.

213 A PowerPoint presentation: 737 MAX Flight Standardization Board, "FAA/Operators Meeting: Return to Service/FSB Information Briefing," April 12, 2019.

214 "I'd say we come": Dominic Gates, "Muilenburg Says Boeing Brings 'A Tone of Humility and Learning' over 737 MAX to Paris Air Show," *Seattle Times,* June 16, 2019.

214 Elwell told Muilenburg: Tangel, Sider, and Pasztor, "'We've Been Humbled.'"

214 The following Saturday: "In Conversation with Boeing CEO Dennis Muilenburg," Aspen Ideas Festival, June 27, 2019. Boeing Century Challenge, June 22, 2019, race results here: https://runsignup.com.

12. BLOOD MONEY

215 "You and your team": Ralph Nader, "Boeing Mismanagers Forfeit Your Pay and Resign: An Open Letter to Boeing CEO Dennis Muilenburg," April 26, 2019, https://nader.org.

216 In late June, they held: A video of the event at the American Museum of Tort Law is available at "Samya Stumo Memorial June 22nd, 2019," https://www.youtube.com.

217 "Good people should": Author interview with Stan Sorscher, November 2019.

218 "I felt that the reason": Author interview with Paul Njoroge, May 2020.

219 "They're not used": Author interview with Michael Stumo, October 2019.

219 "They say 'data-driven'": Author interview with Tarek Milleron, June 2020.

220 "If a student came in": Author interview with Javier de Luis, November 2019.

220 The FAA was running: Dominic Gates, "Newly Stringent FAA Tests Spur a Fundamental Software Redesign of Boeing's 737 MAX Controls," *Seattle Times,* August 1, 2019.

220 "Remember, get right on": U.S. Senate Committee on Commerce, Science, and Transportation, Committee Investigation Report, Aviation Safety Oversight, December 2020, https://www.commerce.senate.gov, p. 44.

221 An FAA inspector: U.S. Senate Committee, p. 44.

221 Those findings spooked even: Author interviews with anonymous sources, October 2020.

222 "my family's flesh": Written Testimony of Paul Njoroge Before the U.S. House Subcommittee on Aviation, July 17, 2019, https://www.congress.gov.

222 After the ValuJet crash: Eric Malnic, "FAA Failure Cited in ValuJet Crash Report," *Los Angeles Times,* August 20, 1997.

223 Minutes before: Boeing statement, "Boeing Dedicates $50 Million of Pledged $100 Million to Near-term Relief for Families of the Victims of the Lion Air Flight 610 and Ethiopian Airlines Flight 302 Accidents," July 17, 2019, https://boeing.mediaroom.com.

223 It was part: "Ahead of Independence Day in the U.S., Boeing [NYSE: BA] announced $100 million in funds to address family and community needs of those affected by the tragic accidents of Lion Air Flight 610 and Ethiopian Airlines Flight 302. These funds will support education, hardship and living expenses for impacted families, community programs, and economic development in impacted communities." Boeing statement, "Boeing Pledges Support to Families, Communities Affected by Lion Air Flight 610 and Ethiopian Airlines Flight 302 Accidents," July 3, 2019, https://boeing.mediaroom.com.

223 "Frankly, that's what": Ali Bahrami's testimony at a Federal Aviation Administration Oversight hearing of the Senate Appropriations Subcommittee on Transportation, July 31, 2019, is available at https://www.c-span.org.

224 She and her son Tor: Author interview with Nadia Milleron, October 2019.

224 Each missing MAX: Darryl Campbell, "The 737 Built Southwest, and the 737 MAX Could Be Its Undoing," *Verge,* October 23, 2019.

225 "deeply disappointed": Natalie Kitroeff and David Gelles, "Inside Boeing, a C.E.O. Stripped of Power and a Top Executive Under Fire," *New York Times,* October 13, 2019.

225 "gay Conquistadores": Ben Wootliff, "Engine of Change at Rolls: Acerbic and Intensely Private, Sir John Rose Has Challenged the Might of US Power and Made Rolls-Royce a Success Again," *Guardian,* August 16, 2003.

225 Muilenburg's placid demeanor: Natalie Kitroeff and David Gelles, "At Boeing, C.E.O.'s Stumbles Deepen a Crisis," *New York Times,* December 22, 2019.

225 The lot eventually: Tom Banse, "Moses Lake Airport Close to Maxing Out on Boeing 737 Storage," Oregon Public Broadcasting, January 9, 2020.

225 By October: Julie Johnsson, "Boeing Stirs Fears of Cash Crunch with Tab for 737 Max at $9 Billion and Rising," Bloomberg, October 23, 2019.

225 It had taken: Mike Baker, "FAA Chief: Manuals Should Have Told 737 MAX Pilots More About Boeing's MCAS System," *Seattle Times,* May 15, 2019.

226 One morning: Author interview with anonymous source, November 2019.

226 "This is the smoking gun": David Gelles and Natalie Kitroeff, "Boeing Pilot Complained of 'Egregious' Issue with 737 Max in 2016," *New York Times,* October 18, 2019.

226 "Dear Mr. Muilenburg": Federal Aviation Administration, "Read the Letter—FAA," October 18, 2019, https://www.faa.gov.

226 "You're forcing my hand": Andrew Tangel, Alison Sider, and Andy Pasztor,

" 'We've Been Humbled': Boeing's CEO Struggles to Contain 737 MAX Crisis," *Wall Street Journal*, December 22, 2019.

226 "Strangely enough": Author interview with Peter DeFazio, February 2020.

227 He'd made at least $28 million: The executive compensation was detailed in a lawsuit filed by Seafarers Pension Plan against Boeing and other top executives in the U.S. District Court for the Northern District of Illinois, 19-cv-08095, December 11, 2019.

13. "GO BACK TO THE FARM!"

228 Just before the October: Author interview with Nadia Milleron, October 2019.

228 "In these cost-conscious": Message to customers, Blake Emergency Services website, https://www.blakeemergency.com/about-us.

229 The only way: Author interview with Javier de Luis, November 2019.

229 At one point: Alison Sider and Alexandra Wexler, " 'Sometimes They're Angry with Us and That's OK': Boeing and 737 MAX Families Form Painful Partnership," *Wall Street Journal*, March 5, 2020.

229 "our friends from Boeing": The video of Lion Air CEO Edward Sirait and the lawyers speaking to reporters on October 29, 2019, is available on YouTube.

229 "They were not operating": Author interview with Sanjiv Singh, November 2020.

230 a flat fee: Author interview with Ken Feinberg, May 2021.

230 That was how the photographs: Lia Eustachewich and Aaron Feis, "Families Confront Boeing CEO Dennis Muilenburg on Capitol Hill with Photos of 737 MAX Crash Victims," *New York Post*, October 29, 2019.

230 "Mr. Muilenburg, as I watched": "Boeing CEO and Government Officials Testify on 737 MAX Safety," Senate Commerce Committee, October 29, 2019, available at https://www.c-span.org.

233 In fact, the lawyer: Author interviews with anonymous sources, May 2020.

234 Barr told subordinates: Author interview with anonymous source, April 2021.

235 When Michael walked in: David Slotnick, "Boeing's CEO Met with Families of 737 Max Crash Victims After His Senate Testimony. Here's What Happened Behind Closed Doors," *Business Insider*, October 29, 2019.

235 "They're not human beings": Author interview with Paul Njoroge, May 2020.

236 "You're the captain": David Shepardson and Tracy Rucinski, "Boeing CEO Resists Multiple Calls for Resignation," Reuters, October 30, 2019.

237 "As students, we must": "Muilenburg's Actions Reflect Poorly on Iowa State," editorial, *Iowa State Daily*, December 12, 2019.

237 A call went out: Author interview with anonymous former Boeing executive, March 2020.

237 Dickson said he'd look: Natalie Kitroeff and David Gelles, "At Boeing, C.E.O.'s Stumbles Deepen a Crisis," *New York Times*, December 22, 2019.

237 Boeing put out a statement: Boeing, "737 MAX Progress Report," November 11, 2019, https://boeing.mediaroom.com.

237 He sent a memo: David Shepardson and Eric M. Johnson, "U.S. FAA Regulator Head Tells Team to 'Take Whatever Time Is Needed' on 737 MAX," Reuters, November 15, 2019.

237 The next month: David Schaper, "FAA Chief Pushes Back on Boeing Pressure to Return 737 Max Jets to Service," NPR, December 12, 2019.

237 Muilenburg at last: Boeing, "Boeing Statement Regarding 737 MAX Production," December 16, 2019, https://boeing.mediaroom.com.

238 Walking away with $59 million: The executive compensation was detailed in a lawsuit filed by Seafarers Pension Plan against Boeing and other top executives in the U.S. District Court for the Northern District of Illinois, 19-cv-08095, December 11, 2019.

238 A board member since 2009: Seafarers Pension Plan vs. Boeing, U.S. District Court for the Northern District of Illinois, 19-cv-08095, December 11, 2019.

14. "THE GUY MOST LIKE JACK"

240 It would have been: Author interview with Frank McCormick, May 2019.

240 In 2019, some former: Author interview with Rick Ludtke, May 2019.

240 On the first Sunday: Author interview with anonymous source, March 2020.

240 Weeks earlier, Boeing's top: Jamie Freed and Tim Hepher, "Airline Growth Hit as Virus Depletes Singapore Airshow," Reuters, February 9, 2020.

241 One resident: Peter Robison and Dina Bass, "Quarantine Motel, Cached Food: Seattle Confronts a Deadly Virus," Bloomberg, March 2, 2020.

241 Asked that question: "CNBC Transcript: Boeing CEO Dave Calhoun Speaks with CNBC's Phil LeBeau Today," CNBC, January 29, 2020.

241 "I get a lot": "Boeing Co (BA) Q4 2019 Earnings Call Transcript," *Motley Fool*, January 29, 2020.

241 A month later: Author interview with anonymous source, March 2020.

241 The messages were part: Peter Robison, Julie Johnsson, and Alan Levin, "Boeing Suspends Co-Workers of Pilot at Center of Max Scrutiny," Bloomberg, February 21, 2020.

242 "the guy who was really": Bill Lane, *Jacked Up: The Inside Story of How Jack Welch Talked GE into Becoming the World's Greatest Company,* 272.

242 his "framework" for everything: Geoffrey Colvin, "Rising Star: David Calhoun, General Electric," *Fortune,* January 24, 2006.

242 When their foursome: Jack Welch, *Jack: Straight from the Gut,* 403.

242 One strike against him: Lane, *Jacked Up,* 272.

242 The lure was $100 million: Geoffrey Colvin, "Going Down the Talent Drain: Public Companies Are Losing Execs to Deep-Pocketed Private Firms," *Fortune,* September 5, 2006.

242 In 2007 the company: Associated Press, "Tata Consultancy Wins Record $1.2 Billion Outsourcing Contract," October 18, 2007.

243 "making a joke": Patrick Thibodeau, "Tax Break Fuels Anger over Outsourcing-Related Layoffs in Fla.," *Computerworld,* July 1, 2008.

243 orchids were scattered: Michael J. de la Merced, "Inside Stephen Schwarzman's Birthday Bash," *New York Times,* February 14, 2007.

243 "For five years": Blackstone Group, "Blackstone Group LP Meeting Investor Day Teleconference," June 12, 2014.

243 "tremendous productivity engine": Barr Seitz, "How Nielsen Fixates on Value Creation to Drive Growth: An Interview with Steve Hasker," *McKinsey on Marketing and Sales,* February 2018, https://www.mckinsey.com.

244 "It's real": "Private Equity a Jobs Creator?" Fox Business, September 15, 2016, https://video.foxbusiness.com.

246 "If we're paying": Author interview with anonymous source, March 2021.

246 "Oh yeah, I remember": Author interview with anonymous source, March 2021.

247 A Boeing press release: "Boeing Enlists Ken Feinberg and Camille Biros to Oversee $50 Million Boeing Community Investment Fund to Support Communities Affected by Lion Air Flight 610 and Ethiopian Airlines Flight 302 Accidents," February 17, 2020, https://boeing.mediaroom.com.

247 "It felt like": Author interview with anonymous source, March 2021.

247 "All I will tell you": Author interview with Ken Feinberg, May 2021.

247 Days before, Calhoun had: Natalie Kitroeff and David Gelles, " 'It's More Than I Imagined': Boeing's New C.E.O. Confronts Its Challenges," *New York Times,* March 5, 2020.

248 On March 10: David Gelles, "The Emotional Wreckage," *New York Times,* March 9, 2020.

248 "They're terrified": Author interview with Nadia Milleron, March 2021.

249 Early that month: Author interviews with anonymous sources, March 2020.

249 Boeing finally said: Dominic Gates, "Boeing Worker at Everett Plant Dies from Coronavirus Infection," *Seattle Times,* March 22, 2020.

249 Boeing had to: Paula Seligson, "Boeing Plans Full Drawdown of $13.825 Billion Loan," Bloomberg, March 11, 2020.

249 Calhoun even considered: Douglas MacMillan, "Nikki Haley Quits Boeing Board, Citing Disagreement with Company's Bailout Request," *Washington Post,* March 19, 2020.

250 The company ultimately: Molly Smith and Julie Johnsson, "Boeing Rules Out Federal Aid After Raising $25 Billion of Bonds," Bloomberg, April 30, 2020.

250 The air force: Valerie Insinna, "Boeing to Get $882M in Withheld KC-46 Funds Back for COVID-19," *Defense News,* April 2, 2020.

250 "We'll never have": Julie Johnsson, "Boeing Mulls Revamped Factory Footprint for Shrinking Jet Market," Bloomberg, July 29, 2020.

252 Calhoun raised hell: Author interview with anonymous source, April 2020.

252 The CEO and his board: Author interview with anonymous source, April 2020.

252 As part of a new: Eric M. Johnson, "Exclusive: Boeing Hires Pilots for Airlines to Help Relaunch 737 MAX," Reuters, December 16, 2020.

253 The effort was led: Author interviews with anonymous former Boeing pilots.

253 "The loss of this critical": SPEEA, "SPEEA Comments on Boeing Eliminating customer Flight Training Airplane pilots, sending jobs to overseas contract house," Business Wire, September 21, 2020.

EPILOGUE

255 Isom sat in: Andrew Tangel, "Boeing's 737 MAX Returns to U.S. Commercial Service with American Airlines Flight," *Wall Street Journal,* December 29, 2020; Ryan Ewing, "What It's Like to Fly the 737 MAX Post-Grounding," *Airline Geeks,* December 31, 2020.

255 The Boeing team: Author interview with anonymous source, June 2020. The flights are detailed in Ashley Burke, "Canada Allowed Grounded Boeing 737 Max Jets to Fly—Without Passengers—at Least 160 Times," CBC, February 3, 2020.

256 One of the most: Federal Aviation Administration, "2019-NM-035-AD The Boeing Company Model 737-8 and 737-9 (737 MAX) airplanes," https://beta.regulations.gov.

256 American had another reason: Author interview with anonymous source, December 2020.

256 That first week: Edward Russell, "American Airlines Finds Travelers Not Avoiding the 737 Max as Many Feared," *Skift,* January 5, 2021.

257 "And they're not": Author interview with Floyd Wisner, May 2020.

257 A law passed: U.S. Senate Committee on Commerce, Science and Transportation, "Congressional Aviation Leaders Applaud Comprehensive Bipartisan, Bicameral Aircraft Safety & Certification Reforms Passed as Part of Omnibus Funding Bill," December 22, 2020, summary available at https://www.commerce.senate.gov.

257 Those new powers: Author interview with Michael Stumo, March 2021.

257 Some of the families: Author interviews with anonymous sources, June 2021.

258 "With its unique systems": Federal Aviation Administration, "2019-NM-035-AD The Boeing Company Model 737-8 and 737-9 (737 MAX) airplanes," https://beta.regulations.gov.

259 Thirty years after: Howard Berkes, "Challenger Engineer Who Warned of Shuttle Disaster Dies," NPR, March 21, 2016.

259 "I said, 'Bob'": Author interview with Allan McDonald, July 2019.

259 Answering questions: Andy Pasztor and Andrew Tangel, "FAA, Boeing Blasted over 737 MAX Failures in Democratic Report," *Wall Street Journal,* September 16, 2020.

260 "I guess I'm not": House Committee on Transportation and Infrastructure, Interview of Ali Bahrami, December 5, 2019, https://transportation.house .gov, p. 136.

260 consider the program a success: House Committee on Transportation and Infrastructure, Interview of Keith Leverkuhn, May 19, 2020, https:// transportation.house.gov, p. 118.

260 The direct cost: Chris Isidore, "Boeing's 737 Max Debacle Could Be the Most Expensive Corporate Blunder Ever," *CNN Business,* November 17, 2020.

261 "Winning is good": The 2017 JWMI MBA Graduation Ceremony, May 31, 2017, https://www.strategiceducation.com.

261 two adjoining multimillion-dollar: Bob Goldsborough, "Retired Boeing CEO Jim McNerney Sells Lake Forest Mansion for $3.98 Million—About Half Its 2006 Buying Price," *Chicago Tribune,* August 12, 2020.

261 built a second mansion: Patti Payne, "Ex-Boeing Chief Phil Condit Opens Fall City Home to Event Bookings (Slide Show)," *Puget Sound Business Journal,* May 28, 2013.

261 The former McDonnell: John Le, "Couple Files Suit against Biltmore Forest in Dispute over Their Twelve Cats," *ABC 13 News,* August 29, 2016, https:// wlos.com.

261 He's an investor: Julie Johnsson, "Boeing's Ousted CEO Resurfaces at Silicon Valley Tractor Maker," Bloomberg, December 14, 2020.

261 The amount of the criminal: From the Justice Department's deferred prosecution agreement: "The base fine is $243,600,000 (representing Boeing's cost-savings, based on Boeing's assessment of the cost associated with the implementation of full-flight simulator training for the 737 MAX)." The agreement didn't say how the amount was calculated, but Southwest— recipient of the $1 million–per–airplane promise of no simulator training— had 246 firm MAX orders as of October 2019. The assessment was likely only a direct cost, not taking into account the possibility of future lost orders if airlines considering the MAX against the Airbus A320neo judged additional needs for simulator training a disadvantage. United States of America v. The Boeing Company, United States District Court for the Northern District of Texas, 4:21-CR-005-O, https://www.justice.gov/, p. 10.

262 It would say: Author interview with anonymous former Boeing pilot, January 2021.

SELECTED BIBLIOGRAPHY

Bauer, Eugene E. *Boeing: The First Century*. Enumclaw, WA: TABA Publishing, 2000.

Berge, Dieudonnee Ten. *The First 24 Hours: A Comprehensive Guide to Successful Crisis Management*. Cambridge, MA: Blackwell, 1990.

Boeing. *Boeing World Headquarters: Our Home in Chicago*. Chicago: Privately printed, 2003.

Byrne, Jerry. *Flight 427: Anatomy of an Air Disaster*. New York: Springer-Verlag, 2002.

Clearfield, Chris, and Andras Tilcsik. *Meltdown: What Plane Crashes, Oil Spills, and Dumb Business Decisions Can Teach Us About How to Succeed at Work and at Home*. New York: Penguin Books, 2018.

Collins, James C., and Jerry I. Porras. *Built to Last: Successful Habits of Visionary Companies*. New York: HarperBusiness, 1994.

Dornseif, Dan. *Boeing 737: The World's Jetliner*. Atglen, PA: Schiffer Publishing, 2017.

Evans, Harold. *Good Times, Bad Times*. London: Weidenfeld & Nicolson, 1983.

Grunberg, Leon, and Sarah Moore. *Emerging from Turbulence: Boeing and Stories of the American Workplace Today*. Lanham, MD: Rowman & Littlefield, 2016.

Johnston, A. M. "Tex," with Charles Barton. *Tex Johnston: Jet-Age Test Pilot*. Washington, D.C., and London: Smithsonian Press, 1991.

Johnston, Moira. *The Last Nine Minutes: The Story of Flight 981*. New York: William Morrow, 1976.

Lane, Bill. *Jacked Up: The Inside Story of How Jack Welch Talked GE into Becoming the World's Greatest Company*. New York: McGraw-Hill, 2008.

————. *Losing It! Behaviors and Mindsets That Ruin Careers: Lessons on Protecting Yourself from Avoidable Mistakes.* Upper Saddle River, NJ: FT Press, 2012.

Mansfield, Harold. *Vision: A Saga of the Sky.* New York: Duell, Sloan and Pearce, 1956.

Michaels, Kevin. *Aerodynamic: Inside the High-Stakes Global Jetliner Ecosystem.* Reston, VA: American Institute of Aeronautics and Astronautics, 2018.

McMartin, Joseph A. *Collision Course: Ronald Reagan, the Air Traffic Controllers, and the Strike That Changed America.* New York: Oxford University Press, 2011.

Newhouse, John. *The Sporty Game.* New York: Knopf, 1982.

————. *Boeing Versus Airbus: The Inside Story of the Greatest International Competition in Business.* New York: Knopf, 2007.

O'Boyle, Thomas F. *At Any Cost: Jack Welch, General Electric, and the Pursuit of Profit.* New York: Knopf, 1998.

Petzinger, Thomas, Jr. *Hard Landing: The Epic Contest for Power and Profits That Plunged the Airlines into Chaos.* New York: Times Books, 1995.

Rodgers, Eugene. *Flying High: The Story of Boeing and the Rise of the Jetliner Industry.* New York: Atlantic Monthly Press, 1996.

Rosen, Robert H., with Paul B. Brown. *Leading People: Transforming Business from the Inside Out.* New York: Viking Penguin, 1996.

Sabbagh, Karl. *Twenty-First-Century Jet: The Making and Marketing of the Boeing 777.* New York: Scribner, 1996.

Serling, Robert J. *Legend and Legacy: The Story of Boeing and Its People.* New York: St. Martin's Press, 1992.

Slater, Robert. *Jack Welch and the GE Way: Management Insights and Leadership Secrets of the Legendary CEO.* New York: McGraw-Hill, 1999.

Sutter, Joe, with Jay Spenser. *747: Creating the World's First Jumbo Jet and Other Adventures from a Life in Aviation.* New York: Smithsonian Books, 2006.

Tapscott, Don, and Anthony C. Williams. *Wikinomics: How Mass Collaboration Changes Everything.* New York: Portfolio, 1996.

Verhovek, Sam Howe. *Jet Age: The Comet, the 707, and the Race to Shrink the World.* New York: Penguin Group, 2010.

Welch, Jack, with John A. Byrne. *Jack: Straight from the Gut.* New York: Warner Books, 2001.

INDEX